OSCAR HANDLIN is Professor of History at Harvard University. In 1952, Dr. Handlin received the Pulitzer Prize for history. Notable among his published works are *This Was America* (1949); *The Uprooted* (1951), the definitive work on the social plight of the immigrant in America; *The American People in the Twentieth Century* (1954); *Readings in American History* (1957); and *American Principles and Issues* (1961).

Immigration

AS A FACTOR IN

American History

Immigration
AS A FACTOR IN
American History

OSCAR HANDLIN

Professor of History
Harvard University

A SPECTRUM BOOK

Englewood Cliffs, N. J.

PRENTICE-HALL, INC.

Current printing (last digit):

14

For

DELMORE SCHWARTZ

Contents

Immigration
AS A FACTOR IN
American History

Introduction

IMMIGRATION
had so long been a familiar aspect of American development that
it was not until the end of the nineteenth century that any question was raised as to the propriety of its continuance. The whole
history of the peopling of the continent had been one of immigration. The seventeenth century movement of population had
brought the first settlements to the Atlantic seacoast. The eighteenth century newcomers had pushed those beyond the Alle-
ghenys. And in the nineteenth century, a continued flow of new
Americans had helped open the West and, at the same time, had
contributed to the development of urban life and the growth of
an industrial economy.

The nineteenth century migration to the United States had
begun almost immediately after the restoration of peace in 1815.
The first great, wave-like movement gathered strength steadily
through the 1830's and 1840's, sweeping displaced Irish, German,
and English peasants and laborers from the Old World to the
New. Falling off in magnitude after 1854, the volume of new
entries touched a low point in the mid-1860's. Then a second
wave, made up primarily of Germans, Scandinavians, and Englishmen, reached its peak in 1882. Before the century was over,
still a third wave was gathering momentum with a speed that was
hardly checked when the outbreak of world war in 1914 brought
it to a halt.

1

Throughout the process of settlement immigrants raised troublesome problems of adjustment. Largely peasants, they had not the background or skills to make their way in the economy of the New World. Whether they became farmers or laborers in industry, they found places for themselves only with difficulty. Bringing with them cultures markedly different from that of the United States, it was long before they could create for themselves the forms of expression that would give satisfaction to their lives here. They brought with them religious systems theretofore strange in America, and had to build churches and institutions from afresh. Unfamiliar with the forms of democracy, they learned only slowly how to act as voters and how to participate in the government.

On all these counts, they often found themselves in conflict with other Americans longer in the land. Sometimes the newcomers seemed to take jobs away from the earlier inhabitants. In the cities they drifted into slums, appeared frequently as the clients of charitable agencies, and seemed partially responsible for the increase in crime and intemperance. In a variety of ways they were a burden; the rising tax rate was often traced to their presence. Religious differences, under certain circumstances, aroused bitter hatreds on the part of Protestants toward Catholics and Jews. And as the newcomers developed their own forms for participating in politics, they came to be blamed for bossism and for the corruption associated with the city machines.

On the other hand, the immigrants made a decided contribution to American civilization. Their labor was an important factor in economic expansion. The foreign-born played a critical role in the growth of both American agriculture and American industry. Constant addition of new hands lent the whole productive system a fluid quality, supplied the workers to build both the communications network of canals, railroads, roads, telephone and telegraph lines, and the factories of the new industrial society. Immigration also endowed the social structure with fluidity. In an expanding culture it was difficult to preserve fixed forms, to establish rigid class distinctions that might limit opportunities. Diversity and mobility became characteristic features of life in the United States.

For a long time, such social gains, Americans reckoned, more than paid the cost entailed by the difficulties of absorbing the newcomers. The nation was young, and the expectation that it would expand indefinitely furnished a blanket guarantee that immigrants could continue to establish new homes here.

It was only as the century drew to a close that significant doubts were raised. In the 1890's the critics of immigration were no longer content to charge the newcomers with shortcomings in particular phases of the adjustment to life in America. The demand was also made with increasing vigor that the whole movement be curtailed or indeed brought at once to a halt.

Those who upheld the new exclusive doctrines justified the departure from traditional policy by two lines of argument. They feared that the era of unrestrained expansion had come to a close and that there would thereafter no longer be room for newcomers. They also argued that the character of immigration had changed and that the people then arriving were not as capable of adjusting to the life of the United States as their predecessors earlier in the century.

The demand for restriction touched off a bitter debate that continued for a quarter-century. The immediate objective of those who wished to alter the traditional policy was a literacy test that would bar adult immigrants incapable of reading, under the impression that the bulk of the newcomers would thereby be excluded. At last, in 1917, over the veto of President Wilson and under the influence of excited wartime passions, the measure was enacted. When the resumption of immigration after the restoration of peace showed the ineffectiveness of the literacy test, the restrictionists shifted their support to the quota system by which each nationality (except the Orientals who were altogether barred) became entitled to a fixed number of admissions each year. The various peoples of the world were to be ranked according to their presumed racial proportion to the ancestry of the peoples of the United States, and the size of the quota of each would be determined by its place in the rank. In 1921 and 1924, such provisions became part of American law and in addition the total entries annually were set at about 150,000. A century of migration then came to an end.

The men who made these decisions conceived they were acting in response to changing conditions over which they had little control. In their reasoning they assumed they were responding logically and dispassionately to the curtailment of expansion and to a change in the racial type of newcomers. Were they?

Or were other kinds of motives involved, less conscious and less rational, but nevertheless reflecting a profound change in the nature of the Americans and of the society in which they lived?

The selections which follow will attempt to illustrate the immigrant contribution to American civilization and the forces which brought the movement to a close.

·§ 1 ··

The Dimensions of the Problem

often found it difficult to judge the migration of Europeans to America because the numbers involved were of such a magnitude and the forces at work of such broad scope as to stagger imagination. In the century after 1820 some thirty-five million people were displaced by the collapse of an age-old social order in Europe and were transported to the new world. To understand the transition calls for a comprehension of at least five factors. The early colonial experience developed among Americans an attitude favorable to free immigration. The kinds of forces at work dislodging the Europeans after 1820 would explain who went and who remained behind. Fluctuations in volume from time to time would aid or hinder settlement. Changes in the source of the emigration would affect the nature of the cultural reaction on this side of the ocean. And the motives through which individuals undertook the migration would influence the way in which they accepted the life they discovered in the United States.

The Lessons of the Colonial Experience

In 1819, just as the first great wave of nineteenth century immigration began, a citizen of Philadelphia examined the colonial experience for the light it could throw on future policy. He concluded that immigration ought to be voluntary, not compulsory or induced, and that it ought to bring the newcomer into the United States on terms of complete equality with the old residents.[1]

Migration may be divided into that which is the effect of compulsion, and that which is voluntary.

Of the former there once were two kinds, both of them detrimental and disgraceful to us. In the infancy of our provincial establishments, when the mother country (as it was affectionately termed by us) exercised without opposition, a strong and sometimes injudicious domination over us, she thought proper, perhaps without much maternal feeling, to export a certain description of her convicts, to intermingle with her faithful and industrious colonists. . . .

This transmission of profligacy and vice was . . . soon discovered to be an evil. . . . The wretch whose criminal propensities and habits were little altered by the voyage, submitted with repugnance on his arrival, to the obligations of servitude and the necessity of labor; . . . efforts to escape were common, and often successful; and . . . neither the colonies nor the parent country, were ultimately benefited by the practice. . . .

At what time the second class of compelled migration, the importation of slaves, commenced, we are not exactly able to say. . . . That Pennsylvania . . . permitted this unnatural addition to its plain and sober population, cannot be doubted. In the year seventeen hundred, William Penn, addressing the monthly meeting of friends, expresses anxiety for the Christian instruction of the Negroes. In seventeen hundred and five, a special judicature was erected for their trial, and measures were taken indicating some alarm and apprehension, at the number and conduct of those who had been manumitted. . . .

---

[1] William Rawle, *An Address Delivered before the Philadelphia Society for Promoting Agriculture* (Philadelphia, 1819), 6-10, 16, 19-28.

The first species of forced migration ceased at the commencement of the war of the revolution. The second ought to have terminated in 1808. Congress then received the constitutional power to prohibit the importation of slaves, but there is too much reason to believe, that their laws have been frequently and shamefully evaded.

I turn from subjects on which the statesman cannot meditate without surprise, nor the philosopher without regret, to the more pleasing and more useful consideration of voluntary migration. . . .

There is an obvious distinction, between admitting and inviting emigration. A nation in a state of peace and safety, ought not to deny a hospitable reception to the fugitive from oppression or misfortune at home. This is the debt of humanity. But considerations of a different structure press upon us, when we examine whether it is now expedient, to take pains to invite the inhabitants of other nations to join our community. . . . From these considerations it seems to follow, that this country is not required to make any material alteration in its polity, for the purpose of alluring strangers to join it.

But without inviting, we are ready to receive, and hence arises the liberty to inquire and decide what description of foreigners it is desirable to receive, and to whom it would be useful, were it practicable, to render access difficult. It must be repeated that from this enumeration we are always to except those, whom tyranny and oppression of any kind, public grievances or personal afflictions, may give a claim on our humanity.

When we proceed on the principles assumed, to ascertain the value of the emigrant, we must consider the nature of his occupation. The first, and most useful class, consists of those who bring with them the moral and physical habits and capacity of productive labor. The husbandman, the grazier, the gardener; those who till the earth, or raise the quadruped, should be foremost in the ranks of hospitable reception.

Next to these we place the artist. Not the fabricator of the frivolous gratifications of luxury, but of solid and substantial articles, either of the first necessity, or conducive to the sober and wholesome comforts of middle life.

It is doubtful whether the third, that is, the commercial class form a desirable accession to us. Every reflecting mind must perceive that too large a portion of our citizens is already engaged in commerce for their own interests or those of the nation. . . . Commerce . . . adds nothing to the national stock; its office is to exchange the surplus product of one country, or part of a country, for that of another.

Every nation will always find a sufficient portion of its own citizens ready to engage in it, . . . and it may be laid down as an axiom that the sudden establishment of a large class of foreign merchants, in an agricultural society, will always prove injurious to it. A healthy industrious farmer is a more valuable accession to the political strength than a mercantile house with a large capital from a foreign country.

Considering then the first and certain portions of the second class, as the description of foreigners whom it is for the national interest to receive into our population, the next inquiry is, in what mode and to what extent their migration may be facilitated and encouraged.

In respect to the passage across the Atlantic, there is no doubt that the mercenary views of some owners of ships or their captains, operating on the general ignorance of peasantry in respect to naval matters, have produced sickness and death to many of their passengers. This is a cause of public interference as well on the part of the nation from which the migration takes place, as on the part of that to which it is directed. . . .

The next step in our inquiries is the process of receiving the emigrant into our community.

It may be reduced to four general heads: 1st. Personal safety and protection; 2d. Freedom of religious opinion; 3d. Acquisition of property; [and] 4th. Participation in political rights. . . .

Every stranger is entitled, at the moment of landing, to the protection of the law. The alien, the naturalized and the native citizen, are alike the objects of its care, and alike the subjects of its power. Human society presents its loveliest aspect when, as with us, no discrimination exists but that between virtue and vice; when the only rule, to which conformity is required, is that which levels all distinctions of rank, and all inequalities of property; presenting to the good the even surface of the lake, but exhibiting to the guilty the storm of the ocean. . . .

The freedom of religious opinions is now secured to all, provided their practice does not disturb the peace of the Commonwealth. The history of some of the eastern colonies was, for a time, disfigured by religious persecution; the more extraordinary as they fled from intolerance at home to practice it abroad. . . .

That the acquisition of property should be free, and the protection of it certain, is essential to our own interests. We cannot otherwise convert the emigrant into a useful citizen. But the feudal origin of our laws . . . has drawn a distinction, not perhaps well founded in the intrinsic character of property itself; and forming, in reference to the agricultural class, an unnecessary impediment to the animation and success of their labor. While personal property, to any extent, might be acquired and enjoyed, the ownership of an acre of land was in some colonies withheld from the alien. A long interval succeeded his arrival before he could cease to labor for the benefit of another, and attain that enviable condition, the value of which is less estimated here because it is so common, the possession of an independent freehold. Yet this is precisely the sort of property which it is for the interest of the nation to allow the agricultural emigrant immediately to acquire.

If the artist may open his workshop, fabricate and dispose of his wares; the merchant, with a small additional charge of tonnage duty, purchase and employ ships, or fill his stores with his own goods on their respective arrivals, surely the husbandman should not be compelled to remain years, before he is allowed to become the proprietor of the very subject which he migrates to obtain. . . . The old feudal principles, are now merely nominal. . . . The non-resident owner . . . tends to increase the national stock; and he will export the produce, or consume it here, on precisely the same principles as those which actuate the proper citizen; that is by ascertaining which will be most profitable to himself, and whatever is most profitable to him, will be so to the nation.

But the removal of legal obstacles, is not alone sufficient. When the state has no longer any lands of its own to grant, the facility of acquisition depends on the will of the private owners. Large tracts are often withheld for a long time, from erroneous fixtures of price. In truth it is the interest of such proprietors to dispose of their lands to actual settlers on moderate terms, and to grant freehold estates in preference to leases. And even with low prices, long credits must frequently be allowed, or the means of subsistence and cultivation will be exhausted, before the improvements have been carried so far as to form that attachment to the spot, which will render its cultivation most useful to the nation.

A mode of enabling the traveler to ascertain without difficulty, both the owner, and the price of the land, is desirable. Some sort of local register for this purpose might be convenient. We may perhaps account for so much of our fertile land in Pennsylvania being passed over by those who proceed annually in great numbers to the westward, from this want of information as to the owners.

It remains only to admit the stranger, thus liberally protected and secured in person, in property and in religion, to equal enjoyment of political privileges, and thus render him completely a citizen. A residence of five years, a good moral character and an attachment to the constitution of the United States, entitle him to this admission.

THE WESTWARD FLOW OF PEOPLES

Marcus Lee Hansen, the most distinguished recent historian of immigration, attempts in the selection which follows to outline the main elements in the nineteenth century movement.[2]

Though the thirteen American colonies owed their growth and prosperity largely to the recurrent additions of population from Europe, the century from 1815 to 1914 marked the most significant period in the foreign peopling of the United States. The years from the fall of Napoleon to the outbreak of the World War spanned exactly one hundred seasons of migration in which a great flood of humanity rolled westward across the Atlantic and swept over the waiting continent. To that flood every nation, every province, almost every neighborhood, contributed its stream. Beginning in Ireland and the valley of the Rhine, the fever of emigration extended toward the north and east, gripping the English midlands, the Scandinavian countries and the north of Germany, spread southward through the Baltic provinces, Poland and Austria into Italy and, before it finally ran its course, afflicted the Balkans and the Near East. Only France and Spain proved immune so far as the United States was concerned. It is clear that the cause of so vast an exodus was wider than race or nationality and deeper than legislation or politics. It was not the mania of a single generation, nor of ideas that prevailed for a mere decade or two. The cause was as universal as the movement itself.

---

[2] Reprinted by permission of the publishers from Marcus Lee Hansen, *Atlantic Migration 1607-1860* (Cambridge, Harvard University Press, 1940), 8-13.

Quite as marked as its universality was the periodicity of the movement. It advanced in a series of waves, each greater than the preceding. After a period of flow there followed an interval during which the current hesitated or seemed to reverse itself, only to be followed by a sudden rush of even greater volume. For an understanding of the underlying factors the ebb is no less important than the flow. The source of each gives the significant clue to a solution of the puzzling problem of cause.

Three distinct stages of migration marked the nineteenth century. The first, of special interest for the present volume, began in the 1830's and continued until 1860, reaching its crest in the years 1847-1854. To this exodus the adjective "Celtic" may properly be applied. The emigrants came from Ireland, the Highlands of Scotland and the mountains of Wales—regions where the language and blood were predominantly Celtic and where the land system grew directly out of the agrarian customs of the early tribes. Though many came also from the upper Rhine Valley of Germany and the adjoining districts, these newcomers may in a sense also be regarded as Celtic, for the first peoples to cultivate their hills and valleys had been Celts and, when the conquering German tribes occupied the villages and fields, they took over the divisions and the customs which in primitive times formed such an important feature of the agricultural routine. As elsewhere, the centuries had wrought changes; but the transformed rural economy had more in common with the prevailing system in Ireland than it did with the conditions in the purely German lands to the east. The Belgian and Dutch farmers who sought America also had inherited an economic organization descended from the Celts, and even the Norwegian pioneers of the time came from the districts along the coast to which the Celts had clung long after being expelled from the Continent as a whole.

The next great period of migration covered the decades between 1860 and 1890. Now Englishmen predominated numerically—yeoman farmers and their sons, and agricultural laborers—but the biggest Scandinavian emigration of all time took place within these years, and Germany was represented by Prussians and Saxons, and Austria by Bohemians. As before, the diverse national groups possessed a common denominator, and again that denominator was the system by which land was held. Its origin was Germanic, for the emigrants came from regions where the early Teutonic tribes had fixed the customs that governed agricultural practice and land succession. These Germanic regions stand out on the map with distinct prominence: England from north of the Thames to the Scotch Highlands, Germany east of the Elbe, Austria west of the mountain range that divides its territories, the plains of Denmark and southern Sweden, and the interior valleys of Norway. This exodus was Teutonic in blood, in institutions, and in the basis of its language, forming the most homogeneous of all the migrations to America.

In the third period, that from 1890 to 1914, two distinct geographic regions mingled their diverse currents in the New World. One was Mediterranean in origin, the other Slavic. The latter possessed the same unifying element of land as had the Celtic and Germanic newcomers. Finns, Latvians, Lithuanians, Poles, Karelians and Ukrainians —most of them were subjects of the Russian Empire and all of them enjoyed a common agricultural inheritance. But the Mediterranean peoples present a more complex spectacle, one impossible to simplify. Too many civilizations and cultures had flourished one after the other, too many populations had been swept away by wars and pestilence, to leave intact and distinct the original agrarian unity that may once have existed in Italy and Greece and the countries of the Near East. Commerce and politics remained as binding threads.

The magnitude of this century-long movement, involving the transplantation of thirty-five million people, becomes even more impressive when viewed at the moments of greatest intensity. In the first of the three periods fully half of the migrants arrived in America between 1847 and 1854; in the second, the decade from 1880 to 1890 accounted for a similar percentage; in the third, the years 1909 to 1914 brought an equal proportion. More than seventeen millions crossed the sea in the space of these twenty-five years! This horde of human beings overshadows all other population movements in peace or war. The barbarian invasions of the late Roman Empire and the transportation of American troops in the World War fade into numerical insignificance.

But along with the characteristic of size, attention should be given to the individual aspect and the unofficial nature of the movement in which these multifarious peoples participated. Mankind had moved before this time—as conquering tribes, as organized bands of settlers, as companies of traders. In such migrations the individual had been a cog in a mechanism greater than himself. A section of an established society, detached from its environment, was transferred to the edge of a wilderness or to the midst of a strange and perhaps hostile people. The adventurers brought with them the institutions to which they had been accustomed, and a trained group among them was charged with the sole duty of preserving and developing those institutions, no matter how alien they were to the new surroundings.

But the European of 1815 or 1914 left the Old World and settled in the New usually as an individual. A human atom wrenched itself from an old society and attached itself to a new. In his unfamiliar home he felt no conscious mission or urge to reproduce any but the most personal features of the life to which he was habituated. No patriotic considerations prompted him to remove to America; and whether the culture of his native country was forever restricted within its existing limits or spread to the ends of the earth did not concern him. To be sure, he brought with him the germs of institutions—a preference for the forms of association, worship and pleasure to which he had been accustomed. This sometimes meant that, if he were thrown with fellow immigrants upon his arrival and if the environment were not definitely hostile, they would reproduce a part of the homeland and found a "colony." But in time the chemistry of the new scene dissolved even such Old-World attachments.

With this mass exodus of individuals, governments had little or nothing to do, apart from legislative efforts early in the nineteenth century to ameliorate the sufferings of passengers who sought the cheapest mode of conveyance. Such attempts, inspired by humanitarian motives, sought merely to improve the conditions of transportation, leaving the transported to go when and where they wished. Not until the last years of the century did any European country adopt a policy of emigration or the United States a policy of immigration, and then the legislation came too late to change appreciably the nature of the movement. Though this outflow of people altered many of the fundamental relationships of the modern world, no nation interfered to direct it along a course profitable to itself.

This migration does not constitute an isolated story. It touches the stream of human history at many points. It forms part of the agrarian development which revolutionized the European countryside. It is related to the hygienic progress that doubled the population in the course of three generations. It helped to bring about a new era in Atlantic transportation by furnishing merchant vessels with one of their most reliable wares. Not least important was its contribution to the westward movement in the United States.

SOME INDICATIONS OF VOLUME

The sheer magnitude of the nineteenth century migrations is the basic starting point in the comprehension of its character. Fortunately in 1820 the federal government began to keep an account of aliens entering the ports of the United States. While these enumerations undoubtedly were not exact in the early years, they nevertheless give a good indication of the over-all changes in volume. In the charts reproduced, the statistics have been given graphic form. The first shows the fluctuations in number of total entrants; the second the distribution from decade to decade as among the various types of newcomers; and the Table shows the fluctuating importance in the total movement of the more important nationality groups.[3]

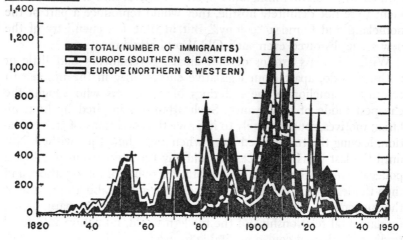

THOUSANDS

Legend:
- TOTAL (NUMBER OF IMMIGRANTS)
- EUROPE (SOUTHERN & EASTERN)
- EUROPE (NORTHERN & WESTERN)

---

[3] Reproduced by permission of the publishers from Francis J. Brown and Joseph S. Roucek, *One America* (Englewood Cliffs, N. J.: Prentice-Hall, Inc., 1946), 6, 7, 636.

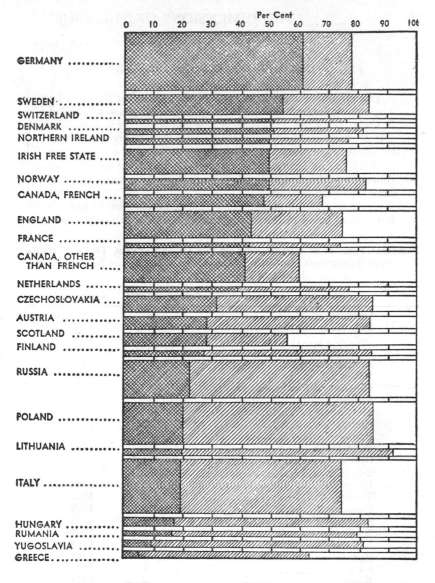

Per Cent

| | 0 | 10 | 20 | 30 | 40 | 50 | 60 | 70 | 80 | 90 | 100 |

GERMANY ....

SWEDEN ....
SWITZERLAND ....
DENMARK ....
NORTHERN IRELAND

IRISH FREE STATE .....

NORWAY ....
CANADA, FRENCH ....

ENGLAND ....

FRANCE ....

CANADA, OTHER
   THAN FRENCH .....

NETHERLANDS ....
CZECHOSLOVAKIA ....

AUSTRIA ....
SCOTLAND ....
FINLAND ....

RUSSIA ....

POLAND ....

LITHUANIA ....

ITALY ....

HUNGARY ....
RUMANIA ....
YUGOSLAVIA ....
GREECE..............

▨ 1900 or earlier   ▨ 1901–1914   ☐ Since 1914

15

Some Indications of Motive

The migration must be viewed in the mass. But it would be a mistake to forget it was made up of individuals, each motivated in undertaking the journey by hopes and fears of his own. The first illustration of such motivation comes from the reminiscences of Samuel Gompers, an English Jew who came as a young man in 1863 to the United States where he was long to lead the American Federation of Labor. The first selection below is taken from Gompers' memoirs.[4]

Other sentiments moved the Polish peasants who, in the letters quoted below in the second selection, told a protective asso-

Principal Sources of Immigration to the United States, Total Immigration Therefrom, and Peak Year, During 130 Years Beginning 1820 and Ending June 30, 1950

Country	Total 130 Years	Peak Year
Germany	6,248,529	1882
Italy	4,776,884	1907
Ireland	4,617,485	1851
Great Britain	4,386,692	1888
Austria-Hungary	4,172,104	1907
Russia	3,343,895	1913
Canada and Newfoundland	3,177,446	1924
Sweden	1,228,113	1882
Mexico	838,844	1924
Norway	814,955	1882
France	633,807	1851
West Indies	496,686	1824
Greece	439,581	1907
Poland	422,326	1921
China	398,882	1882
Turkey	362,034	1913
Denmark	340,418	1882
Switzerland	306,227	1883
Japan	279,146	1907
Netherlands	268,619	1882
Portugal	263,467	1921
Spain	173,021	1921
Belgium	170,374	1913
Romania	158,021	1921
South America	143,133	1924
Czechoslovakia	128,360	1921

[4] Quoted by permission of the publisher, from Samuel Gompers, *Seventy Years of Life and Labor* (New York, E. P. Dutton, 1925), I, 18, 19.

ciation in Warsaw what they expected from the New World. These letters were written shortly before the First World War.[5]

(A). Gompers

It became harder and harder to get along as our family increased and expenses grew. London seemed to offer no response to our efforts toward betterment. About this time we began to hear more and more about the United States. The great struggle against human slavery which was convulsing America was of vital interest to wage-earners who were everywhere struggling for industrial opportunity and freedom. My work in the cigar factory gave me a chance to hear the men discuss this issue. Youngster that I was, I was absorbed in listening to this talk and made my little contribution by singing with all the feeling in my little heart the popular songs, "The Slave Ship" and "To the West, To the West, To the Land of the Free."

It was typical of the feeling among English wage-earners of my boyhood days that the two most popular songs were "The Slave Ship" and "To the West." I learned both and sang them with a fervor in which all my feeling quivered and throbbed. I could throw back my head and sing:

> To the west, to the west, to the land of the free
> Where mighty Missouri rolls down to the sea;
> Where a man is a man if he's willing to toil,
> And the humblest may gather the fruits of the soil.
> Where children are blessings and he who hath most
> Has aid for his fortune and riches to boast.
> Where the young may exult and the aged may rest,
> Away, far away, to the land of the west.

The song expressed my feeling of America and my desire to go there rose with the ringing chorus:

> Away! far away, let us hope for the best
> And build up a home in the land of the west.

Years afterward Andrew Carnegie told me this song had inspired his father with a desire to come to America.

---

[5] W. I. Thomas and F. Znaniecki, *Polish Peasant in Europe and America* (Boston, The Gorham Press, 1920), V, 25-27.

(B). Polish Peasants

I have a very great wish to go to America. I want to leave my native country because we are 6 children and we have very little land, only about 6 morgs [acres] and some small farmbuildings, so that our whole farm is worth 1200 roubles at the highest. And my parents are still young; father is 48 and mother 42 years old. So it is difficult for us to live. Father got me married and gave me a dowry of 200 roubles, and I received 200 roubles with my wife. So father has given me my share and now I am alone with my wife. I have no children yet. Here in our country one must work plenty and wages are very small, just enough to live, so I would like to go in the name of our Lord God; perhaps I would earn more there. I will leave my wife with her father, i.e., my father-in-law. I have 200 roubles for the journey. I am a healthy boy 24 years old. I do not fear any work. [Asks advice.]

I have served as farm-steward 4 years in a single place. Formerly I served as farm-clerk in other places. I am a bachelor 32 years old. I am very economical and I have put aside nearly 150 roubles, which ought to suffice for my journey. I shall be obliged to leave my parents, who are already old, without any means to live. My father served for more than 30 years in a single place and during this time was never noticed for bad behavior. Even now he is sometimes employed, if his health allows him, to make a levy on a debtor, or as overseer of workmen. Nevertheless, he lives in a poor cabin rented from a peasant and if his children did not sustain him he would probably die from cold and hunger. . . . The life of a manor-official has become very difficult at the present time.

I am not afraid of any physical work. I understand builder's and carpenter's work perfectly. . . . It is true that agriculture is the most pleasant occupation to one who has grown up in it, but considering the slavery which binds one when serving and the solitude within four walls, as in a prison, which I have here, it is impossible to hold out any longer. And about marriage one does not even dare to think!

I want to go to America, but I have no means at all because I am poor and have nothing but the ten fingers of my hands, a wife and 9 children. I have no work at all, although I am strong and healthy and only 45 years old. I cannot earn for my family. I have been already in Dombrowa, Sosnowiec, Zawiercie and Lodz, wherever I could go, and nowhere could I earn well. And here they [the children] call for food and clothing and more or less education. I wish to work, not easily only but even hard, but what can I do? I will not go to steal and I have no work.

So I beg the Protective Association to accept me for this journey and not only me, but I should like to take with me two of my children, a boy 16 and a girl 18 years old. And I beg the Association. There are still other people who would readily go to America. They are also poor.

I live in the district of Zytomierz. I have no land of my own. I am not a craftsman and it is very difficult for me to live here. I rent some desiatinas [a desiatina is about 2 acres] of land from an estate-owner. I have to pay 15 roubles rent for each desiatina. . . . And now I cannot pay the rent to the proprietor; therefore I must soon leave this place. But where can I find a piece of bread with a wife and two children? Because of this difficulty, having no work, I address myself to the respected directors with the request that they advise and protect me in my journey to America. . . . I do not intend to go with my whole family because I have too little money. I am merely looking for work for some time.

2

The Old World Background

THE IMMIGRANTS
were not immediately transformed by coming to the New World
for they had already been molded and influenced by the environment of the Old. Their life in America would be subtly conditioned by the necessity of adjusting ways of behavior and habits
of thought shaped in an entirely different context to the necessities of the promised land. In understanding the character of that
adjustment, it is essential to know something about the circumstances under which the newcomers departed from the lands of
their birth.

The men and women who arrived in the United States in the
century after 1820 brought with them a varied heritage. Since
they came from every part of Europe, there were immense differences among them. They had in common, however, discontent
with their status at home and the desire to improve their conditions. Some entered upon their exodus under the pressure of a
great disaster, as did the Irish after 1846. Others were moved by
the force of more gradual economic and social changes. All were

influenced in their settlement by the memory of what had brought them to the New World.

It is necessary too to remember that between the New World and the Old there lay a great ocean and a long perilous voyage. The dangers and hardships of the crossing also influenced the adjustment of those who survived it.

THE FLIGHT FROM FAMINE IN IRELAND

The murderous famine that spread across Ireland for two years after 1846 found that unhappy island in an already weakened condition. Overpopulated, ruled by alien masters, and living on the margin of existence even in normal times, it was overwhelmed by the disaster. Hundreds of thousands died and millions lost their claims to the tiny plots of land which had been their sole hope for survival. Under these circumstances emigration became the only alternative to death. The commander of a relief ship sent from the United States with supplies received letters from a Catholic parish priest and a Landlord which described conditions in their districts.[1]

(A). *Father John O'Sullivan*

The people . . . had some little means, some resources up to the present. Those are all gone now for the purchase of food; and famine, with its invariable attendant, disease, is making fearful inroads on the unfortunate victims of both.

It is not long since I was called in to prepare a poor fellow, whose mother lay beside him dead two days, and he was burning with rage to think she should have come to such an end, as to die of starvation. I was called in a few days after to a miserable object, beside whom lay a child dead, for the twenty-four hours previous; two others lay beside her just expiring, and, horrible to relate, a famished cat got upon the bed, and was about to gnaw the corpse of the deceased infant, until I prevented it. At another time I accompanied a Captain of one of her Majesty's steamers, who was authorized to report upon

---

[1] Robert Bennet Forbes, *The Voyage of the Jamestown on Her Errand of Mercy* (Boston, 1847), cviii-cix, cxviii-cxx.

the state of the country; Captain Williams, a gentleman, a Christian, and a sailor. He, too, could scarcely believe the accounts of the famine, until I brought him to their hovels, and showed five or six lying in fever, huddled together on the damp, cold ground, with scarce a wisp of straw under them; and, in another cabin, four or five unfortunate beings just risen from fever, crouched over a small pot of seaweed boiling on the fire, that one of them had crawled to the shore, to collect for their dinner.

Such is the mortality, that I do not think I exaggerate, when I give it as my opinion *that a third of the population has been already carried away. Every morning four or five corpses are to be found on the street,* dead, the victims of famine and disease.

Flesh and blood cannot bear up against it. The frightful objects that pursue me during the day, actually haunt me in my dreams at night, and, I do sincerely assure you, that my first prayer in the morning, and my last at night, is, that God Almighty may speedily take me to himself, rather than be longer a witness to such an accumulation of misery.

(B). Lord Mountcashell

This extensive district, (comprising two poor law districts,) contains four parishes, with a population of about 9,800 souls. Some of this district belongs to me, but more than three-fourths to others. As a resident I witness the sufferings of all, and feel for the misery they are exposed to. I need not here detail the sacrifices and exertions I have made, to assist the overwhelming mass of pauperism around me, during the last inclement winter. The poor know it, and are grateful; but my resources are at an end, and most of my tenants unable to pay me anything they owe me, so that I can do little more for them, although their situation daily becomes more critical.

Out of this population of 9,800 souls, according to the most accurate computation made by the clergy of the parishes, there are at this moment over 7,000 in the greatest state of misery and distress, out of which 5,000 have not, unless given them, a single meal to provide for their wants tomorrow. This has arisen from the total failure of the potato, upon which the people solely relied, and also, the unproductive nature of the oat crop last harvest, in these districts. Herewith, I enclose a list of the names of 118 unfortunate beings, who died, either from actual starvation or its effects since the first day of January in this place. Some have been found in the fields dead, others have dropped by the side of the roads, but the great majority have expired in their miserable cabins from cold, hunger, and nakedness.

The typhus fever, the effect of last winter's sufferings, is now raging with fearful virulence, and hundreds are at this moment struggling here on the brink of eternity. In the town of Kilworth, not to speak of the rural parts, upwards of 50 families are lying on beds of straw, attacked by the contagion. Dysentery has also carried off several heads of families, leaving the younger branches in a state of complete destitution. I have only named 118 persons, who have died from famine or its effects, but let it not be supposed that I have been able to ascertain anything like the number who have been carried off, or dropped in the more distant or mountainous parts of this extensive district.

For some time past we have given up the practice of holding coroners inquests, in consequence of the coroner, (who resides in this district,) being unable to attend to the numerous calls made upon him. About three days ago, one inquest was, however, held, and the case may be considered not unworthy of notice. A poor man named James Carthy, in the last stage of weakness and exhaustion, having been given a small quantity of meal took it home, where his unfortunate wife was confined to her bed of straw by want and fever. Having made a fire, he attempted to cook some "stir-about," but his strength failed him; he grew giddy, and fell with his face into the fire. The poor wife perceiving that he could not extricate himself, in vain attempted to leave her bed to assist him. She had not the strength to move. She heard the crackling of the fire, and she saw her husband expire. The effect was too much for her mind and body to bear, and an hour afterwards she also was a corpse. The verdict given by the jury was, that both died from the effects of exhaustion, caused from starvation.

It would be an endless task, as well as a most painful one, to note down the details of individual suffering. Every day furnishes victims, and the living hear, and endeavor to drive from their minds, as soon as they can, the horrifying particulars that are related. I have this day, returning to my house, witnessed more than one person dying by the road side. I have been informed that there are dead bodies lying in our district at this moment unburied. I have known of bodies here remaining in the mountainous parts, neglected for more than eight days; and I am at this time giving food to a girl of twelve years old, the only remnant of a family, consisting of eight persons, her father and mother included, all of whom were alive one fortnight ago. Need I say more to rouse your sympathy?

MIGRATION OUT OF GERMANY

Emigration from Germany included not only fugitives from famine as in Ireland, but also farmers and artisans with enough funds to start life in the New World, and some political refugees. A writer in a British periodical describes the early stages of that movement.[2]

Germany is the only other country, besides Great Britain, from which emigration takes place on a great scale, and is likely to lead to important results. Since the year 1840, she has sent out annually 60,000 settlers, about our own average. In the present year [1846], the number is stated in the English papers at 80,000. It is very probable that this number will continue for the future, and even increase, as the predisposing causes are not occasional, but permanent, in the subsisting state of the country. The reasons which are all-powerful there, are not the same as actuate us. The results, too are very different. . . .

The chief emigration to America at present is from the Upper and Middle Rhine, the Grand Duchy of Baden, Würtemberg, the two Hesses, and Bavaria. In Bavaria especially, whole village communities sell their property for whatever they can get, and set out, with their clergyman at their head. "It is a lamentable sight," says a French writer, "when you are travelling in the spring or autumn on the Strasburg road, to see the long files of carts that meet you every mile, carrying the whole property of the poor wretches, who are about to cross the Atlantic on the faith of a lying prospectus. There they go slowly along; their miserable tumbrils—drawn by such starved, drooping beasts, that your only wonder is, how they can possibly hope to reach Havre alive—piled with the scanty boxes containing their few effects, and on the top of all, the women and children, the sick and bedridden, and all who are too exhausted with the journey to walk.

---

[2] *Chambers's Edinburgh Journal*, V (June 13, 1846), 387-389.

One might take it for a convoy of wounded, the relics of a battlefield, but for the rows of little white heads peeping from beneath the ragged hood." These are the emigrants from Bavaria and the Upper Rhine, who have no seaport nearer than Havre. Those from the north of Germany, who are comparatively few in number, sail mostly from Bremen. The number of these likewise is increasing. From 1832 to 1835 inclusive, 9,000 embarked every year from Bremen; from 1839 to 1842, the average number was 13,000; which increased to 19,000 in the year 1844

Society in Germany is so much more rudimentary than in England, that it is remarkable to see this same tendency exhibiting itself in the two nations. In Germany population is comparatively sparse, in Great Britain it is dense; in the one there is great wealth and profound poverty, in the other the extremes of property rarely exist; the one has a large and dominant town population, the other has fewer towns in proportion than any country in Europe; the one teems with political activity, in the other political activity is not, or at least has not yet taken to itself a practical presence and a name.

The dread of destitution is a motive to emigrate in Germany, as in England; but not a principal motive. This is clear from the fact that the emigration does not take place in those districts where there is most want, but exists equally where population is dense, and where it is thinly distributed. In Westphalia, for instance, a great number of small proprietors have lately sold their lands, and sailed for America —each of whom, it is reckoned, has taken with him at least thirty pounds' worth of goods and money. The Bavarians emigrate alike from the Rhine country, where population is thickly clustered together, and from the upland districts, where there are not eighty inhabitants to the square mile.

The one great cause of this almost national movement is the desire for absolute political and religious freedom; the absence of all restrictions upon the development of society; and the publication of opinions which cannot be realized at home. The great agitation in society, caused first by the French domination, and then by the convulsive rise against it, has never passed away. In that gigantic struggle, when everything rested on the popular soul, the bonds of privilege and class were tacitly abandoned, and could never thenceforth be reunited as before. The promises of having constitutional governments, at that time made by the sovereigns to their subjects, have been but partially fulfilled. There is nothing that can be called oppression on the part of the government; . . . but there are many restrictions, and the young, the restless, and the imaginative thirst for their ideal freedom, and many of them seek for the realization of Utopia in America.

Complete religious equality is a still more powerful want in a country where Catholics and Protestants are so nearly balanced, and where the state of parties is such, that the minority in faith, though nominally equal in law, must always live under the cold shade of an alien creed. This of itself has urged many across the Atlantic. . . .

Another motive has been the great success of some of the earlier settlers. The Moravians and Shakers, who have emigrated from Germany, have worked wonders in some parts. In 1815, the Separatists, another religious body, sometimes called Rappists, from their head, M. Rapp, sailed from Würtemberg with a capital only of £1,200, and formed a settlement on the Ohio. At the present time, the real property in land belonging to the society is reckoned at £340,000, exclusive of personal property, and a large sum of money in the funds. The success of the colony of Zoar has been equally striking. It was founded twenty years ago by a few families with a scanty capital, and now possesses 40,000 acres of land, a disposable capital of £100,000 and an immense quantity of machinery and stock, foundries, tan-pits, and mills in abundance. This extraordinary affluence is because these two colonies were founded on the principle of a community of property, and have been throughout under a strict religious government. But the present emigrants forget this; and looking only at the prosperity achieved, they think that as the Moravians and Rappists have succeeded, they must succeed to the same extent, without either the same capital or self-denial.

The Disruption of the East European Economy

Large-scale emigration from central and eastern Europe began toward the end of the nineteenth century. The Germanic and Slavic peoples who moved from this part of the continent sought economic improvement and greater freedom as had those who had earlier moved out of the West. This migration was everywhere accompanied by a disruption of traditional peasant communities. A distinguished American social scientist, who had the

*opportunity to study and to observe these developments in east-
ern Europe, explains the connection between emigration and the
collapse of the peasant economy.*[3]

The old peasant economy was almost self-sufficing. House industry
eked out the farm production. The earthenware for cooking and the
pretty flowered crockery, the wooden utensils for stall and house, the
farm tools—fork and rake and plough,—the products of spinning-
wheel and loom and needle and dye-pot, all were homemade, and
few were the articles that must be bought for money.

This old self-sufficient household economy was, however, gradually
broken in upon from many sides as industry developed at the expense
of agriculture. Even in places where no industry arose the effect of
that which was growing up in other countries, afar or nearby, made
itself powerfully felt. As a money economy, with purchase and sale,
extended, the dependence on household production diminished.
Money was needed for taxes. The obvious economy of cheap factory
textiles, the superiority of iron pots to earthen ones, indeed the temptation of novel wares of various kinds at low prices, all made new
demands for money. With these changes went a rise in standards of
living; new goods were available and new desires were contagious.

At the same time with this rise in demands, growth of population
without growth of industry made an increased pressure on the
land. . . .

The old peasant economy had represented a fairly stable economic
equilibrium. Population was kept more or less at a level by it, since
only one son could take his father's place, and consequently it was
difficult for more than one to establish a family, unless, indeed, he
went away to seek his fortune. It was the expectation that everything
should go on as it had done. That is the essence of custom, and the
peasant world is the world of custom.

The results of the breakup of the old system of land holding were
often disastrous. The peasant being free to divide his land and feeling
that his children all had equal claims, cut up land which was only
sufficient to support one household among a number of descendants.
The landholder unable to support himself from his own plot sought
to eke out his living by working for wages in a population where few

---

[3] Emily Green Balch, *Our Slavic Fellow Citizens* (New York, 1910), 47-50.

could afford to hire labor. In some districts debts, contracted under circumstances which put the borrower at the mercy of a creditor, worked havoc.

Thus the peasant with mortgage payments which he could not meet or with children for whom he could not provide an adequate patrimony, saw himself face to face with an intolerable decline of social status for himself or for his children; namely, reduction to the position of a propertyless day laborer. This is the sting which induces many a man among the Slovaks, the Poles, the Ruthenians, to fare overseas or to send out his son to the new land from which men come back with savings.

In some cases the countryside had never supported its population; there had always been an exodus, permanent or seasonal, of some of the men and boys, as for instance in some Slovak counties. As the dislocation of the old economy became more serious, and as mobility of population increased, there was further overflow,—to Germany for the summer farm work, to the cities, to less closely settled districts, (e.g. to Southern Hungary), to Russia, to Brazil, to the United States. Quicker transportation, and above all, knowledge of the facts, opened the way across the sea, and all the requisites for a heavy emigration movement were present. Sometimes the head of a family goes to retrieve the family fortunes, sometimes he sends the most promising son. Or a brother goes hoping to earn enough to pay off the inheritance of his co-heirs and buy the sole right to the land which cannot support more than one family.

While the grounds of emigration are in the main economic, it is a mistake to suppose that poverty is its cause in the sense that the greater the poverty of a man or district, the greater the impulse to emigration. Poverty, especially a settled poverty to which people have adjusted themselves, and which finds expression in a low standard of living and perhaps in physical deterioration, is not an initiating force. Rather, it means stagnation and lack of any margin of energy for new undertakings.

It is when the habitual balance of family budgets is disturbed that a sense of poverty incites to emigration. The maladjustment may be due to a cutting down of income by some disaster, or it may be due to an increase of wants. The result is the same. And this awakening of new wants is a characteristic of our time, affecting one backward and lethargic region after another. It is extremely contagious, and the news that it is anywhere possible to earn more and to live better calls slumbering forces of energy and unrest into sudden life. Emigration will then result if there is any opening which promises improved circumstances.

THE SOURCE OF ITALIAN LABOR

Migration out of Italy began to assume large proportions in the last decade of the nineteenth century at about the same time as the movement out of eastern Europe. The causes were identical, except that the poverty of the soil and overpopulation made the situation of the Italian peasant even more difficult than that of his Slavic counterpart. A thoughtful American writer described the process while it was at its height.[4]

Profound dissimilarities make sweeping generalities about Italians impossible. Yet in one point every province is alike. The poor everywhere are all crushed by heavy taxes for maintenance of the large army and navy which make Italy a first-class European power. More serious than the exactions of the tax-gatherer is the long-continued agricultural depression that has reduced a large part of the South to poverty. Nor is this all. The peasant's lot is made infinitely worse by an "Irish question" that is the blight of nearly all southern Italy, Sicily, and Sardinia. There are the same huge entailed estates and the same lazy, reactionary, and absentee landlords. Throughout large sections great tracts of fertile soil support only one shepherd or one farmer per square mile. To these idle lands must be added the vast stretches of barren mountains, and the malaria-infested fifth of the entire surface of the peninsula. No new territory has been added to the kingdom, while the population has been increasing within twenty years from twenty-eight and one-half to thirty-two and one-half millions—an average density for the whole country of 301 per square mile. And the excess of births over deaths amounts to nearly 350,000 a year—the population of a province. Through whole districts in this overcrowded land Italians have to choose between emigration and starvation.

A definite economic cause drives the poor *Meridionale* [southerner]

---

[4] John Foster Carr, "The Coming of the Italian," *Outlook*, LXXXII (1906), 420-422, 426-428.

from his home, and a definite economic cause and not a vague migratory instinct brings him to America. He comes because the country has the most urgent need of unskilled labor. This need largely shapes the character of our Italian immigration, and offers immediate work to most of the newcomers. Almost eighty per cent of them are males; over eighty per cent are between the ages of fourteen and forty-five; over eighty per cent are from the southern provinces, and nearly the same percentage are unskilled laborers, who include a large majority of the illiterates. These categories overlap, so that the bulk of our Italian immigration is composed of ignorant, able-bodied laborers from the South. They come by the hundred thousand, yet their great numbers are quickly absorbed without disturbing either the public peace or the labor market. In spite of the enormous immigration of Italians in 1903 and 1904, the last issue of the United States Labor Bulletin shows that the average daily wage of the laborer in the North Atlantic States—the "congested" district at the very gates of Ellis Island—had increased within the year from $1.33 to $1.39. And 1904 was not a particularly prosperous year. Equally significant, in view of the unprecedented Italian immigration of the first six months of this year, is the announcement in the last number of the Bulletin of the New York State Department of Labor that the improvement in the conditions of employment has been so marked, and "the proportion of idle wage-earners has diminished so rapidly, that the second quarter of 1905 surpasses that of 1902, the record year."

The demand of the East for labor is first heard by the new arrival who needs to look for work, and probably a majority of Italian *braccianti* [laborers] never go more than a hundred and fifty miles away from New York. Immediate work and high wages, and not a love for the tenement, create our "Little Italies." The great enterprises in progress in and about the city, the subways, tunnels, water-works, railroad construction, as well as the ordinary building operations, call for a vast army of laborers. . . .

This same inborn conservatism that risks nothing makes of southern Italians the most mobile supply of labor that this country has ever known. Migratory laborers, who come here to work during eight or nine months of the year, and return between October and December, are a very large part of the annual immigration. They form a stream of workers that ebbs and flows from Italy to America in instant response to demand; and yet the significance of the movement has gone almost entirely unnoticed. More than 98,000 Italians—laborers and others, but chiefly laborers—went back to Italy in 1903. In 1904, owing to a temporary lull in our prosperity and the general business uncertainty during a Presidential campaign, the demand slackened. The common laborer, who ordinarily pays a padrone [boss or contractor] fifty cents as a fee for employment, was offering as high as five dollars for a job in the summer of 1904. In the end, more than 134,000 Italians returned to Italy within the year, and we were saved the problem of an army of unemployed. . . .

So far from being a scum of Italy's paupers and criminals, our Italian immigrants are the very flower of her peasantry. They bring healthy bodies and a prodigious will to work. They have an intense love for their fatherland, and a fondness for old customs; and both are deepened by the hostility they meet and the gloom of the tenements that they are forced to inhabit. The sunshine, the simplicity, the happiness of the old outdoor ways are gone, and often you will hear the words, "Non c'é piacere nella vita"—there is no pleasure in life here. But yet they come, driven from a land of starvation to a land of plenty. Each year about one-third of the great host of industrial recruits from Italy, breaking up as it lands into little groups of twos and threes, and invading the tenements almost unnoticed, settles in the different colonies of New York. This is a mighty, silent influence for the preservation of the Italian spirit and tradition.

The Perils of the Crossing

For a long time, the difficulties of the voyage between Europe and America exerted a deep influence upon all immigrants. Death claimed many who left their homes with hope in their hearts; and fear of the dangers kept others at home. But even those who came safely off the ships for years thereafter were marked by the trying experience.

As if the perils of the ocean and the weather were not enough, the passengers were also at the mercy of greedy captains and shipowners. In the early years, when many immigrants were redemptioners who had signed contracts as servants, they were sub-

ject to ruthless exploitation, as Andreas Geyer, Jr. discovered in 1805.[5] But sixty years later, the New York State Commissioners of Emigration revealed, even free passengers who paid their own way were helpless.[6]

Toward the end of the nineteenth century, the steamship shortened the length of the journey and mitigated some of its perils. But Robert Louis Stevenson found that immigration was still a difficult process.[7]

(A). Geyer

I went to visit those unfortunate people, and in truth they may be called unfortunate. And I must confess I have seen a number of vessels at Philadelphia with redemptioners, but never did I see such a set of miserable beings in my life. Death, to make use of the expression, appeared to be staring them in the face. The complaints were numerous which they made against the captain respecting the bad treatment they received from him on and during the passage. . . .

They left Hamburg some time in November last, and arrived at Tönningen, where lay the ship *General Wayne*, John Conklin, Master, bound for New York, with whom they entered into a certain agreement, on the condition that he, the said Conklin, would take them to New York, that during the passage they should be allowed a certain quantity of bread, meat, peas, fish, vinegar, butter, potatoes, tobacco, etc., as also a dram in the morning, as will appear by a reference to the agreement itself, each passenger having one.

About fourteen days after they left Tönningen they put into an English port near Portsmouth, where they remained about four weeks. . . . During that time a British recruiting officer came on board the ship, when the captain informed them that they now had an opportunity of enlisting, that those who so chose to do might, as the recruiting officer was on board the ship. Ten men consented, and entered their names, giving to the other passengers their reasons for so

---

[5] Andreas Geyer, Jr., "Letter to the German Society of Philadelphia," quoted in Friedrich Kapp, *Immigration and the Commissioners of Immigration* (New York, 1870), 183-185.

[6] Quoted in Kapp, *Immigration and the Commissioners of Immigration*, 189-192.

[7] Robert Louis Stevenson, *The Amateur Emigrant* (Chicago, 1895), 39-42, 44-48, 50-55.

doing, namely, that, having been already put on allowance by the
captain, they were apprehensive that, should they stay on board the
ship, they should be starved before they arrived in America. Amongst
those that enlisted was a man who had a wife and child on board the
ship. . . . Eight days after they had thus entered their names they
were taken from the ship by the recruiting officer, although some of
them wished to withdraw their names, but to no effect; go they must.
The woman and her child are now at Amboy, lamenting the loss of
the husband and father.

On the last day of their remaining in this British port, the same
recruiting officer came the third time on board the ship, when the
mate called four or five of the passengers by name, and told them, in
the presence of the captain, they must be soldiers and go with the
officer. They replied they had no intention of being soldiers, they
wished to go to America. Whereupon the captain and mate seized
one of them by name Samuel Vogel, and threw him into the boat
belonging to the recruiting officer, which was alongside of the ship.
However, Vogel got back again into the ship, went below, and hid
himself, but was again compelled to come forward with his clothes,
when the recruiting officer, observing him weep, declared he would
not have him, and left the ship, mentioning that he should not have
come on board had not the captain, the day before, pressed him so to
do. The captain was highly dissatisfied with these men for refusing to
go, and declared that they should not have anything to eat on board
the ship, that they might starve, and ordered one of them to be
flogged for refusing, which was performed, too, in a cruel manner.
. . . The whole of the passengers, when at this British port, complained to the captain that the treatment they received was not such
as was agreed to between them at Tönningen. He replied they were
not then in Tönningen, neither were they in America, but in England.

They then set sail, and after fourteen days had elapsed the captain
informed them that they would get nothing to eat except bread and
meat. After this each person received two biscuits, one pint of water,
and the eighth part of a pound of meat per day. This regulation continued for two or three weeks, when they one and all declared they
could not any longer exist on the small allowance they received; that
they must, without doubt, perish. The hunger and thirst being at this
time so great, and the children continually crying out for bread and
drink, some of the men, resolved, at all events to procure bread, broke

open the apartment wherein it was kept, and took some. This was discovered by the captain, as were also those who did the same, when each of them was ordered to, and actually did, receive, after being first tied, a number of lashes on their bare backs well laid on. The whole of the passengers were also punished for this offence. The men received no bread, the women but one biscuit.

This continued for nine days, when the men were again allowed one biscuit per day; however, the captain would at least make or proclaim a fast day. In this situation their condition became dreadful, so much so that five and twenty men, women and children actually perished for the want of the common necessities of life, in short, for the want of bread. The latter were ten in number, all at the time at the breasts of their mothers. The hunger was so great on board that all the bones about the ship were hunted up by them, pounded with a hammer and eaten; and what is more lamentable, some of deceased persons, not many hours before their death, crawled on their hands and feet to the captain, and begged him, for God's sake, to give them a mouthful of bread or a drop of water to keep them from perishing. But their supplications were in vain; he most obstinately refused, and thus did they perish. The cry of the children for bread was, as I am informed, so great that it would be impossible for man to describe it.

(B) New York State Commissioners of Emigration

The Leibnitz, originally the Van Couver, is a large and fine vessel, built at Boston for the China trade, and formerly plying between that port and China. She sold some years ago to the house of Robert M. Sloman, and has since sailed under her present name.

We were informed that her last trip was her second with emigrants on board. Last summer, she went to Quebec with about seven hundred passengers, of whom she lost only a few on her passage; this time, she left Hamburg, November 2, 1867, Capt. H. F. Bornhold, lay at Cuxhaven, on account of head-winds, until the 11th, whereupon she took the southern course to New York. She went by the way of Madeira, down to the Tropics, 20th degree, and arrived in the Lower Bay on January 11, 1868, after a passage of 61 days, or rather 70 days—at least, as far as the passengers are concerned, who were confined to the densely crowded steerage for that length of time.

The heat, for the period that they were in the lower latitudes, very often reached 24 degrees of Réaumur, or 94 degrees of Fahrenheit. Her passengers 544 in all—of whom 395 were adults, 103 children, and 46 infants—came principally from Mecklenburg, and proposed to settle as farmers and laborers in Illinois and Wisconsin; besides them, there were about 40 Prussians from Pomerania and Posen, and a few Saxons and Thuringians. . . .

Of these 544 German passengers, 105 died on the voyage, and three in port, making in all 108 deaths—leaving 436 surviving.

The first death occurred on November 25th. On some days, as for instance on December 1, nine passengers died, and on December 17, eight. The sickness did not abate until toward the end of December, and no new cases happened when the ship had again reached the northern latitudes. Five children were born. During the voyage some families had died out entirely; of others, the fathers or mothers are gone; here, a husband had left a poor widow, with small children; and there, a husband had lost his wife. We spoke to some little boys and girls, who, when asked where were their parents, pointed to the ocean with sobs and tears, and cried, *"Down there!"*

Prior to our arrival on board, the ship had been cleansed and fumigated several times, but not sufficiently so to remove the dirt, which, in some places, covered the walls. Mr. Frederick Kassner, our able and experienced Boarding Officer, reports that he found the ship and the passengers in a most filthy condition, and that when boarding the *Leibnitz* he hardly discovered a clean spot on the ladder, or on the ropes, where he could put his hands and feet. He does not remember to have seen anything like it within the last five years. . . .

As to the interior of the vessel, the upper steerage is high and wide. All the spars, beams, and planks which were used for the construction of temporary berths had been removed. Except through two hatchways and two very small ventilators, it had no ventilation, and not a single window or bull's-eye was open during the voyage. In general, however, it was not worse than the average of the steerages of other emigrant ships; but the lower steerage, the so-called orlop-deck, is a perfect pesthole, calculated to kill the healthiest man. It had been made a temporary room for the voyage by laying a tier of planks over the lower beams of the vessel, and they were so supported that they shook when walking on them. The little light this orlop-deck received came through one of the hatchways of the upper-deck. Although the latter was open when we were on board, and although the ship was lying in the open sea, free from all sides, it was impossible to see anything at a distance of two or three feet. On our enquiring how this hole had been lighted during the voyage, we were told that some lanterns had been up there, but on account of the foulness of the air, they could scarcely burn. It had, of course, much less than the upper-deck draft or ventilation, and was immediately over the keel, where the bilge-water collects, and adjoining part of the cargo, which consisted of wool and hides. And in this place about 120 passengers were crowded for 70 days, and for a greater part of the voyage in a tropical heat, with scanty rations and a very inadequate supply of water, and worse than all, suffering from the miasma below, above, and beside them, which of itself must create fever and pestilence!

The captain himself stated to us that the passengers refused to carry the excrements on the deck, and that "the urine and ordure of the upper-steerage flowed down to the lower." As the main-deck was very difficult of access from the orlop-deck, the inmates of the latter often failed to go on deck even to attend to the calls of nature. There were only six water-closets for the accommodation of all the passengers. They have been cleansed, of course; but the smell that emanated from them was still very intense, and corroborates the statement of the above-named officers—that they must have been in an extraordinary frightful condition.

When the ship *Lord Brougham*, belonging to the same line, arrived on the 6th of December last, from Hamburg, and had lost 75 out of 383 passengers, we personally examined the majority of the survivors, and found them not only healthy and in good spirits, but, at the same time, in every respect satisfied with the treatment they had received on board.

The present case, however, is different. There was not a single emigrant who did not complain of the captain, as well as of the short allowance of provisions and water on board. As we know, from a long experience, that the passengers of emigrant ships, with a very few exceptions, are in the habit of claiming more than they are entitled to, we are far from putting implicit faith in all their statements. There is as much falsehood and exaggeration among this class of people as among any other body of uneducated men. We have, therefore, taken their complaints with due allowance, and report only so much thereof as we believe to be well founded.

All the passengers concur in the complaint that their provisions were short, partly rotten, and that, especially, the supply of water was insufficient, until they were approaching port. We examined the provisions on board, and found that the water was clear and pure. If the whole supply during the voyage was such as the samples handed to us, there was no reason to complain as to quality. But, in quantity, the complaint of the passengers are too well founded; for they unanimously state, and are not effectually contradicted by the captain, that they never received more than half a pint of drinkable water per day, while by the laws of the United States they were entitled to receive three quarts. Some of the biscuit handed to us were rotten and old, and hardly eatable; other pieces were better. We ordered the steward to open a cask of corned-beef and found it of ordinary good quality. The butter, however, was rancid. Once a week herrings were cooked instead of meat. The beans and sauerkraut were often badly cooked, and, in spite of hunger, thrown overboard.

The treatment of the passengers was heartless in the extreme. The sick passengers received the same food with the healthy, and high prices were exacted for all extras and comforts. A regular traffic in wine, beer, and liquors was carried on between the passengers on the one side and the steward and crew on the other. . . .

When the first deaths occurred, the corpses were often suffered to remain in the steerage for full twenty-four hours. In some cases the bodies were covered with vermin before they were removed.

There was no physician on board. Although we found a large medicine-chest, it was not large enough for the many cases of sickness, and was, in fact, emptied after the first two weeks of the voyage.

The captain seems to have been sadly deficient in energy and authority in matters of moment, while he punished severely small offences; as, for instance, he handcuffed a passenger for the use of insulting words; but he did not enforce the plainest rules for the health and welfare of his passengers. Instead of compelling them, from the first, to come on deck and remove the dirt, he allowed them to remain below, and to perish among their own excrements. Of the whole crew, the cook alone fell sick and died, as he slept in the steerage. Three passenger girls who were employed in the kitchen, and lived on deck, enjoyed excellent health, during the whole voyage.

The physicians . . . to whose report we refer for particulars, most positively declare that it was not the Asiatic cholera, but intestinal and stomach catarrh . . . more or less severe, and contagious typhus, which killed the passengers. From what we saw and learned from the passengers, we likewise arrive at the conclusion that the shocking mortality on board the *Leibnitz* arose from want of good ventilation, cleanliness, suitable medical care, sufficient water, and wholesome food.

(C). *Stevenson*

Down one flight of stairs there was a comparatively large open space, the center occupied by a hatchway, which made a convenient seat for about twenty persons, while barrels, coils of rope, and the carpenter's bench afforded perches for perhaps as many more. The canteen, or steerage bar, was on one side of the stair; on the other, a no less attractive spot, the cabin of the indefatigable interpreter. I have seen people packed into this space like herrings in a barrel, and many merry evenings prolonged there until five bells, when the lights were ruthlessly extinguished and all must go to roost.

It had been rumored since Friday that there was a fiddler aboard, who lay sick and unmelodious in Steerage No. 1; and on the Monday forenoon, as I came down the companion, I was saluted by something in Strathspey time. A white-faced Orpheus was cheerily playing to an audience of white-faced women. It was as much as he could do to play, and some of his hearers were scarce able to sit; yet they had crawled from their bunks at the first experimental flourish, and found better than medicine in the music. Some of the heaviest heads began to nod in time, and a degree of animation looked from some of the palest eyes. . . . This fellow scraped away; and the world was positively a better place for all who heard him. We have yet to understand the economical value of these mere accomplishments. I told the fiddler he was a happy man, carrying happiness about with him in his fiddle-case, and he seemed alive to the fact. . . .

That night I was summoned by *Merrily Danced the Quaker's Wife* into the companion of Steerage No. 4 and 5. This was, properly speaking, but a strip across a deck-house, lit by a sickly lantern which swung to and fro with the motion of the ship. Through the open slide-door we had a glimpse of a grey night sea, with patches of phosphorescent foam flying, swift as birds, into the wake, and the horizon

rising and falling as the vessel rolled to the wind. In the center the
companion ladder plumped down sheerly like an open pit. Below, on
the first landing, and lighted by another lamp, lads and lasses danced,
not more than three at a time for lack of space, in jigs and reels and
hornpipes. Above, on either side, there was a recess railed with iron,
perhaps two feet wide and four long, which stood for orchestra and
seats of honor. In the one balcony, five slatternly Irish lasses sat
woven in a comely group. In the other was posted Orpheus, his body,
which was convulsively in motion, forming an odd contrast to his
somnolent, imperturbable Scots face. His brother, a dark man with a
vehement, interested countenance, who made a god of the fiddler,
sat by with open mouth, drinking in the general admiration and
throwing out remarks to kindle it. . . .

The dancing was but feebly carried on. The space was almost im-
practicably small; and the Irish wenches combined the extreme of
bashfulness about this innocent display with a surprising impudence
and roughness of address. Most often, either the fiddle lifted up its
voice unheeded, or only a couple of lads would be footing it and
snapping fingers on the landing. And such was the eagerness of the
brother to display all the acquirements of his idol, and such the
sleepy indifference of the performer, that the tune would as often as
not be changed and the hornpipe expire into a ballad before the
dancers had cut half a dozen shuffles.

In the meantime, however, the audience had been growing more
and more numerous every moment; there was hardly standing-room
around the top of the companion; and the strange instinct of the race
moved some of the newcomers to close both the doors, so that the
atmosphere grew insupportable. It was a good place, as the saying is,
to leave.

The wind hauled ahead with a head sea. By ten at night heavy
sprays were flying and drumming over the forecastle; the companion
of Steerage No. 1 had to be closed, and the door of communication
through the second cabin thrown open. Either from the convenience
of the opportunity, or because we had already a number of acquaintances in that part of the ship, Mr. Jones and I paid it a late visit.

Steerage No. 1 is shaped like an isosceles triangle, the sides opposite the equal angles bulging outward with the contour of the ship.
It is lined with eight pens of sixteen bunks apiece, four bunks below
and four above on either side. At night the place is lit with two lan-

terns, one to each table. As the steamer beat on her way among the rough billows, the light passed through violent phases of change, and was thrown to and fro and up and down with startling swiftness. You were tempted to wonder, as you looked, how so thin a glimmer could control and disperse such solid blackness. When Jones and I entered we found a little company of our acquaintances seated together at the triangular foremost table. A more forlorn party, in more dismal circumstances, it would be hard to imagine. The motion here in the ship's nose was very violent; the uproar of the sea often overpoweringly loud. The yellow flicker of the lantern spun round and round and tossed the shadows in masses. The air was hot, but it struck a chill from its foetor. From all round in the dark bunks, the scarcely human noises of the sick joined in a kind of farmyard chorus. In the midst, these five friends of mine were keeping up what heart they could in company. Singing was their refuge from discomfortable thoughts and sensations. One piped, in feeble tones, *Oh Why Left I My Hame?* which seems a pertinent question in the circumstances. Another, from the invisible horrors of a pen where he lay dog-sick upon the upper shelf, found courage, in a blink of his sufferings, to give us several verses of the *Death of Nelson*; and it was odd and eerie to hear the chorus breathe feebly from all sorts of dark corners, and "this day has done his dooty" rise and fall and be taken up again in this dim inferno, to an accompaniment of plunging, hollow-sounding bows and the rattling spray-showers overhead. . . .

I heard a man run wild with terror beseeching his friend for encouragement. "The ship's going down!" he cried with a thrill of agony. "The ship's going down!" he repeated, now in a blank whisper, now with his voice rising towards a sob; and his friend might reassure him, reason with him, joke at him—all was in vain, and the old cry came back, "The ship's going down!" There was something panicky and catching in the emotion of his tones; and I saw in a clear flash what an involved and hideous tragedy was a disaster to an emigrant ship. If this whole parishful of people came no more to land, into how many houses would the newspaper carry woe, and what a great part of the web of our corporate human life would be rent across for ever!

The next morning when I came on deck I found a new world indeed. The wind was fair; the sun mounted into a cloudless heaven; through great dark blue seas the ship cut a swathe of curded foam.

The horizon was dotted all day with companionable sails, and the sun shone pleasantly on the long, heaving deck. . . .

This Tuesday morning we were all delighted with the change of weather, and in the highest possible spirits. We got in a cluster like bees, sitting between each other's feet under lee of the deck-houses. Stories and laughter went around. The children climbed about the shrouds. White faces appeared for the first time, and began to take on color from the wind. I was kept hard at work making cigarettes for one amateur after another, and my less than moderate skill was heartily admired. Lastly, down sat the fiddler in our midst and began to discourse his reels, and jigs, and ballads, with now and then a voice or two to take up the air and throw in the interest of human speech.

Through this merry and good-hearted scene there came three cabin passengers, a gentleman and two young ladies, picking their way with little gracious titters of indulgence and a Lady-Bountiful air about nothing, which galled me to the quick. I have little of the radical in social questions, and have always nourished an idea that one person was as good as another. But I began to be troubled by this episode. It was astonishing what insults these people managed to convey by their presence. They seemed to throw their clothes in our faces. Their eyes searched us all over for tatters and incongruities. A laugh was ready at their lips; but they were too well-mannered to indulge it in our hearing. Wait a bit, till they were all back in the saloon, and then hear how wittily they would depict the manners of the steerage. We were in truth very innocently, cheerfully, and sensibly engaged, and there was no shadow of excuse for the swaying elegant superiority with which these damsels passed among us, or for the stiff and waggish glances of their squire. Not a word was said; only when they were gone Mackay sullenly damned their impudence under his breath; but we were all conscious of an icy influence and a dead break in the course of our enjoyment.

3

The Economic Adjustment

THE EXPERIENCE of the immigrants in becoming a part of the society of the New World had a double significance. It influenced markedly the whole course of American development and it became a subject of controversy as the movement to restrict immigration provoked attempts to evaluate the effects upon the United States of the traditional liberal policy.

The controversy ranged over every aspect of American life, because everywhere there were traces of the influence of the immigrants. But the economic aspects of the adjustment particularly aroused discussion. Had the American economy profited by free immigration or had the result been simply an unhealthy rapid industrialization achieved by depressing the standards of the working class? Had the host of foreign-born laborers caused the evils of urban life? Had the great mass of newcomers really served to increase the population of the United States, or had they simply crowded out the native-born stock?

During the great debate over immigration restriction it was difficult to pull the facts apart from the prejudices with which they were handled. In retrospect now it may be easier. The selections which follow supply the material for a judgment of some of the consequences of immigration for the society of the United States.

THE IMMIGRANT AND AMERICAN AGRICULTURE

Given the availability of land and the necessity of conquering an empty continent, there was little dispute but that the immigrant farmer made a useful contribution to American life. Writing after the close of the movement, the historian, Marcus Lee Hansen, attempts to assess the effects of constant immigration upon agriculture and the expansion of the frontier;[1] and a contemporary guidebook shows some of the conditions foreign-born farmers encountered.[2]

(A). Hansen

What hastened settlement was the mobility of the Americans as compared with other peoples. . . . Two reasons for this mobility have been advanced: a migratory habit which characterized the people, and the kind of agriculture they practiced. Undoubtedly both reasons operated, and each deserves fuller consideration. Evidence of the migratory habit derives principally from anecdotes recorded by none too friendly visitors. The instinct urging the Yankees to move on was reported to be so irresistible as to warrant the saying: "If hell lay in the west they would cross heaven to reach it." Aversion to neighbors encouraged the impulse. . . . With so much land to choose from, one could never be content with what he happened to possess. Somewhere was a perfect hundred-and-sixty-acre tract: the right balance of meadow, arable and forest, a clearer spring, a more sheltered spot for his home, more wild game in the woods and fewer snakes and crows. . . .

For Yankee youth, migration became the normal experience.

[1] Reprinted by permission of the publishers from Marcus Lee Hansen, *The Immigrant in American History* (Cambridge, Harvard University Press, 1940), 60-68, 72-76.
[2] Calvin Colton, A.M., *Manual for Emigrants to America* (London, 1832).

Therein lies an essential difference between native and foreign-born. The ambition of the German-American father, for instance, was to see his sons on reaching manhood established with their families on farms clustered about his own. To take complete possession of a township with sons, sons-in-law and nephews was a not unrealizable ideal. To this end the would-be patriarch dedicated all his plodding industry. One by one, he bought adjacent farms, the erstwhile owners joining the current to the farther West. Heavily timbered acres and swamp lands which had been lying unused were prepared for cultivation by patient and unceasing toil. "When the German comes in, the Yankee goes out," was a local proverb that varied as Swedes, Bohemians or other immigrant groups formed the invading element. But the American father made no such efforts on behalf of his offspring. To be a self-made man was his ideal. He had come in as a "first settler" and had created a farm with his ax; let the boys do the same. One of them perhaps was kept at home as a helper to his aging parents; the rest set out willingly to achieve beyond the mountains or beyond the river what the father had accomplished in the West of his day. Thus mobility was fostered by family policy.

Equally important as a predisposing factor was the type of agriculture that prevailed. The pioneer farmers burned down the trees because it was the easiest way to make a clearing. They planted the same crop, season after season, largely because they were mentally too sluggish to experiment with new products. As a result, the soil became impoverished and no attempt was made, either by scientific rotation or by fertilizing, to restore or maintain its productivity. The land was mined, not farmed, and when the surface treasures had been skimmed off, the process was repeated in another place where Nature's bounty was as yet untouched.

Wasteful though these methods may seem today, a good word should be said for the pioneers. In the onward sweep of population they performed an indispensable task. Without their services as a vanguard, the great army in the rear could not have occupied the two and a half thousand miles from the Alleghenies to the Pacific in less than a century. . . .

To these two basic causes for mobility—national tradition and agricultural methods—a third should be added: foreign immigration. Without the influx of millions of Europeans, this clocklike progression across the continent could not have occurred. The population would not have been so mobile. There would have been a frontier, to be sure, but not the kind of frontier that produced the now accepted historical consequences. At what point did the immigrant of the nineteenth century contribute his capital, his strength and his skill? The European newcomer was not, in the American sense, a frontiersman. He had, in fact, an innate aversion to the wilderness with its solitude and loneliness and primitive mode of life. Moreover, the job of frontiersman was a highly skilled profession, involving a thousand knacks and devices by which Nature's raw materials were transformed to satisfy the demand for food and shelter. It called for aptitudes that were not developed in the European village. Neither by experience nor temperament was the immigrant fitted for pioneering.

If many at first intended to emulate the backwoodsmen of whose thrilling exploits they had read in American works of fiction, the resolve generally faded upon the first acquaintance with the strange new world and upon learning that the backwoods lay far from the port of debarkation. Those who nevertheless pursued their original intention soon regretted their temerity. The boundless forest was a disheartening sight, and the American ax a dangerous instrument in the hands of a novice. . . . Of the immigrants who ventured into the wilds few made a success. The majority drifted back to civilization; and their advice, spread by word of mouth, by letters and by printed guidebooks, was emphatic: let the Americans start the clearing; they alone possess the specialized technique. . . .

But if the immigrants were not frontiersmen, did they not constitute a large proportion of the second class, those who have been described as pioneer farmers? Among these later comers a number were found, but not a large percentage and only a few of these were recent arrivals in America. At this stage backwoods duties still predominated; handling the ax was more important than holding the plow. Nor did the German or the Irishman know how to preserve meat for the New Orleans market, or how to pilot a flatboat over river rapids. Therefore he tended to avoid this stage of frontier development, leaving it to the natives or at least to those foreigners who had served an apprenticeship on an American border farm, where they had forgotten everything about European agriculture and learned much that was new.

It was when the pioneer farmers departed that the immigrant farmers made their appearance. In the 1820's and 1830's they took over the evacuated lands in western New York, Pennsylvania and Ohio. In the 1840's they swarmed into Missouri, Illinois and southern Wisconsin. In the 1850's and 1860's they occupied eastern Iowa and Minnesota and consolidated their position in the older states. By the 1870's they had reached the prairies. And while the immigrants were moving in, the Americans were moving out—not all of them, but enough to give the invaders an opening wedge which they spread quietly and steadily in the subsequent decades. . . .

By 1870, when the policy enacted in the homestead law was beginning to operate, new material conditions and mental attitudes governed the process of expansion. The powerful appeal of free farms overshadowed caution and lured the immigrants at once to the frontier, for they wanted to get there before the land was all gone. Broadly speaking, the homestead area corresponded with the great triangle that is included between the upper Mississippi and the Missouri rivers, with an extension westward of the latter in its lower reaches. South of this region there was some public land, but it was either in the hands of the Indians or of poor quality; to the west lay barren plains and the mountains; to the east much of the country was already occupied under previous laws. Hence within this triangle occurred the principal concentration of immigrants during the seventies and eighties: the Scandinavians, the Germans and the English. That most of them survived to people this section with their descendants today is no indication of the struggle they passed through as pioneer settlers. . . .

In summary, just what was the influence of immigration upon American expansion? By nature and habit the American was restless. Undoubtedly he was destined to inherit the earth from the Atlantic to the Pacific. But, as the evidence shows, he was hastened into his inheritance. When an Englishman or a German came with gold in his hand and asked, "Will you sell?" there was no hesitation in the reply. He took the gold and went. Thus the immigrants were the "fillers in," and by virtue of the numbers and speed with which they came they helped to give the movement of expansion its disorganized and reckless character.

(B). *Colton's Manual*

Advice to those, who wish to purchase Land, or Farms.

There are always improved plantations and farms in the market, in every State and in every settled part of the Union, from the changes which are constantly taking place in society by the deaths of proprietors, or by the motives which some find to remove from one place to another. And he who chooses to purchase an improved farm, or plantation, must of course pay for the fair value of the improvements, buildings, &c.—and also for the adventitious value of its vicinity to market, to large towns, and for other relative considerations, which vary so much in different places and circumstances, that it is impossible to specify the price, abstracted from such considerations.

If an emigrant wishes to settle in an older and well-organized community, and has money to purchase an improved farm, larger, or smaller;—and if he has not decided in what particular State, or district of a State, he will take his position,—let him provide transient accommodations for his family, if he has one, and get upon a horse, and ride over the land, in its length and breadth, if he chooses, and survey the country to his satisfaction. Let him pass over different States and Territories, and the almost endless variety of choice, that will be presented, will abundantly reward him for all his pains and expense. If he spends three, or six months, or a year, and travels thousands of miles, he may be a gainer by it—especially, if he has a few hundred pounds to invest in such property. He had better not be too hasty, nor listen to the first casual adviser, that may happen to come in his way. The new establishment of a family, in a new country, for the future generations of one's posterity, is an important step;—and in such a country as the United States, there is a wide field of choice, a thousand circumstances to be considered, and sufficient motives for an extensive and thorough inspection.

THE IMMIGRANT ARTISAN

For a long time, there was also no disagreement as to the need for skilled foreign-born artisans in the growing towns of Amer-

ica. Another immigrant guidebook suggests the trades in which there was most room.[3]

Industrious men need never lack employment in America. Laborers, carpenters, masons, bricklayers, stonecutters, blacksmiths, turners, weavers, farmers, curriers, shoemakers, and tailors, and the useful mechanics generally, are always sure of work and good wages. Stone-cutters now receive, in New York, two dollars a day, equal to nine shillings sterling; carpenters, one dollar and 87½ cents; bricklayers, two dollars; laborers, from one dollar to one and a quarter; others in proportion. At this time, house-carpenters, bricklayers, masons, and stonecutters, are paid three dollars per day in Petersburgh (Virginia). The town was recently consumed by fire, but it is now rising from its ashes in more elegance than ever.

Artisans receive better pay in America than in Europe, and can live with less exertion, and more comfort; because they put an additional price on their work, equal to the cost of freight and commission charged by the merchant on importation. . . .

Men of science, who can apply their knowledge to useful and practical purposes, may be very advantageously settled; but mere literary scholars, who have no profession, or only one which they cannot profitably practice in this country, do not meet with much encouragement,—in truth, with little or none, unless they are willing to devote themselves to the education of youth. The demand for persons who will do this, is obviously increasing; and, although many excellent preceptors are everywhere to be found among the native Americans, there is still considerable room for competition on the part of well qualified foreigners. In the seminaries for classical education, it is common to find the preceptors natives of Ireland; and the same may be said of the mathematical schools.

In the southern states, where a thin population is spread over an extensive country, good schools are comparatively few; but there are rich planters in those districts, in whose families foreigners of genteel address, and good knowledge of the classics, English, and arithmetic, will find employment and a good salary, as private tutors. It does not detract from a man's personal respectability to have been thus employed. The Americans are too wise to treat that condition as mean,

---

[3] S. H. Collins, *The Emigrant's Guide to and Description of the United States of America* (Hull, 1830), 110-111, 112-113.

which is essential to the honor and prosperity of the nation, and which supposes in its professor natural talents and acquired knowledge. It is not unusual, in this country, to see young men who taught school until they had accumulated some property, and who then turn to the professions of law, physic, or divinity, or else become farmers or merchants. The practice and feelings of the Americans, in this particular, may be judged from the fact, that many gentlemen, who begin their career as schoolmasters, pass through all the gradations of state honors, are appointed to foreign embassies, promoted to the head of departments of the federal government, and have as good prospects as others of attaining the presidency.

THE IMMIGRANT BUSINESSMAN

A few immigrants by dint of hard labor were also able to earn their livelihood by trade. Usually they lacked capital, however, and were compelled to make humble starts as peddlers. Some rose from such positions to places at the head of great enterprises, but the majority, no doubt, never surmounted the hardships described in the diary of a young German-Jewish merchant in New England in 1842 and 1843.[4]

On the eve of the [Jewish] New Year I found myself with a new career before me. What kind of career? "I don't know," the American's customary reply to every difficult question. . . .

I was in New York, trying in vain to find a job as clerk in a store. But business was too slow, and I had to do as all the others; with a bundle on my back I had to go out into the country, peddling various articles. This, then, is the vaunted luck of the immigrants from Bavaria! O misguided fools, led astray by avarice and cupidity! You have left your friends and acquaintances, your relatives and your parents, your home and your fatherland, your language and your customs, your faith and your religion—only to sell your wares in the wild places of America, in isolated farmhouses and tiny hamlets. . . .

In such an existence the single man gets along far better than the father of a family. Such fools as are married not only suffer themselves, but bring suffering to their women. How must an educated

---

[4] Abraham Kohn, "A Jewish Peddler's Diary" (translated from the German by Abram Vossen Goodman), *American Jewish Archives*, III (1951), 96-106.

woman feel when, after a brief stay at home, her supporter and shel-
terer leaves with his pack on his back, not knowing where he will find
lodging on the next night or the night after? On how many winter
evenings must such a woman sit forlornly with her children at the
fireplace, like a widow, wondering where this night finds the head of
her family, which homestead in the forests of Ohio will offer him a
poor night's shelter? O, that I had never seen this land, but had remained in Germany, apprenticed to a humble country craftsman!
Though oppressed by taxes and discriminated against as a Jew, I
should still be happier than in the great capital of America, free from
royal taxes and every man's religious equal though I am! . . .

Last week in the vicinity of Plymouth I met two peddlers, Lehman
and Marx. Marx knew me from Fürth, and that night we stayed
together at a farmer's house. After supper we started singing while I
felt melancholy and depressed. O, how I thought of my dear mother
while I sang! . . .

Today, Sunday, October 16th, we are here in North Bridgewater
[Massachusetts], and I am not so downcast as I was two weeks ago.
The devil has settled 20,000 [2,000?] shoemakers here, who do not
have a cent of money. Suppose, after all, I were a soldier in Bavaria;
that would have been a bad lot. I will accept three years in America
instead. But I could not stand it any longer.

As far as the language is concerned, I am getting along pretty well.
But I don't like to be alone. The Americans are a peculiar people.
Although they sit together by the dozen in taverns, they turn their
backs to each other, and no one talks to anybody else. Is this supposed
to be the custom of a republic? I don't like it. Is this supposed to be
the fashion of the nineteenth century? I don't like it either. . . .

On Wednesday, November [9th, my brother] . . . Moses and I
went to Holden, where we stayed until Sunday . . . with Mr. How.
On Monday we went on, arriving on Tuesday at Rutland. In the
morning our packs seemed very heavy, and we had to rest every half-
mile. In the afternoon a buggy was offered to us and, thank Heaven,
it was within our means. We took off our bundles and anticipated
thriving business. Wednesday we proceeded to Barre by horse and
carriage, and on Thursday went to Worcester to meet [our brother]
Juda. Here we stayed together until Friday, November [25th], when
we left for West Boylston, staying for the night at Mr. Stuart's, two
miles from Sterling. We stayed on Saturday night and over Sunday

at the home of Mr. Blaube, where I met the most beautiful girl I have ever seen. Her name is Helena Brown and she is from Boston. But despite this girl, I do not yet like America as well as I might wish. But if Heaven causes us to prosper we may yet be entirely satisfied.

Last Thursday was Thanksgiving Day, a general holiday, fixed by the governor for the inhabitants of Massachusetts. Yet it seems to be merely a formal observance, coldly carried through with nothing genuine about it. To the American one day is like another, and even Sunday, their only holiday, is a mere form. They often go to church here, but only to show the neighbor's wife a new veil or dress.

Winter has come, because there is much snow and wind since Thursday, the 24th. We were at Sterling and Leominster on Monday, November 28th, and went from there to Lunenburg.

Not far from here we were forced to stop on Wednesday, November 30th, because of the heavy snow. We sought to spend the night with a cooper, a Mr. Spaulding, but his wife did not wish to take us in. She was afraid of strangers, she might not sleep well; we should go our way. And outside there raged the worst blizzard I have ever seen. O God, I thought, is this the land of liberty and hospitality and tolerance? Why have I been led here? After we had talked to this woman for half an hour, after repeatedly pointing out that to turn us forth into the blizzard would be sinful, we were allowed to stay. She became friendlier, indeed, after a few hours, and at night she even joined us in singing. But how often I remembered during that evening how my poor mother treated strangers at all times. Every poor man, every traveler who entered the house, was welcomed hospitably and given the best at our table. Her motto, even for strangers, was: "Who throws stones at me shall be, in turn, pelted by me with bread." Now her own children beg for shelter in a foreign land. . . .

Thursday was a day of rest owing to twelve inches of snow. On Friday and Saturday business was very poor, and we did not take in $2 during the two days. . . .

On Monday morning, December 5th, we set out, in God's name, for Groton in a sleigh and at night stayed with an old farmer, about two miles from that place. It was a very satisfactory business day, and we took in about $15. On Tuesday we continued through much snow, via Pepperell, to Hollis, in New Hampshire. Towards evening the good Moses managed to overthrow the sleigh, and me along with it, into the snow. I am sure that, should I ever come this way in future years, I shall always be able to recognize the spot where I lay in a snowdrift.

After spending Wednesday in Milford, we traveled beyond on Thursday and Friday, spending Saturday at Amherst and Sunday at the home of Mr. Kendall in Mount Vernon. Business, thanks be to God, is satisfactory, and this week we took in more than $45. We rode horseback for pleasure on Sunday.

> Things will yet go well.
> The world is round and must keep turning.
> Things will yet go well.

So goes an old German song which I once heard an actor sing in Fürth in a play, which one, I don't remember.

On Monday the 12th to Lyndeborough; Tuesday to Wilton; Wednesday to Mason Village; Thursday, New Ipswich; Friday, Ashburnham. On Saturday, we came to Westminster, where we stayed over Sunday, the eighteenth of December. It was extremely cold this week, and there was more snow than we had ever seen in our lives. At some places the snow was three to four feet deep, and we could hardly get through with the sleigh. How often we thanked the good God that we did not have to carry our wares on our backs in this cold! To tramp with a heavy pack from house to house in this weather would be terrible. . . .

The weather is very bad, and the sleigh sinks two feet into the snow. Money is scarce, but, God be thanked, sleeping quarters have been good. There is much work for little profit, yet God in heaven may send better times that all our drudgery will not have been in vain. . . .

Thursday, January 12th, was one of the hardest days of my entire life. I shall never forget it. In the morning we drove to a solitary house, three miles from Hancock in the direction of Nelson. The sleigh went on fairly well. After we had driven five or six miles there was, suddenly, no more snow to be seen. It was three o'clock in the afternoon and we were among the high hills. No snow appeared before us, not a single white patch behind us, great hills surrounded us; there was no prospect of trade or of a night's shelter. Where could we go? In such a situation the intellect is powerless; faith in God alone can help. And the situation was not improved by my brother Juda, who had been in depressed spirits all day. Well, "Forward," said Napoleon, and forward it went. I proceeded ahead two miles, Juda slowly following with the sleigh as best he could. At the home of some very poor people, such a home as I had not yet seen in America, I found lodging for the night. My worries, however, kept me from sleeping that night.

On Friday morning . . . we drove slowly back to Hancock, making difficult progress. We spent the night in the same house we had visited yesterday . . . and set out for Brookline on Monday. . . . On Tuesday, in low spirits, we went to Hollis, on Wednesday . . . to Groton, and on Thursday to Lunenburg, where we exchanged the sleigh for the wagon. After spending Friday, the twentieth, at West Boylston, we came on Saturday to Worcester once more, arriving only an hour before Moses. We thanked God at finding him in good health, although he did not appear quite as hearty as he had four weeks before. He had been sleeping poorly, poor devil, and I knew how he felt, for I have had these experiences too.

We spent Saturday, Sunday, and Monday in Worcester. The joy of being together for a few days always costs money. . . . We are so pleased to see each other well again that it is very hard to leave. Dear mother, how I wish you too could join our reunions! God will aid us and lead us back again to you.

On Tuesday morning at ten I left Worcester, it being my turn to travel alone for seven weeks. A thousand thanks to God, I felt far stronger than when I first left my brothers in Boston. Now I have become more accustomed to the language, the business, and the American way of life.

The Immigrant and the Labor Market

The sharpest disputes over the economic effects of immigration came after 1880 with reference to the role of newcomers as industrial laborers. This was one of the subjects of investigation of a federal immigration commission that studied the matter between 1907 and 1910. The fact that the most influential technical director of the commission, J. W. Jenks, was a bitter foe of immigration may have influenced the conclusions of its summary report.[5]

[5] United States Immigration Commission, "Reports," 61st Congress, 3rd Session, *Senate Document*, No. 747, I, 37-39.

*In 1912 Isaac A. Hourwich, himself an immigrant, questioned
the conclusions of the Immigration Commission. He reexamined
the data and drew from it a radically different estimate of the
relationship of immigration to labor conditions.[6]*

(A). Immigration Commission

A large proportion of the southern and eastern European immigrants of the past twenty-five years have entered the manufacturing and mining industries of the eastern and middle western States, mostly in the capacity of unskilled laborers. There is no basic industry in which they are not largely represented and in many cases they compose more than 50 per cent of the total number of persons employed in such industries. Coincident with the advent of these millions of unskilled laborers there has been an unprecedented expansion of the industries in which they have been employed. Whether this great immigration movement was caused by the industrial development, or whether the fact that a practically unlimited and available supply of cheap labor existed in Europe was taken advantage of for the purpose of expanding the industries, can not well be demonstrated. Whatever may be the truth in this regard it is certain that southern and eastern European immigrants have almost completely monopolized unskilled labor activities in many of the more important industries. This phase of the industrial situation was made the most important and exhaustive feature of the Commission's investigation, and the results show that while the competition of these immigrants has had little, if any, effect on the highly skilled trades, nevertheless, through lack of industrial progress and by reason of large and constant reinforcement from abroad, it has kept conditions in the semiskilled and unskilled occupations from advancing.

Several elements peculiar to the new immigrants contributed to this result. The aliens came from countries where low economic conditions prevailed and where conditions of labor were bad. They were content to accept wages and conditions which the native American and immigrants of the older class had come to regard as unsatisfactory. They were not, as a rule, engaged at lower wages than had been paid to the older workmen for the same class of labor, but their pres-

---

[6] *Immigration and Labor* (2nd ed., New York, B. W. Huebsch, Inc., 1922), 4-6, 9-12, 19, 20, 23, 35.

ence in constantly increasing numbers prevented progress among the older wage-earning class, and as a result that class of employees was gradually displaced. An instance of this displacement is shown in the experience in the bituminous coal mines of western Pennsylvania. This section of the bituminous field was the one first entered by the new immigrants, and the displacement of the old workers was soon under way. Some of them entered other occupations and many of them migrated to the coal fields of the Middle West. Later these fields also were invaded by the new immigrants, and large numbers of the old workers again migrated to the mines of the Southwest, where they still predominate. The effect of the new immigration is clearly shown in the western Pennsylvania fields, where the average wage of the bituminous coal worker is 42 cents a day below the average wage in the Middle West and the Southwest. Incidentally, hours of labor are longer and general working conditions poorer in the Pennsylvania mines than elsewhere. Another characteristic of the new immigrants contributed to the situation in Pennsylvania. This was the impossibility of successfully organizing them into labor unions. Several attempts at organization were made, but the constant influx of immigrants to whom prevailing conditions seemed unusually favorable contributed to the failure to organize. A similar situation has prevailed in other great industries.

Like most of the immigration from southern and eastern Europe, those who entered the leading industries were largely single men or married men unaccompanied by their families. There is, of course, in practically all industrial communities a large number of families of the various races, but the majority of the employees are men without families here, and whose standard of living is so far below that of the native American or older immigrant workman that it is impossible for the latter to successfully compete with them. They usually live in cooperative groups and crowd together. Consequently, they are able to save a great part of their earnings, much of which is sent or carried abroad. Moreover, there is a strong tendency on the part of these unaccompanied men to return to their native countries after a few years of labor here. These groups have little contact with American life, learn little of American institutions, and aside from the wages earned profit little by their stay in this country. During their early years in the United States they usually rely for assistance and advice on some member of their race, frequently a saloon keeper or grocer, and almost always a steamship ticket agent and "immigrant banker," who, because of superior intelligence and better knowledge of American ways, commands their confidence. Usually after a longer residence they become more self-reliant, but their progress toward assimilation is generally slow. Immigrant families in the industrial centers are more permanent and usually exhibit a stronger tendency toward advancement, although, in most cases, it is a long time before they even approach the ordinary standard of the American or the older immigrant families in the same grade of occupation. This description, of course, is not universally true, but it fairly represents a great part of the recent immigrant population in the United States. Their numbers are so great and the influx is so continuous that even with the remarkable expansion of industry during the past few years there has been created an over supply of unskilled labor, and in some of the industries this is reflected in a curtailed number of working days and a consequent yearly income among the unskilled workers which is very much less than is indicated by the daily wage rates paid; and while it may not have lowered in a marked degree the American standard of living, it has introduced a lower standard which has become prevalent in the unskilled industry at large.

(B). Hourwich

The real agents who regulate the immigration movement are the millions of earlier immigrants already in the United States. It is they that advance the cost of passage of a large proportion of the new immigrants. When the outlook for employment is good, they send for their relatives, or encourage their friends to come. When the demand for labor is slack, the foreign-born workman must hold his savings in reserve, to provide for possible loss of employment. At such times no wage-earner will assume the burden of providing for a relative or friend, who might for a long time be unable to secure employment. It is in this way that the business situation in the United States reacts upon the volume of immigration. The fluctuating supply of immigrant labor, like that of any other commodity, may sometimes outrun the demand and at other times lag behind it, yet, if we compare the totals for industrial cycles, comprising years of panic, of depression, and of prosperity, within the past sixty years, we find that the ratio of immigration to population has been well-nigh constant. In the long run immigration adjusts itself to the demand for labor. . . .

Still, the labor market being normally overstocked, it sounds plausible that the immigrant, who is accustomed to a lower standard of living at home than the American workman, will be able to underbid and displace his American competitor. If this view were correct, we should find, in the first place, a higher percentage of unemployment among the native than among the foreign-born breadwinners. Statistics, however, show that the proportion of unemployment is the same for native and foreign-born wage-earners. The immigrant has no advantage over the native American in securing or retaining employment. In the next place, we should find more unemployment in those sections of the United States where the immigrants are most numerous. In fact, however, the ratio of unemployment in manufactures is the same in the North Atlantic States with a large immigrant population as in the South Atlantic States where the percentage of foreign-born is negligible. Coal miners are thought to have suffered most from immigration. Yet it appears that Pennsylvania, which is among the States with the highest percentages of foreign-born miners, has the second lowest percentage of unemployment. The highest ratio of unemployment, according to the latest published census data, was found in West Virginia, where the percentage of foreign-born miners was next to the lowest. A similar relation between unemployment and the proportion of immigrants is observed among cotton-mill operatives and common laborers: immigrants are not attracted to those States where opportunities for regular employment are less favorable. . . .

The effect of immigration upon labor in the United States has been a readjustment of the population on the scale of occupations. The majority of Americans of native parentage are engaged in farming, in business, in the professions, and in clerical pursuits. The majority of the immigrants, on the other hand, are industrial wage-earners. Only in exceptional cases has this readjustment been attended by actual displacement of the native or Americanized wage-earner. In the course of industrial evolution some trades have declined owing to the introduction of new methods of production. In such cases there was naturally a decrease of the number of native as well as of foreign-born workers. As a rule, however, the supply of immigrant labor has been absorbed by the increasing demand for labor in all industries without leaving a surplus sufficient to displace the native or older immigrant wage-earner. There were but a few occupations which showed an actual, not a relative decrease of native Americans of native stock. This decrease was due to the disinclination of the young generation to follow the pursuits of their fathers; the new accessions from native stock were insufficient to replace the older men as they were dying off, and the vacancies were gradually filled up by immigrants. But for every position given up by a native American there were many new openings filled by native American wage-earners. . . .

The effect of immigration upon the occupational distribution of the industrial wage-earners has been the elevation of the English-speaking workmen to the status of an aristocracy of labor, while the immigrants have been employed to perform the rough work of all industries. Though the introduction of machinery has had the tendency to reduce the relative number of skilled mechanics, yet the rapid pace of industrial expansion has increased the number of skilled and supervisory positions so fast that practically all the English-speaking employees have had the opportunity to rise on the scale of occupations. This opportunity, however, was conditioned upon a corresponding increase of the total operating force. It is only because the new immigration has furnished the class of unskilled laborers that the native workmen and older immigrants have been raised to the plane of an aristocracy of labor. . . .

The objection to the unskilled immigrant is based upon the belief that because of his lower standard of living he is satisfied with lower wages than the American or the older immigrant. It is therefore taken for granted that the effect of the great tide of immigration in recent years has been to reduce the rate of wages or to prevent it from advancing. . . .

The primary cause which has determined the movement of wages in the United States during the past thirty years has been the introduction of labor-saving machinery. The effect of the substitution of mechanical devices for human skill is the displacement of the skilled mechanic by the unskilled laborer. This tendency has been counteracted in the United States by the expansion of industry: while the ratio of skilled mechanics to the total operating force was decreasing, the increasing scale of operations prevented an actual reduction in numbers. Of course this adjustment did not proceed without friction. While, in the long run, there has been no displacement of skilled mechanics by unskilled laborers in the industrial field as a whole, yet at certain times and places individual skilled mechanics were doubtless dispensed with and had to seek new employment. The unskilled laborers who replaced them were naturally engaged at lower wages. The fact that most of these unskilled laborers were immigrants disguised the substance of the change—the substitution of unskilled for skilled labor—and made it appear as the displacement of highly-paid native by cheap immigrant labor. . . .

There is consequently no specific "immigration problem." There is a general labor problem, which comprises many special problems, such as organization of labor, reduction of hours of labor, child labor, unemployment, prevention of work-accidents, etc. None of these problems being affected by immigration, their solution can not be advanced by restriction or even by complete prohibition of immigration.

THE INDUSTRIES MANNED BY IMMIGRANTS

It will be helpful in understanding some of these general problems to look at a number of specific industries in which immigrants provided an essential labor force. In each, the employment of the foreign-born presented problems; yet each could expand only with the aid of the newcomers. A newspaper account of 1834 reveals some of the difficulties in the management of the Irish workingmen, essential in the immense tasks of construction that supplied the United States with canals, railroads, and buildings.[7] A reporter's account in 1895 shows the type of Jewish labor that enabled the clothing industry to develop.[8] A letter by an experienced superintendent in 1875 explains the preference of the owners of steel mills for immigrant hands.[9] And, an economist in 1901 notes the importance of Eastern European miners in the coal industry.[10]

[7] *Hagerstown (Maryland) Torch-Light,* January 30, 1834.
[8] John DeWitt Warner, "The 'Sweating System' in New York City," *Harper's Weekly,* XXIX (February 9, 1895), 135-136.
[9] W. R. Jones to E. V. McCandless, February 25, 1875, quoted in James Howard Bridge, *The Inside History of the Carnegie Steel Company* (New York, 1903), 81-82.
[10] Peter Roberts, *The Anthracite Coal Industry* (New York, 1901), 103-106, 108.

(A). *The War on the Canal*

The cause of the above battle was a beating received by one man, a Fardown, on the Thursday previous, from some of the opposing party, on the section attacked. This individual, named John Irons, has since died of the wounds received, and an inquest been held over the body—the verdict, "he came to his death from blows received on several parts of his body & head, from persons unknown."

Since the foregoing event, great commotion has existed among the hands. Very little work has been done, and a state of alarm and warlike preparation has taken place. On Thursday last, we are informed, a party of Corkonians committed excesses along the line above this place. Yesterday morning a small party were seen approaching this place from above, and were met on the Aqueduct and driven back by an opposing party of their countrymen in the town. In this affray one man was very seriously beaten and wounded. The citizens of the town, with commendable alacrity, soon put themselves in military order, under arms for the protection of the peace of the place, and remained under arms for the balance of the day, and the greater part of the night.

This scene was soon followed by another which resulted in a disastrous battle and several deaths. A party of Fardowns or Longfords, consisting of about three hundred men, headed by intrepid leaders, were announced as approaching from below. Their design they stated to be, to pass up the line of the Canal to the upper dam, for the purpose of exhibiting their strength, and not to commit a breach of the peace unless attacked. They were armed in part with guns, but principally with helves, clubs, etc. They passed up quietly over the Aqueduct, and on their way, as we learn, three or four hundred more of the same party fell into their ranks. At the upper dam, in a field on the other side of Middlekauff's, they met the enemy in battle array, drawn up on top of a hill about three hundred in number, and armed, in part, with military weapons. The information we have is, that the attack, or at least a challenge to the combat, was made by the latter party. Volleys of shot were exchanged; some men were seen to fall, and the party above began to fall back and disperse before the superior forces of their enemy. A pursuit ensued through the woods, where frequent firing was heard, and no doubt many lives were taken. Persons who traversed the field after the battle was over observed five men in the agonies of death, who had been shot through the head, several dead bodies were seen in the woods, and a number wounded in every direction.—Those who observed the battle describe it as one of great rage and most deadly violence.—All the deaths and wounded are reported to have been of the Corkonians.

About 10 o'clock last night, the victorious party returned, and passed quietly through this place, after halting a few moments in one of the public streets, to their respective sections and shantees below the town.—Quiet was restored for the balance of the night.

We have thus attempted merely a sketch of the horrid barbarities committed in this neighborhood through the past week. The public peace has been outraged, and the civil authority contemned. It remains for the officers of justice, to take the necessary steps to repair these gross violations of the law.

Postscript.—Since writing the above, a principal leader of one of the parties has been arrested for examination. The volunteer companies have arrived from Hagerstown, commanded by Col. Wm. H. Fitzhugh, who is also Sheriff of the county, and are now in readiness to act in aid of the civil authority. An express has been dispatched to the seat of government for a sufficient regular force to be sent on and stationed here or at other suitable points along the line of the Canal, to preserve order among the laborers, and for purposes of general protection.

Nothing of importance occurred on Sunday.—On Monday a deputation of four gentlemen left Williamsport and proceeded down the line of the canal, as far as Hollman's dam, and a similar deputation proceeded up the line simultaneously, as far as Middlekauff's dam, for the purpose of persuading the contending parties to appoint deputies to a Convention, proposed to be held in Williamsport that day, for the purpose of bringing about an adjustment of their differences, and concluding a treaty of peace. About dusk the two deputations returned to town, bringing with them deputies from the respective sections above and below. These deputies had been appointed by their assembled countrymen on the various contracts, and were fully empowered and authorized to enter into an adjustment of the differences existing between the adverse parties. Accordingly, in the course of the evening, they met, in conjunction with the two deputations which had gone out for them, the magistrates and some of the gentlemen of Williamsport, at the tavern of Mr. Lyles, and agreed upon an amicable adjustment of their disputes; the substance of which agreement will be found in the following:—

Proceedings of a meeting, held at Williamsport, on Monday evening, January 27, 1834.

On motion of Col. Dall—Gen. Otho H. Williams was appointed Chairman, and Thos. Purcell was appointed Secretary.—

The Chairman then addressed the Irish deputies from the Cork and Longford parties. He stated the object of the meeting, and urged on the parties concerned the necessity of a speedy and complete reconciliation of the difficulties and disagreements that led to the late riotous proceedings on the Canal.

The Secretary then prepared a paper in the form of an agreement, the object of which is not only to remove the misunderstandings that have already occurred but to prevent like results in future; to this was attached a recognizance to keep the peace. This agreement was then signed by the deputies from each party.

On motion of W. D. Bill, Esq. it was resolved, that a written copy of the articles of agreement be furnished forthwith to each party thereto.

On motion of Mr. Warfield it was resolved, that one hundred copies of the foregoing agreement be printed for distribution along the canal.

It was further resolved, that the proceedings of this meeting be published in the public prints of the county.

Gen. O. H. Williams again addressed the Irish deputies. He explained to them the solemnity of the obligation they had just executed in the presence of the magistrates. The necessity of their preserving inviolate the pledge they had thus entered into; and at the same time he apprised them that in case the agreement was violated, it was the determination of the citizens and the military to unite with the opposite side and drive entirely from the county the party who were guilty of the infraction. . . .

O. H. Williams, *Chairman*.

T. F. Purcell, *Sec'ry*.

During the day, on Monday, Gen. Williams brevetted Capt. Hollingsworth, Capt. Hollman, and Capt. Allen. Capt. Hollingsworth immediately organized a fine troop of horse—and Captains Hollman and Allen enrolled about one hundred and fifty citizens of Williamsport, in their respective companies—the whole of which force was placed under the command of Col. Dall, and is now ready, on a moment's warning for energetic action.

Early on Tuesday morning, Gen. Williams received intelligence, by express, that a force of upwards of 100 men had passed Harpers Ferry, on Monday evening, on their way up the canal, with a view of reinforcing their friends, the Corkonians, at Middlekauff's dam. Col. Dall was immediately apprised of their movement and caused Captain Hollingsworth to meet this force at Hollman's dam—they were made acquainted with the terms of compromise, gave up their arms, and manifested a willingness to return quietly to their work, down the river.

The prisoners in our jail, connected with the disturbances, amounting to about forty, will probably be recognized to appear at our next county court, and set at liberty without delay. The following is a copy of the Treaty of Peace, made and concluded, at Williamsport, on the 27th day of January, 1834, between the Corkonians and Longford men, the two contending parties on the Chesapeake and Ohio Canal.—

Whereas great commotions and divers riotous acts have resulted from certain misunderstandings and alleged grievances, mutually urged by two parties of laborers and mechanics engaged on the line of the Chesapeake and Ohio Canal, and natives of Ireland; the one commonly known as the Longford men, the other as the Corkonians; and whereas it has been found that these riotous acts, are calculated to disturb the public peace, without being in the least degree beneficial to the parties opposed to each other, but on the contrary are productive of great injury and distress to the workmen and their families—

Therefore, we, the undersigned, representatives of each party, have agreed to, and do pledge ourselves to support and carry into effect the following terms of the agreement:—

We agree for ourselves, that we will not either individually or collectively, interrupt, or suffer to be interrupted in our presence, any person engaged on the line of the Canal, for or on account of a local difference, or national prejudice, and that we will use our influence to destroy all these matters of difference growing out of this distinction of parties, known as Corkonians and Longfords; and we further

agree and pledge ourselves in the most solemn manner to inform on
and bring to justice any person, or persons, who may break the pledge
contained in this agreement, either by interrupting any person passing
along or near the line of the Canal, or by secretly counselling, or as-
sisting any person or persons, who may endeavor to exercise riotous
conduct among the above parties and we further bind ourselves to
the State of Maryland, each in the sum of twenty dollars, to keep
the peace towards the citizens of the State. In witness thereof, we
have hereunto signed our names, at Williamsport, this twenty seventh
day of January, eighteen hundred and thirty four.

(B). *The "Sweating System" in New York City*

Two years since it was my duty, as chairman of a Congressional
committee, to investigate the so-called "sweating system," New York
being one of the several cities visited. The "sweating system" is practically the process by which ready-made clothing is manufactured in
tenement-houses.

Conditions have radically changed during the last twenty-five years.
Formerly the women of each household made up the greater part of
its clothing, the rest being supplied by the local tailor, and made up
on his premises. The "ready-made" business has developed new econ-
omies, especially in divisions of labor and the method of its employment. Middlemen have been given a place between the "manufacturer" and the actual operative, processes have been cheapened and
labor degraded.

The materials are cut and "bunched" for each garment by the
manufacturer. They are then distributed in large lots to special job-
bers, known as "contractors," each a specialist in his line. For example,
one makes coats, another cloaks, another pantaloons, while some
make special grades or sizes. With this distribution the wholesaler
washes his hands of the business, his ignorance of how and where his
goods are actually made up being as ideal as intentional.

Not far from one-half of the goods thus distributed are made up
in the contractors' factories. As to the other half, the first contractor
sublets the work to a "sweater," whose shop is generally one of the
two larger rooms of a tenement flat, accommodating from six to fif-

teen or twenty "sweating" employees—men, women, and children. In the other large room of the flat are his living, sleeping, and cooking arrangements, overflowing into the workroom. Employes whom he boards, who eat at their work, and who sleep on the goods, frequently complete the intimate connection of home and shop. One-fourth of our ready-made and somewhat of our custom-made clothing are thus put together.

The people engaged are those whose families are most prolific, whose sense of cleanliness is least developed, who comprehend no distinction between living and work rooms, whose premises are dirty to the point of filth, and who are found in the most densely populated portions of the city.

But this is not the worst. Single families, inhabiting one or more rooms, generally having a family as sub-tenants, or a number of lodgers or boarders, subcontract work from the tenement "sweaters." Thus by tenement "home-workers" are made another one-fourth of our ready-made clothing and a much larger proportion of our children's clothing. The homes of these home-workers include many of the most wretched in which human beings exist among us. The conditions of squalor and filth are frequently such as to make even inspection impossible, except by one hardened to the work, while the quarters in which this work is centred are those into which tend the most helpless of our population.

From the wholesale manufacturer, handling each year a product of millions, through the contractor to the "sweater," and on to the "home-worker," the steps are steadily downward—of decreasing responsibility, comfort, and compensation. The profit of each (except the wretch at the bottom) is "sweated" from the next below him.

The contractors' shops are much like other factories—the large proportion of foreign labor and a tendency toward long hours being their main distinctions. In the tenement "sweat shops" unhealthy and unclean conditions are almost universal, and those of filth and contagion common. The employes are in the main foreign-born and newly arrived. The proportion of female labor is large, and child labor is largely used. Wages are from a fourth to a third less than in the larger shops. As to hours, there is no limit except the endurance of the employes, the work being paid for by the "task," and the task so adjusted as to drive from the shop any employe who, whenever he is given a bench, will not work to the limit of physical endurance, the hours of labor being rarely less than twelve, generally thirteen or fourteen, frequently from fifteen to eighteen, hours in the twenty-four.

The lot, however, of these "sweat-shop" workers is luxury compared to that of those engaged in tenement home work. The homeworker is generally a foreigner just arrived, and frequently a woman whose husband is dead, sick, or worthless, and whose children keep her at home. Of these tenement home-workers there are more women than men, and children are as numerous as both. The work is carried on in the one, two, or three rooms occupied by the family, with its subtenants or boarders. No pretence is made of separating shop work from household affairs. The hours observed are those which endurance alone limits. Children are worked to death beside their parents. Contagious diseases are especially prevalent among these people; but even death disturbs from their occupation only the one or two necessary to dispose of the body.

As to wages in this "tenement home-work," there is nothing which can properly be so called. The work is secured by underbidding of tenement sweat shops, and is generally piece-work, one process of which may be attended to by the head of the family, and the rest by its other members according to their capacity. Those engaged are so generally compelled to accept rather than to choose their work that it is taken without reference to the possibility of gaining a livelihood therefrom, the miserable workers earning what they can, begging to supplement it, and dying or being supported as paupers when they fail.

A large proportion—nearly, if not quite, one-half—of all the clothing worn by the majority of our people is thus made under conditions revolting to humanity and decency, and such as to endanger the health of the wearer.

(C). *Advice from Captain Jones*

Now I will give you my views as to the proper way of conducting these works.

1st. We must be careful of what class of men we collect. We must steer clear of the West where men are accustomed to infernal high wages. We must steer clear as far as we can of Englishmen who are great sticklers for high wages, small production and strikes. My experience has shown that Germans and Irish, Swedes and what I denominate "Buckwheats"—young American country boys, judiciously mixed, make the most effective and tractable force you can find. Scotsmen do very well, are honest and faithful. Welsh can be used in limited numbers. But mark me, Englishmen have been the worst class of men I have had anything to do with; and this is the opinion of Mr. Holley, George and John Fritz.

2nd. It should be the aim of the firm to keep the works running steadily. This is one of the secrets of Cambria low wages. The workmen, taking year in and year out, do better at Cambria than elsewhere. On steady work you can calculate on low wages.

3rd. The company should endeavor to make the cost of living as low as possible. This is one bad feature at present but it can be easily remedied.

These are the salient points. The men should be made to feel that the company are interested in their welfare. Make the works a pleasant place for them. I have always found it best to treat men well, and I find that my men are anxious to retain my good will by working steadily and honestly, and instead of dodging are anxious to show me what a good day's work they have done. All haughty and disdainful treatment of men has a very decided and bad effect on them.

Now I have voluntarily given you my views. I have felt this to be a necessity on my part; for I am afraid that unless the policy I have marked out is followed we need not expect the great success that is obtainable. These suggestions are the results of twenty-five years' experience obtained in the most successful iron works in this country:— Crane and Thomas Iron Works, Port Richmond Iron Works, and the Cambria works.

You are at liberty to show this letter to your father and Mr. Coleman; otherwise regard it as a confidential letter.

Yours truly,

W. R. Jones

(D). Roberts

Thirty years ago the employes of the anthracite coal fields were chiefly English, Irish, Scotch, Welsh and German. To-day, in addition to representatives of these nations, are Poles, Little Russians, Hungarians, Magyars, Lithuanians, Slovacks, Bohemians, Italians, and Swiss, employed in and around the mines.

In the town of Shenandoah twenty different languages are spoken. The complexion of the anthracite mining towns has changed wholly in the last thirty years. On the streets foreign tongues are heard; the tall, dark-complexioned and dolichocephalic Anglo-Saxon is largely supplanted by the thick-set, light-haired, brachycephalic Slav; the Polish and Russian Jew have accompanied these peoples; they hold possession of prominent business sites in mining towns and do a thriving business. The Slavs have brought their religion with them, and have erected imposing church edifices which they liberally support. The Slav has come to stay, and a generation hence the vast majority of laborers in the anthracite mines will be of that character.

Cheap labor was first introduced into these coal fields because of friction between capitalists and laborers. Before the Civil War amicable relations prevailed between the coöperative forces. Then in the majority of collieries employer and employes lived side by side and could peacefully adjust their differences. But as concentration of capital went on, and the disturbing influences, due to scarcity of labor, checked immigration and increased demand for coal, were felt, distrust supplanted confidence, antagonism took the place of coöperation, and for a decade, from 1865-1875, strikes, lock-outs, suspensions, prevailed everywhere. The operators naturally looked for relief. Labor has largely passed beyond their control. Superintendent Kulich, of Coxe & Co., is said to have been the first to bring over some of his fellow countrymen from Hungary, in the year 1870. The following is the statement of T. V. Powderly in his "Thirty Years of Labor" (pages 428-429). "The immigration from Poland began to make itself felt in 1872, and though the Poles were poor and ignorant of our laws they were anxious to learn, and soon began to improve their condition. The tide began to set in from Hungary in 1877. The railroad strike of that year created a desire on the part of the railroad operators to secure the services of cheap, docile men, who would tamely submit to restrictions and impositions. Hungary was flooded with advertisements which set forth the great advantages to be gained by emigration to America. The Italian immigration had been going on for several years, but no authentic record of the actual hiring of men abroad for service in the United States is obtainable beyond the year 1880."

The expressed purpose of introducing these peoples into the anthracite coal fields was to break the power of Anglo-Saxon employes, who had become, during the years of prosperity, intolerably arrogant and arbitrary.

There is to-day in the anthracite coal fields a population of nearly 100,000 Slavs. Statistics taken of 150 shafts in 1897, employing 59,832 persons, showed 23,402 native born, 13,521 native citizens and 22,860 aliens. In three shafts in Lackawanna county, over 75 per cent. of the employes are Slavs. Under the Delaware and Hudson Company, 40 per cent. of the mining force is of this class. Under the Reading from 20 to 25 per cent. of the force underground are Slavs.

In 1898, out of 294 miners' certificates issued in the Fourth District, 183, or 62.24 per cent., were given to this class of laborers. In stripping mining in the Fifth District not a single English-speaking employe, except the foreman, is engaged. In three shafts in Schuylkill county operated by individuals, the force underground was over 70 per cent. Slav. If we leave out the breaker boys, who form about 13 per cent. of the anthracite employes, and count only laborers over 16 years of age, from 25 to 30 per cent. of the employes in the anthracite coal fields are Slavs, or between 30,000 and 35,000 in all. They are not uniformly distributed. In the Lykens and Panther Creek Valleys very few are to be found, while in Shenandoah and Nanticoke they are largely in the majority. Scores of collieries to-day cannot work when the Slavs observe a religious holiday. Anthracite mining cannot at present get along without the Slav.

The anthracite industry seems to have been always afflicted with surplus labor. In 1849, the Pottsville *Miners' Journal* says that half the number of collieries in Schuylkill could supply the market demand. Now-a-days also, the general complaint is that there are too many men.

This surplus labor has been able to exist in the anthracite coal fields because of the unnecessary increase in the number of collieries, which was partly due to the desire for gain, and partly to the system of distribution of railroad cars adopted by the carrying companies. The annual tonnage to be marketed is, during years when a community of interests exists between the railroads, divided between the various carrying companies according to the capacity of the breakers in the territory controlled by them. According to this system of distribution the larger the capacity of the collieries of any corporation or individual operator, the larger share can he claim of the tonnage to be produced. This induced many operators to open collieries which were not necessary to meet the market demand, and which they could not, in years when prices were kept at a remunerative point, hope to operate more than half or two-thirds time. All these collieries, however, employed a force adequate to operate them to the full extent of their capacity, but the demand for coal not permitting this, the necessary result was intermittent labor. The number of men employed could produce at half time the supply the market demanded at remunerative prices.

The nature of the coal trade also favors surplus labor. Anthracite is chiefly used for domestic consumption, which varies with the seasons of the year. A hard winter will enable all the mines to work nine hours a day for possibly three or four months in succession. Then comes a falling off in the demand as the weather grows milder, and the result is intermittent labor. Coal cannot, to any large extent, be produced in summer and stored away for winter. It is best stored in the mines. It is too bulky for yards in close proximity to cities, and the work of loading and unloading is expensive. These difficulties make it impossible to regulate production, so as to give the employes regular work the year round. Hence, when a rush of orders comes, all hands are employed. When demand is at its lowest ebb, the breakers are put on half time.

The table . . . [of coal production] shows the annual increase or decrease in the number of employes and of tons produced from the year 1870 to 1899 inclusive. The accompanying chart also shows how labor during these years fluctuated with production. All through these years there has been surplus labor. More labor is needed to produce coal from the deeper seams, but improvement in the art of mining has more than offset the extra demand for labor on this account.

The table shows that the average net increase per year for the 29 years in the number of employes was 4.92 per cent.; while the average net increase per year in the amount of production was 6.154 per cent. A conservative estimate of the increased production due to improvement in machinery during the last quarter of a century is put at 50 per cent. This is the reason why the number of tons produced and the number of men employed have been kept at about the same ratio, notwithstanding the increased difficulties to be contended with in mining. . . .

Old miners say that the real wages of men in the coal fields are as high to-day as they have ever been. In this estimate they compute the amount of commodities men can procure with the money they earn. The history of the wages paid in this industry during the last sixty years shows great fluctuation; but the difference during this period in the purchasing power of the dollar makes the difference in the amounts received by the workmen far less significant than at first would appear. Three periods of twenty years each stand out distinctly in the chart: From 1840 to 1860, wages were low, averaging about $1.05 a day. From 1860 to 1880, great variation existed, and the fluctuations were remarkable. The maximum was reached in 1869 when wages were $18.18 a week and the minimum, in 1861 when $6.48 was paid. The third period, from 1880 to 1900, presents greater uniformity than the previous one. Wages were adjusted in 1880, and since that date to last October, no reduction or advance was made in the Northern coal field, and the changes in the Middle and Southern fields were due to the sliding scale, which was in vogue there for thirty years, and abandoned last fall at the request of the men.

THE IMMIGRANT AND AMERICAN POPULATION

A sharp debate followed the challenging assertion by Francis A. Walker, a noted statistician, that the immigrants had not really added to the population. Instead, Walker explained, the newcomers had merely driven down the birth rate of the native Americans and had thus replaced a superior with an inferior racial stock. The argument was most strikingly presented in an article in 1891 in The Forum, an extract from which makes up the first selection printed below.[11]

Walker's thesis was repeatedly challenged in the decades after he asserted it. A dispassionate analysis of the whole problem, made in 1940 by the demographer, Walter Willcox, is printed in the second selection that follows.[12]

[11] Francis A. Walker, "Immigration and Degradation," *Forum*, XI, 637-644.
[12] Walter F. Willcox, *Studies in American Demography*. (Ithaca, Cornell University Press, 1940), 395-404.

(A). *Walker*

From 1790 to 1800, the population of the United States increased 35.10 per cent, or at a rate which would have enabled population to be doubled in twenty-three years; a rate transcending that maintained, so far as is known, over any extensive region for any considerable period of human history. And during this time the foreign arrivals were insignificant, being estimated at only 50,000 for the decade. Again, from 1800 to 1810, population increased by 36.38 per cent. Still the foreign arrivals were few, being estimated at only 70,000 for the ten years. Again, between 1810 and 1820 the rate of increase was 33.07 per cent, and still immigration remained at a minimum, the arrivals during the decade being estimated at 114,000. Meanwhile the population had increased from 3,929,214 to 9,633,822. . . .

Between 1820 and 1830, population grew to 12,866,020. The number of foreigners arriving in the ten years was 151,000. Here, then, we have for forty years an increase, substantially all out of the loins of the four millions of our own people living in 1790, amounting to almost nine millions, or 227 per cent. Such a rate of increase was never known before or since, among any considerable population, over any extensive region.

About this time, however, we reach a turning point in the history of our population. In the decade 1830-40 the number of foreign arrivals greatly increased. . . . The question now of vital importance is this: Was the population of the country correspondingly increased? I answer, No! The population of 1840 was almost exactly what by computation it would have been had no increase in foreign arrivals taken place. Again, between 1840 and 1850, a still further access of foreigners occurred, this time of enormous dimensions, the arrivals of the decade amounting to not less than 1,713,000. . . . Again we ask, Did this excess constitute a net gain to the population of the country? Again the answer is, No! Population showed no increase over the proportions established before immigration set in like a flood. In other words, as the foreigners began to come in larger numbers, the native population more and more withheld their own increase. . . .

But what possible reason can be suggested why the incoming of the foreigner should have checked the disposition of the native toward the increase of population at the traditional rate? I answer that the best of good reasons can be assigned. Throughout the northeastern and northern middle States, into which, during the period under consideration, the new-comers poured in such numbers, the standard of material living, of general intelligence, of social decency, had been singularly high. Life, even at its hardest, had always had its luxuries; the babe had been a thing of beauty, to be delicately nurtured and proudly exhibited; the growing child had been decently dressed, at least for school and church; the house had been kept in order, at whatever cost, the gate hung, the shutters in place, while the front yard had been made to bloom with simple flowers. . . . Then came the foreigner, making his way into the little village, bringing—small blame to him!—not only a vastly lower standard of living, but too often an actual present incapacity even to understand the refinements of life and thought in the community in which he sought a home. Our people had to look upon houses that were mere shells for human habitations, the gate unhung, the shutters flapping or falling, green pools in the yard, babes and young children rolling about half naked or worse, neglected, dirty, unkempt. Was there not in this, sentimental reason strong enough to give a shock to the principle of population? But there was, besides, an economic reason for a check to the native increase. The American shrank from the industrial competition thus thrust upon him. He was unwilling himself to engage in the lowest kind of day labor with these new elements of the population; he was even more unwilling to bring sons and daughters into the world to enter into that competition. For the first time in our history the people of the free States became divided into classes. Those classes were natives and foreigners. Politically the distinction had only a certain force, which yielded more or less readily under partisan pressure, but socially and industrially that distinction has been a tremendous power, and its chief effects have been wrought upon population. Neither the social companionship nor the industrial competition of the foreigner has, broadly speaking, been welcome to the native. . . .

If the foregoing views are true, or contain any considerable degree of truth, foreign immigration into this country has, from the time it first assumed large proportions, amounted not to a re-enforcement of our population, but to a replacement of native by foreign stock. . . .

Whatever view may be taken of the past, no one surely can be enough of an optimist to contemplate without dread the fast rising flood of immigration now setting in upon our shores. During the past ten years, five and a quarter millions of foreigners entered the ports of the United States. We have no assurance that this number may not be doubled in the current decade. Only a small part of these newcomers can read, while the general intelligence of the mass is even below what might be assumed from such a statement. By far the greater part of them are wholly ignorant of our institutions, and, too often, having been brought up in an atmosphere of pure force, they have no symapthy with the political ideas and sentiments which underlie our social organization; often not even the capability of understanding them.

What has just now been said would, of course, have been true in some degree of the body of immigrants in any preceding period. But the immigration of the present time . . . is tending to bring to us no longer the more alert and enterprising members of their respective communities, but rather the unlucky, the thriftless, the worthless. . . . There is no reason why every stagnant pool of European population, representing the utterest failures of civilization, the worst defeats in the struggle for existence, the lowest degradation of human nature, should not be completely drained off into the United States. So long as any difference of economic conditions remains in our favor, so long as the least reason appears for the miserable, the broken, the corrupt, the abject, to think that they might be better off here than there, if not in the workshop, then in the workhouse, these Huns, and Poles, and Bohemians, and Russian Jews, and South Italians will continue to come, and to come by millions.

(B). Willcox

The evidence on which Walker relied . . . was never published, I believe, in any fuller form. His assertion remains an assertion, although, coming as it did from the leading authority in the field of Federal statistics, it has deservedly carried great weight.

In the 40 years since his statements were made, new evidence and improved methods of analysis have been introduced. With these helps, it is timely to ask again: Were the rates of decennial increase in the population of the United States between 1790 and 1860, as Walker claimed, approximately uniform? . . .

Walker's statement, "the decline of this rate of increase among Americans began at the very time when foreign immigration first assumed considerable proportions," is not established by this evidence, because neither then nor now is it possible to distinguish the "rate of increase among Americans" in the first half of the nineteenth century from the general rate. . . .

The main inferences, however, are that the population of each part of the United States grew in response to its own conditions at the time, and that the apparent uniformity in the rates of growth before 1850, upon which Walker rested his theory, disappears as soon as the different parts of the country are studied separately. His theory had its value as a challenge of the current belief that immigration regularly increased the population by an amount equal to its number. But it is almost equally incorrect to maintain that it did not increase the population at all. In view of the meager evidence obtainable about the growth of population in the United States in the earlier part of the nineteenth century, it may be doubted whether it will ever be possible to determine where between these two extreme views, both of them apparently incorrect, the truth actually lies. It may be noted, however, that the birth rate as roughly measured by the proportion of children under 5 years of age to 1,000 women of child-bearing age at each census began to fall as early as 1810 and has fallen ever since with one exception, the decade 1850-60, probably due to the large immigration just before 1850 and to the high birth rate among the immigrants which more than balanced whatever fall in the birth rate may have occurred among the native population. In the light of the present evidence, it may be surmised that the approximate uniformity in the rate of increase during the early decades of the last century was due largely to the cheapness and accessibility of good agricultural land on the frontier. This conjecture perhaps some future student will be able to confirm or refute.

4

Immigrant Organization

country or the city, the immigrants faced immense problems of adjustment. The majority who became and remained unskilled laborers met with endless material hardships. But even those who solved satisfactorily the problem of earning a livelihood had to learn the ways of life of the New World.

The whole process was complicated for all of them by the fact that migration did not simply wipe away their earlier experiences. They could not simply acquire fresh habits; they were tied to old ones which they had to adapt to novel conditions. This applied equally to language, ways of thought and of worship and to patterns of family behavior.

Confronted by such difficulties, the immigrants turned to one another for assistance. They had no wish to be alone but sought out the company and aid of their fellows. The later arrivals profited by the mistakes and experiences of those who had come before them. In every sphere of life in which these problems appeared, there arose also organizations of newcomers to ease the difficulties.

76

The one form of organization all carried across with them from the Old World was the church. The immigrants in departing had no desire to abandon their religion; and most of them struggled earnestly to reconstruct the familiar ways of worship in the New World. Their attachment was not simply theological; it was as much a matter of form as of substance. Each newcomer wished to see exactly re-created what he had left behind and could not therefore accept the existing churches whether of the native Americans or of the other immigrant groups. All established their own.

The New World also made unexpected demands that called for novel efforts to educate the children, to provide mutual assistance against illness or disease, and to supply helpless men with the means for social action. The result was a great flowering of voluntary organizations which played an important role in helping the immigrant to adjust to his new life as an American.

THE CHURCHES

Each immigrant group insisted upon building its own churches, because these institutions played an intimate part in their lives. They were familiar places of worship; but they were also integral elements of the way of life of their old homes. The strength of this sentiment is revealed in a contemporary account of a group of Hollanders who had come to Iowa;[1] and also in a description by a historian of the festivals of the Italian immigrants in New York, some thirty years after their migration.[2] Therefore, newcomers to America were not satisfied with the institutions created by others even though they shared an identical religious affiliation. This sentiment was expressed in a letter to the Pope by the St. Raphael Societies who desired the American Catholic Church to recognize the separate character of the German and other immigrant groups, a sentiment which was crystallized in the Cahenslyite Movement.[3]

[1] Stuart, *Zes Maanden in America*, Part II, pp. 25-27, as translated by Jacob Van der Zee, *The Hollanders of Iowa* (Iowa City, 1912), 299-301.

[2] W. P. A. Federal Art Project, *The Italians of New York* (New York, 1938), 86-87, 87-91.

[3] Letter of February, 1891, in *New York Herald*, May 28, 1891; also in Colman J. Barry, *Catholic Church and German-Americans* (Milwaukee, 1953), 313-315.

(A). *Stuart*

'Twas Sunday, and a Sunday which I shall not soon forget. What a quiet, almost holy Sabbath rest brooded over that scene! . . . Such space, and such stillness, seriousness, and peace! How well does the fresh, youthful, simple life of the little colony harmonize with that quiet, pure, virgin nature! About the little settlers' town with its widely-scattered wooden houses, and beyond, here and there, at a great distance, a little blue cloud of smoke rising from the green field of this or that farm hidden in the folds of the undulating prairie.

But see, gradually there comes a stir! Miles away we see them approaching from all directions, churchgoers of this morning: here a light buggy or an open wagon, yonder a slow-moving ox cart, or a horseman, also a single amazon, a stout, young farmer's daughter who comes galloping over the fields, a delightful sight to see. But whether they come fast or slow, they arrive in time: those who must travel long distances are seldom late.

We too betook ourselves to the large "public square," as the place is proudly called, on which the settlers already imagine they see noble buildings but which is now nothing more than a sketch, an open plot of land surrounded by a few small dwellings and four rows of trees which can stand in *our* shadows. But for the moment we see a big stir there. Horses and oxen, unhitched, are tied to posts or allowed to graze, and little groups of men and women form here and there in front of blacksmith shop and church.

Of that church entertain no lofty expectation! It is indeed the most unsightly structure in which I have ever preached. Imagine a small rectangular building of boards, perhaps ten metres long and five metres wide, with a stove in the center and benches around it. That is the school.— Perpendicular to this school-room at one end, like the upper part of the capital letter T, there is a shed with a few rough, unplaned boards on supports to serve as pews, and against the back wall opposite the entrance stand a chair and a table for the minister. This shed and the school-room turned into one form the church. During the week on school-days, the partition between the two rooms is closed, but on Sunday for church services boards are removed from the upper part and the church is then ready to receive an audience.

To be sure this is something quite different from a stately gothic cathedral or the beautiful marble church edifices of New York, but it appeals no less to the emotions; yes, I even dare assert, it is no less picturesque to the eye. It reminds me of Schwartz's picture of the barn where the Pilgrim Fathers in America first worshipped God. Would that my friend Bosboom, who understands so well the charm of light and brown and knows how to put feeling and even poetry into a stable or a view, would that he were here for a short quarter of an hour to catch the ray of light which the pale winter's sun causes to play through the little open side-window against the dark wainscot and upon so many quiet and pious upturned faces; or would that Rochussen could reproduce that audience with a few of his ingenious, characteristic figures; men with quiet power and strength written in their bearing and upon their faces, and women, some of whom were nursing children, with hands clasped in prayer which was none the less real although they embraced what to them was most precious on earth. I have seldom if ever been more inspired by an audience than by the one in the midst of which I was permitted to stand that morning, and if I returned any of the inspiration which those hearers unconsciously gave to me, that Sunday morning on the prairies was not entirely lost for eternity.

(B). *The Italians of New York*

In the early days of New York's Italian colony, when most of its inhabitants were illiterate laborers from the extreme south of the Italian Peninsula, the observance of church holidays and saints' days bore a quaint and picturesque character. The immigrants had brought with them their native costumes, in many cases their only possessions of value, and they wore these costumes on every festive occasion. Their enthusiasm and innocence prevented them from feeling that self-consciousness which by now has destroyed some of the spontaneity and childlike abandon of the old Italian festival spirit. As time goes on the festival attendance grows smaller, the enthusiasm ebbs. . . .

There are, however, certain feast days and saints' days of extraordinary popularity. The Neapolitans come out in full force to honor San Gennaro (St. Januarius), their martyred patron; Sicilians from the vicinity of Palermo glorify Santa Rossilia; and those from the east coast of that island pay homage to Catania's Sant' Agata. Though his miracles were all performed in the North, and he himself was a Frenchman, San Rocco (St. Roch) is nevertheless a favorite with Italians from all provinces, perhaps because his day almost coincides with Ferragosto, as the Southerners call the Feast of the Assumption.

San Rocco is feted in opulent style. Streets are extra-illuminated, bands fill the air with joyous music, fireworks are popped off, and a parade in costume winds its course through the neighborhood. His day, August 16, succeeds Assumption Day. These celebrations usually take place in Elizabeth Street south of Bleecker, in Roosevelt Street and in Hicks Street, Brooklyn.

Then there is the fascinating festival of Our Lady of Mount Carmel. . . . The principal and most solemn rites take place at the Church of Our Lady of Mount Carmel in East One Hundred and Fifteenth Street, where for more than half a century they have set the dominant tone in the religious experience of the neighborhood. On this occasion Little Italy becomes completely transformed. The streets are decorated with flags, banners and flowers. Beautifully illuminated multi-colored arches extend from sidewalk to sidewalk across the roadway. Innumerable stands with pastries, fruits, and souvenirs line the thoroughfares. Worshippers of all classes and ages mill about in dense, jostling crowds. Among the devout Italians who come to the sanctuary to pay homage to Our Lady of Mount Carmel are many living in the remoter parts of the city, and some even from neighboring states who have journeyed here for this occasion. Many of them bring huge, ornate candles to light at the altar. Others bring offerings of gold and silver plaques to the church as tokens of gratitude for favors received at the hands of the Blessed Virgin.

For three days the sanctuary is the objective of a constant pilgrimage. Solemn rites, accompanied by vocal and instrumental music, make up a large part of the festivities. Outstanding preachers deliver fervent sermons. Such is the faith of Our Lady of Mount Carmel followers that there is an endless procession from early morning until late at night. At 10 P.M. the *festa* reaches its climax, with fireworks, music and song. A general gaiety prevails as the thousands of worshippers attest their devotion to the "Queen of Heaven."

The great Neapolitan *festa*, held in Mulberry Street on September 19, honors San Gennaro, who was martyred by the Romans at Pozzuoli in A.D 306. Unlike the celebration in Naples, where the patron's day is observed as a public holiday, the merrymaking here is generally confined (save for the women) to the evening. The narrow street is arched with electric lights of varied colors, and a procession of worshippers follows the effigy of the saint up and down the roadway between booths laden with candies, candles, votive offerings and the like. There are fireworks to top off the festivities.

On Sant' Agata's Day, February 5, her effigy is borne up and down Baxter Street, with several thousand Sicilians following in procession. This saint, the legend has it, performed an unparalleled miracle when, nearly 250 years ago, she deflected with her veil the flow of molten lava from Etna on the very edge of the city of Catania, saving the population from certain death.

Western Sicilians on September 4 turn out on Fourteenth Avenue, between Sixty-second and Sixty-fifth Streets (in Brooklyn) to pay homage to Santa Rosalia, who nearly 300 years ago saved the city of Palermo from a pestilence. It was her bones, her followers believe, that accomplished this miracle, for at the time she herself had been dead for more than four centuries.

There are many other occasions in the church calendar when Italians demonstrate their religious devotion in public. At Christmas, of course, the weather usually forbids any open-air celebration; but the decorations in Italian churches are often elaborate—especially the *presepii* (literally, mangers), which represent miniature scenes of the Nativity with gaily colored figurines of the Holy Family, the Magi, shepherds, sheep and cattle—and of course the Star of the East —all skillfully arranged to represent the Holy Night in Bethlehem. These "mangers" are placed on public view long before Christmas and are held over until Epiphany.

Holy Week, beginning Maundy Thursday afternoon, is also the occasion for parades in those localities where Southern Italians predominate. Lent is ushered in by a carnival on Shrove Tuesday and by a great pre-Lenten ball. Corpus Christi, too, is universally held in high honor and observed on the Thursday following Trinity Sunday.

Feasts are divided, according to the manner of their celebration, into *feste fori*, bearing the double obligation of resting from work and attending mass; and *festi chori*, which are observed only in the liturgy. Besides these there are popular festivals which evoke the carnival spirit among the residents of several Little Italys.

(C). *The St. Raphael Society, 1891*

The above mentioned take the liberty to place before Your Holiness, with deepest respect, the fact that the numerous emigrants constitute a great strength, and could co-operate eminently in the expansion of the Catholic Church in the several states of America. In this way they could contribute to the moral stature of their new homeland, as well as to the stimulation of religious consciousness in the old European fatherlands.

Only the true Church, of which Your Holiness is the highest shepherd, can obtain these happy results because it is the true source of all progress and civilization.

But in order that European Catholics, in their adopted country, preserve and transmit to their children their faith and its inherent benefits, the undersigned have the honor to submit to Your Holiness the conditions, which in the light of experience and in the nature of things, appear to be indispensable for that purpose in the countries of immigration. The losses which the Church has suffered in the United States of North America number more than ten million souls.

1. It seems necessary to unite the emigrant groups of each nationality in separate parishes, congregations, or missions wherever their numbers and means make such a practice possible.

2. It seems necessary to entrust the administration of these parishes to priests of the same nationality to which the faithful belong. The sweetest and dearest memories of their homeland would be constantly recalled, and they would love all the more the holy Church which procures these benefits for them.

3. In areas settled by emigrants of several nationalities who are not numerous enough to organize separate national parishes, it is desirable as far as possible, that a pastor be chosen to guide them who understands the diverse languages of these groups. This priest should

be strictly obliged to give catechetical instruction to each of the groups in its own language.

4. It will be especially necessary to establish parochial schools wherever Christian public schools are not available, and these schools should be separate, as far as possible, for each nationality.

The curriculum of these schools should always include the mother tongue as well as the language and history of the adopted country.

5. It seems necessary to grant to priests devoting themselves to the emigrants all rights, privileges, and prerogatives enjoyed by the priests of the country. This arrangement, which is only just, would have the result that zealous, pious, and apostolic priests of all nationalities will be attracted to immigrant work.

6. It seems desirable to establish and encourage societies of various kinds, confraternities, charitable orgnizations, mutual aid and protective associations, etc. By these means Catholics would be systematically organized and saved from the dangerous sects of Freemasons and organizations affiliated with it.

7. It seems very desirable that the Catholics of each nationality, wherever it is deemed possible, have in the episcopacy of the country where they immigrate, several bishops who are of the same origin. It seems that in this way the organization of the Church would be perfect, for in the assemblies of the bishops, every immigrant race would be represented, and its interests and needs would be protected.

8. Finally the undersigned wish to point out that for the attainment of the objectives which they have enumerated, it would be very desirable, and this they vigorously urge, that the Holy See foster and protect in the emigration countries: a) special seminaries and apostolic schools for training missionaries for emigrants; b) St. Raphael societies for the protection of emigrants, and that it recommend to the Most Rev. Bishops that they establish such societies in the emigration countries where they do not yet exist, and that the Holy See place them under the protection of a Cardinal Protector.

The undersigned hope for the happiest and most immediate results from this organization and these measures. Emigration missionaries trained under the direction of a distinguished Italian Bishop have already gone to America. Others, members of neighboring nations, are waiting, before entering, upon their important and holy calling, for the Supreme Shepherd of the Church, by a decree of his wisdom, to

guarantee the free exercise of their mission. If the Holy See will lend
its indispensable co-operation, wonderful results should follow. The
poor emigrants will find on American soil their priests, their parishes,
their schools, their societies, their language, and thus cannot fail to
extend the boundaries of the Kingdom of Jesus Christ on earth.

Immigrant Organization for Self-Help

*Strangers in an unfamiliar world, the immigrants turned to
one another for help in meeting the numerous problems of adjustment. The result was the spread of an enormous variety of
voluntary associations within which the newcomers organized
their communities. A Massachusetts Commission describes the
range of their activities in 1914.*[4]

The societies which are organized and maintained by the members
of the different nationalities, and which flourish in some form in
every community where there are large groups of immigrants, are a
factor in helping the immigrant through the trials of immigration and
the difficulties of adjustment to new conditions. The chief reason
among all nationalities for the formation of these societies is insurance
against sickness and death, but most of them combine with this some
other objects. Nearly all of them outline an educational and civic
program. They may lack the means to carry this out, yet the statement
of these purposes has an influence upon the members. Cooperation
with these organizations on the part of American agencies would help
the immigrant in solving his own problems, and might mean the carrying out of these larger ideals. The organizations of the Swedes,
French-Canadians and Germans are familiar to Americans, but very
few realize the organized efforts which those who come from Southern and Eastern Europe are making in their own behalf.

A detailed description of the latter cannot be given, but reference
is made to a few of the typical ones among the nationalities which
belong to what is called the new immigration.

There are two organizations among the Greeks in every city or town
in this country where there is a colony of this nationality. The first to
appear is usually the *Greek community*, having as its main purpose the

---

[4] *Report of the Commission of Immigration on the Problem of Immigration in
Massachusetts* (Boston, 1914), 202-207.

building and maintenance of a Greek church, but being also a fraternal organization. In Massachusetts there are nine organized Greek communities; six estimate their membership at over 1,000, one at 10,000. The other three have between 600 and 900 members.

Since 1912 a bread tax of 1 cent for each loaf of bread used has been levied on their members by the Greek communities of Massachusetts. This bread tax, collected each Sunday, is used for the maintenance of the church and of the school, if there is one.

The Pan-Hellenic Union is a national organization with headquarters in Boston. In addition to the payment of sick and death benefits the Union has outlined a comprehensive program for bettering the conditions of Greeks in America by creating a spirit of self-help, by protecting the Greek immigrants and laborers, by aiding in the furtherance of the political ambitions of their much-loved mother country and, at the same time, by instilling in the Greeks of the United States veneration and affection for the laws and the institutions of America. The Pan-Hellenic Union has twenty branches in Massachusetts, one with 1,000 members, three with 500 or over, two with 200 and fourteen with less than 100.

There are several local societies in the large Greek communities whose members are from the same towns in Greece, and whose object is to help each other in time of need and to do something for their town or city in the home land. These societies, however, are rapidly being absorbed into the Pan-Hellenic Union.

Among the Italians the societies are not united, for whatever the object of a society, its membership is usually drawn from those who come from one town or province in Italy. The result is a great number of associations. In Springfield, for example, where the Italian population, according to the census for 1910, is 2,915, there are twelve societies. One society has recently celebrated its twenty-fifth anniversary with great enthusiasm. It reports 400 members, a fund of $3,500 and a record of having paid out, in sick benefits and to destitute families, about $15,000. It is described in its report as a society that "unites us and gives us strength, and will make us more acceptable in the eyes of the American people; that will guide us in all vicissitudes and trouble of life; that will give us work when we are idle; that will succor us with money when we are sick; that will help our families and accompany us with dignified ceremony when we die."

The many Italian mutual benefit societies in Boston are of three slightly different types: first, those which require membership in the Catholic church and are usually named for the patron saint of the vicinity from which the group comes; second, those which do not require membership in the Catholic church and are rather political in their objects; and third, those which have a certain patriotic side and whose members have been soldiers in Italy. All three types have essentially the same benefit features.

The Italian Immigrant Aid Society hardly belongs to this part of the discussion, as it has had much American assistance. Still, since it is subsidized by the Italian government, it is an Italian rather than an American organization. Its objects are to protect the Italian against exploitation and to provide for the return to Italy of those who are sick or discouraged. Its representatives are at the docks to assist those who are entering or leaving the country.

Among the Jews in addition to the large philanthropic societies which are formed by the wealthier to assist in the Americanization of the newcomers and to care for the poor of their faith, there are many smaller societies which are organized and supported principally by the more recently arrived Russian, Polish and Roumanian Jews. The loan societies which have been formed in several cities in Massachusetts seem the most successful of these charities. They are supported by subscription, and they loan, upon the indorsement of a member, small sums without interest. The Hebrew Immigrant Aid Society, to whose work on the docks reference has already been made, is largely supported by Russian Jews. As among the other immigrants so among the Jews mutual benefit associations have been formed; some of these have branches throughout New England. The statement of the objects of these societies usually covers much civic and educational work, but most of them have as yet done very little along these lines.

The Lithuanians have about sixty mutual benefit societies in Massachusetts and about thirty educational societies arranging lectures and classes. Many of these are very closely connected with the church. Distinctive features of the Lithuanian societies of Massachusetts are their "national homes," or club houses, where their clubs can meet, and where a library of Lithuanian books and papers is maintained. There are homes of this kind in three cities, and three more are being built. The Lithuanian Benevolent Society, which was organized to build the home in Boston, is a well-established mutual benefit society with 350 members. The Lithuanian Roman Catholic Alliance has 17 groups in the different industrial centers in Massachusetts, some of the groups having as many as 160 members.

Among Massachusetts Poles there are many branches of the Polish National Alliance. This is one of the largest single societies among the Slavic people in the United States. While it is primarily a mutual benefit society, it is much more than that, for it has special committees for education, agriculture, industry, charity and recreation. The Polish Industrial Association is associated with another large national organization,—the Polish Catholic Alliance. A Polish immigration society has recently been organized which maintains a temporary lodging house where Poles who arrive in Boston and are unable to proceed at once to their destination may stay. It also has a representative to meet the boats in order to protect and help the Polish newcomer. The Polish Young Men's Alliance is a national organization with several branches in Massachusetts; each local branch has a library and a reading room and holds evening classes in English and civics and in gymnastics. The mutual benefit features are the best-developed part of the work.

The Syrian societies are at present at a very early stage of the development of their organizations. In Boston, in connection with the Syrian Orthodox Church, there are two societies,—St. John of Damascus, which supports the church, and the United Greek Orthodox Society, which raises money for the school in connection with the church. This last-named society is managed by a group of men who represent the four societies of Damascus, three active members from each society. There are also organizations in connection with the Syrian Roman Catholic churches. The usual form of organization among the Syrians, however, is to have 13 active members, including the officers, who really constitute the society, whatever the other membership may be. One such society was founded, in the words of one of its members, "to praise the name of the Syrians." The plan is to have those who have been here some time assist the recent arrivals by lectures and informal talks, and so prevent the mistakes and failures which might bring the Syrians into disrepute.

The most interesting organizations, however, found among the foreign-speaking people of Massachusetts are the co-operative societies, usually having stores in which the profits are divided among the members by the giving of interest on shares or dividends of purchases. This form of society lends itself admirably to the uses of the immigrant.

Professor Ford, in his book *Co-operation in New England*, has given a detailed description of these organizations. According to this study there are thirty-one distributive co-operative associations of non-English speaking urban consumers in Massachusetts, of which seven are Lithuanian, six Finnish, five Italian, three Polish, two each French, German, Hebrew and Swedish, one Belgian and one Swedish-Finnish. Of these the Finnish stores, as a whole, show the greatest success. The first one was established twelve years ago; at present there are six. Of these the Kaleva Co-operative Association of Maynard deserves especial mention because it is largely responsible for a movement to federate the Finnish Co-operative societies in New England. According to Mr. Ford, "It was founded in 1907 by Finnish mill hands of that town, and now has over 300 members, only one of whom is not a Finn. The capital stock of $2,900 is in $5 shares. The building in which the store is situated cost $16,000, and $2,300 is received in rents. . . . The store is exceptionally clean, large and attractive, the management experienced and enterprising, and the members interested and loyal. . . . The Kaleva Association is in touch with over fifteen other co-operative stores in this country, a record which is unique. . . . Finnish working men have thus reached a point in co-operation beyond that attained by any other working man's association in New England.

When it is remembered that the members of many of these societies come from countries in which, because of the fear on the part of the dominant race of a revolutionary uprising, they have been practically prohibited from engaging in any form of organized activity, the success of these attempts in America indicates an initiative and an appreciation of the value of association for a common good which are encouraging.

To Preserve the Old Culture

The immigrant organizations were designed not merely to supply existing social needs. They served also to attach newcomers and their children to the cultures of the homeland in which they still found values of importance. The desire to retain such con-

nections was particularly vivid among those who spoke languages not common in America. Each such group attempted through supplementary schools to communicate to the next generation the tongue of its ancestors. A commemorative volume describes the efforts to do so among the Poles of Chicago.[5] An article in a Russian newspaper in New York describes the influence of the press.[6] And a social scientist examines the influence of the Yiddish newspapers upon their readers.[7]

(A). Skibinska

Although very tolerant to all foreign-born people, Americans are perpetually astonished of the Poles' desire to preserve the Polish language and culture among their offspring in America. Some even accuse them of clannishness, of hindering assimilation, of building their own communities, centering their activities, and so on.

It is a pleasure to correct these misapprehensions and to explain to our American friends and neighbors that the Polish language and culture hold endless fascination; not only are they interesting to the Polish immigrant who naturally would wish to preserve Old World custom as much as possible, but to American-born generations as well. There is no element of compulsion in these schools; the children are proud to learn of their parents' country with its 600-year old culture, and fascinating history of knights, warriors and heroes who fought bravely for the independence of their country and then lived at peace with their neighbors when peace was assured. The knowledge of this splendid heritage forms an excellent background for civic pride and endeavor, making the American generations of Poles better citizens in their new homeland.

In nearly every community where Polish people dwell those schools are conducted. The well-trained instructors often vary the two hours of study with folk songs and stories for the children who willingly forfeit a part of their week-end vacations to learn their mother tongue.

---

[5] A. M. Skibinska, "Polish Language Supplementary Schools" in *Poles of Chicago, 1837-1937* (Chicago, 1937), 134-135.

[6] Mark Villchur, article in *Russkoye Slovo* (New York City), June 10, 1919, translated in Robert E. Park, *The Immigrant Press and Its Control* (New York, 1922), 7-9.

[7] Mordecai Soltes, "The Yiddish Press," *American Jewish Year Book*, XXVI (1924), 174-176.

The Polish National Alliance, a fraternal organization with an active, forward-looking youth movement, organized such schools twenty-nine years ago. Madame Mary Sakowska, a prominent woman leader and welfare worker, was the sponsor of this movement. In the year 1908 six schools were organized at such community centers as Kosciuszko Park, Davis Square, Eckhardt Park, Sherman, Mark White and Russell Community Centers. Pioneer teachers in this new field were Janina Dunin and Jadwiga Krassowska-Stopowa. Yearly attendance at these schools reached the total of one thousand pupils. In 1926 under the auspices of the Polish People's University Center, and sponsored by a civil leader, Dr. Wladyslaw Koniuszewski, another school was founded. This was followed by various other centers with a unified program, and by the organizations of the teachers which culminated in the planning of the "Polish School Day" in 1932 with sixteen schools participating in the program with an attendance of three thousand.

The yearly school exhibits of peasant art draw visitors from all parts of the city and many an aspiring young artist has been awarded a scholarship to Poland to study the folklore of his forefathers.

In any summary of the work of the Polish schools it is evident that the knowledge of the Polish language among the American-born youth has created a better contact with their parents who immigrated from oppressed Poland and settled here permanently, building churches, schools, newspapers, and community centers, but who never ceased to long for their newly freed homeland, the Republic of Poland. Knowing that they will not return to ther native land, what is more natural than their desire to pass on to their children this proud and splendid heritage of culture and to make them realize that in making it a part of American culture they are adding to the latter rather than subtracting from its prominence? The immigrant generation is happy to see their youth absorb Polish along with American culture and take pride in the homeland of their forefathers, thus assured of their becoming better and more contented citizens of America.

(B). *Villchur*

Peasants and laborers constitute more than 90 per cent of all the Russian immigrants in the United States. According to the census of

1910, there are 38.4 per cent illiterate among the Russians above fourteen years of age. But even those who are able to read rarely saw newspapers in Russia, and theaters were out of their reach. The Russian village from which the majority of immigrants came had no press and no theater.

Out of 312 correspondents only 16 have regularly read newspapers in Russia; 10 others used from time to time to read newspapers in the *volost,* the village administrative center; 12 were subscribers to weekly magazines.

In America all of them are subscribers or readers of Russian newspapers. *Two hundred of them are theatergoers, and all are visiting the "movies."*

Twenty-five per cent of them read also the American newspapers published in the English language. But some mention the fact that they "understand only one word out five." Others, buying an American daily, just glance over the headlines. "These are easy to understand, and you know all the news," writes one of the correspondents.

The question whether they like American newspapers or not is answered negatively by the majority of Russian readers. Some complain that the newspapers are *too local* in their character. A newspaper in some city like Willimantic is 90 per cent a local paper, and to it the affairs of Willimantic are of more importance than the all-American and the world problems. The Russian readers are used to seeing even in their provincial press an expression of the world's thought. . . . Generally, the responses to the questionnaire paint a picture of a cultural success of the Russians in America. Immigrants from the governments of Grodno, Minsk, and Volyn write that *at home they used newspapers as cigarette papers,* while here they became regular readers of periodicals. An interest in the press creates an interest in the book, in the theater, and the whole outlook of the Russian in America widens. Not only his own interests, the interests of his family and of his circle, become near and dear to him, but also the problems of his country, of the republic in which he resides, and gradually, of the whole wide world.

(C). *Soltes*

The simplification of the Yiddish tongue has helped to spread the Yiddish newspapers among the Jewish masses, the vast majority of whom had not had the benefits of a secular education and had not read any journals in the lands from which they emigrated. The Yiddish press proceeded to develop a generation of readers. Therein lies one of the fundamental reasons for the unusual influence which it exerts upon the mind-content of its large family of readers. It is practically the only source of information to which most of them have access. It guides them in the early stages of their process of adjustment to the new and complex American environment. It has educated the large majority of the immigrant Jews up to the point where they would be in a position to appreciate and read the newspaper as an easy, direct means of keeping in touch with important events which occur in this country as well as throughout the world. To the extent to which it has aroused in the immigrant Jews the demand for Yiddish newspapers, the latter have practically developed their own reading public, and have indirectly prepared their readers for an appreciation of the native press.

The facility and readiness with which the various influences of American life are assimilated by the immigrant in transition, are evident in the manner in which the Yiddish press handles the different features, particularly the news. The utilization of emphatic news headings, frequently bordering on the sensational; the human interest treatment of daily events; the promptness with which the leaders detect changes in conditions and the eagerness with which they adapt themselves to the newly-ascertained desires and interest of their readers; the care, skill and ability with which the newspapers are edited, the spirit of enterprise which characterizes their method of conducting the various departments,—all reflect direct influences of the native press.

In their general features the Yiddish daily newspapers are essentially journals for the masses. Their tendency is towards popularization, with sensationalism as the inevitable culmination. On the other hand, one of the distinctive features of the Yiddish press is the disposition to devote an unusually large proportion of its space to solid reading material such as does not usually find its way into the American newspaper, but which goes rather into the American magazine. The reason for this phenomenon becomes clear when we remember that the Yiddish newspaper is very frequently the only source of information and guidance which the reader has. It is therefore not merely a conveyor of news, but also a sort of literary and popular scientific journal, which deals with a wide range of subjects, supplies a large proportion of miscellaneous reading matter and caters to the needs and interests of the reader of magazine-stuff.

5

The Immigrant in American Politics

AMONG THE PROBLEMS
which immigrants encountered for the first time upon their arrival in the United States was that of the use of political power. The great mass of the newcomers had been peasants or laborers at home; and had therefore been excluded from any share in their governments. None of them had had the experience of living in a democracy; and most of them had been the helpless subjects of despotic masters. They were therefore compelled to learn the ways of a representative political order with little previous preparation.

Naturally they did so only slowly and with difficulty. Their problem was complicated by the fact that American politics was itself changing in the years of their arrival as a rural agrarian society gave way to an urban industrial one. In the decades after the Civil War, especially, when corruption intruded into many areas of government, some immigrants became its unwitting tools.

But more important was the rapidity with which the foreign-born learned to act as free citizens in a democracy. The fact that they acquired citizenship as a right soon after arrival and were thus entrusted with a share of power gave them responsibility; and in time they lived up to it, although there were many difficulties in the process.

Furthermore, the immigrants proved capable of making substantial contributions of their own to the theory and practice of American government. The hardships of their own lives led them to seek a broader scope for government action than some of their native contemporaries. And their ties with their homelands led them to a vision of American principles extending throughout the world, rather than confined to the North American continent.

THE IMMIGRANT AND THE CITY MACHINE

Many observers viewed with anger the deterioration in American political life in the years after the Civil War. Not a few of them were inclined to blame it all upon the immigrant citizens in the growing cities. Their antagonism was particularly directed at the urban political machines which seemed to function with the support of immigrants. Certainly the new voters had new attitudes toward the state. But perhaps the state itself was changing and less responsive than it once had been to the needs of its citizens; and it may be that the machine was the means through which the immigrants sought services no one else performed. In the first selection which follows a reformer examines one such organization critically.[1] In the second a reporter sets down the justification a ward politician gave of himself.[2] And in the final selection a social worker presents an estimate of the attitudes of immigrants to politics. Robert A. Woods, head social worker of the South End House, Boston, a settlement house dedicated to work among the foreign-born in the slums, published his firsthand observations as part of a general study of social conditions in Boston.[3]

---

[1] Lincoln Steffens, "The Shamelessness of St. Louis," *McClure's Magazine*, XX (1902), 546-553.

[2] William L. Riordon, *Plunkitt of Tammany Hall* (New York, 1905), 3-5, 9-10, 46-61.

[3] Robert A. Woods, ed., *Americans in Process* (Boston, 1902), 149-158.

(A). *Steffens*

The convicted boodlers [bribe-takers] have described the system to me. There was no politics in it—only business. The city of St. Louis is normally Republican. Founded on the home-rule principle, the corporation is a distinct political entity, with no county to confuse it. The State of Missouri, however, is normally Democratic, and the legislature has taken political possession of the city by giving to the governor the appointment of the Police and Election Boards. With a defective election law, the Democratic boss in the city became its absolute ruler.

This boss is Edward R. Butler, better known as "Colonel Ed," or "Colonel Butler," or just "Boss." He is an Irishman by birth, a master horseshoer by trade, a good fellow—by nature, at first, then by profession. Along in the seventies, when he still wore the apron of his trade, and bossed his tough ward, he secured the agency for a certain patent horseshoe which the city railways liked and bought. Useful also as a politician, they gave him a blanket contract to keep all their mules and horses shod. Butler's farrieries glowed all about the town, and his political influence spread with his business; for everywhere big Ed Butler went there went a smile also, and encouragement for your weakness, no matter what it was. Like "Doc" Ames, of Minneapolis—like the "good fellow" everywhere—Butler won men by helping them to wreck themselves. A priest, the Rev. James Coffey, once denounced Butler from the pulpit as a corrupter of youth; at another time a mother knelt in the aisle of a church, and during service audibly called upon Heaven for a visitation of affliction upon Butler for having ruined her son. These and similar incidents increased his power by advertising it. He grew bolder. He has been known to walk out of a voting-place and call across a cordon of police to a group of men at the curb, "Are there any more repeaters out here that want to vote again?"

They will tell you in St. Louis that Butler never did have much real power, that his boldness and the clamor against him made him seem great. Public protest is part of the power of every boss. So far, however, as I can gather, Butler was the leader of his organization, but only so long as he was a partisan politician; as he became a "boodler" pure and simple, he grew careless about his machine, and did his boodle business with the aid of the worst elements of both parties. At any rate, the boodlers, and others as well, say that in later years he had about equal power with both parties, and he certainly was the ruler of St. Louis during the Republican administration of Ziegenhein, which was the worst in the history of the city. His method was to dictate enough of the candidates on both tickets to enable him, by selecting the worst from each, to elect the sort of men he required in his business. In other words, while honest Democrats and Republicans were "loyal to party" (a point of great pride with the idiots) and "voted straight," the Democratic boss and his Republican lieutenants decided what part of each ticket should be elected; then they sent around Butler's "Indians" (repeaters) by the vanload to scratch ballots and "repeat" their votes, till the worst had made sure of the government by the worst, and Butler was in a position to do business.

His business was boodling, which is a more refined and a more dangerous form of corruption than the police blackmail of Minneapolis. It involves, not thieves, gamblers, and common women, but influential citizens, capitalists, and great corporations. For the stock-in-trade of the boodler is the rights, privileges, franchises, and real property of the city, and his source of corruption is the top, not the bottom, of society. Butler, thrown early in his career into contact with corporation managers, proved so useful to them that they introduced him to other financiers, and the scandal of his services attracted to him in due course all men who wanted things the city had to give. The boodlers told me that, according to the tradition of their combine, there "always was boodling in St. Louis."

Butler organized and systematized and developed it into a regular financial institution, and made it an integral part of the business community. He had for clients, regular or occasional, bankers and promoters; and the statements of boodlers, not yet on record, allege that every transportation and public convenience company that touches St. Louis has dealings with Butler's combine. And my best information is that these interests were not victims. Blackmail came in time, but in the beginning they originated the schemes of loot and started Butler on his career. Some interests paid him a regular salary, others a fee, and again he was a partner in the enterprise, with a special "rake-off" for his influence. "Fee" and "present" are his terms, and he has spoken openly of taking and giving them. I verily believe he regarded his charges as legitimate (he is the Croker type); but he knew that some people thought his services wrong. He once said that when he had received his fee for a piece of legislation, he "went home and prayed that the measure might pass," and, he added facetiously, that "usually his prayers were answered."

His prayers were "usually answered" by the Municipal Assembly. This legislative body is divided into two houses—the upper, called the Council, consisting of thirteen members, elected at large; the lower, called the House of Delegates, with twenty-eight members, elected by wards; and each member of these bodies is paid twenty-five dollars a month salary by the city. With the mayor, this Assembly has practically complete control of all public property and valuable rights. Though Butler sometimes could rent or own the mayor, he preferred to be independent of him, so he formed in each part of the legislature a two-thirds majority . . . which could pass bills over a veto. These were the "combines." They were regularly organized, and did their business under parliamentary rules. Each "combine" elected its chairman, who was elected chairman also of the legal bodies, where he appointed the committees, naming to each a majority of combine members.

In the early history of the combines, Butler's control was complete, because it was political. He picked the men who were to be legislators; they did as he bade them do, and the boodling was noiseless, safe, and moderate in price. Only wrongful acts were charged for, and a right once sold was good; for Butler kept his word. The definition of an honest man as one who will stay bought, fitted him. But it takes a very strong man to control himself and others when the money lust grows big, and it certainly grew big in St. Louis. Butler used to watch the downtown districts. He knew everybody, and when a railroad wanted a switch, or a financial house a franchise, Butler learned of it early. Sometimes he discovered the need and suggested it. Naming the regular price, say $10,000, he would tell the "boys" what was coming, and that there would be $1,000 to divide. He kept the rest, and the city got nothing. The bill was introduced and held up till Butler gave the word that the money was in hand; then it passed. As the business grew, however, not only illegitimate, but legitimate permissions were charged for, and at gradually increasing rates. Citizens who asked leave to make excavations in streets for any purpose, neighborhoods that had to have street lamps—all had to pay, and they did pay. In

later years there was no other way. Business men who complained
felt a certain pressure brought to bear on them from most unexpected
quarters downtown. . . .

Boodling was safe, and boodling was fat. Butler became rich and
greedy, and neglectful of politics. Outside capital came in, and finding Butler bought, went over his head to the boodle combines. These
creatures learned thus the value of franchises, and that Butler had
been giving them an unduly small share of the boodle.

Then began a struggle, enormous in its vile melodrama, for control
of corruption—Butler to squeeze the municipal legislators and save
his profits, they to wring from him their "fair share." Combines were
formed within the old combines to make him pay more; and although
he still was the legislative agent of the inner ring, he had to keep in
his secret pay men who would argue for low rates, while the combine
members, suspicious of one another, appointed their own legislative
agent to meet Butler. Not sure even then, the cliques appointed "trail-
ers" to follow their agent, watch him enter Butler's house, and then
follow him to the place where the money was to be distributed.
Charles A. Gutke and John K. Murrell represented him in the House
of Delegates, Charles Kratz and Fred G. Uthoff in the Council. The
other members suspected that these men got "something big on the
side," so Butler had to hire a third to betray the combine to him. In
the House, Robertson was the man. When Gutke had notified the
chairman that a deal was on, and a meeting was called, the chairman
would say:

"Gentlemen, the business before us tonight is [say] the Suburban
Railway Bill. How much shall we ask for it?"

Gutke would move that "the price be $40,000." Some member of
the outer ring would move $100,000 as fair boodle. The debate often
waxed hot, and you hear of the drawing of revolvers. In this case (of
the Suburban Railway) Robertson rose and moved a compromise of
$75,000, urging moderation, lest they get nothing, and his price was
carried. Then they would lobby over the appointment of the agent.
They did not want Gutke, or any one Butler owned, so they chose
some other; and having adjourned, the outer ring would send a
"trailer" to watch the agent, and sometimes a second "trailer" to
watch the first. . . . Such, then, is the boodling system as we see it
in St. Louis. Everything the city owned was for sale by the officers
elected by the people. The purchasers might be willing or unwilling

takers; they might be citizens or outsiders; it was all one to the city
government. So long as the members of the combines got the pro-
ceeds they would sell out the town. Would? They did and they will.
If a city treasurer runs away with $50,000 there is a great haloo about
it. In St. Louis the regularly organized thieves who rule have sold $50,-
000,000 worth of franchises and other valuable municipal assets. This is
the estimate made for me by a banker, who said that the boodlers got
not one-tenth of the value of the things they sold, but were content
because they got it all themselves. And as to the future, my boodling
informants said that all the possessions of the city were listed for future sale, that the list was in existence, and that the sale of these
properties was only postponed on account of accident—the occurrence
of Mr. Folk.

Preposterous? It certainly would seem so; but watch the people of
St. Louis as I have, and as the boodlers have—then judge.

(B). Plunkitt

Everybody is talkin' these days about Tammany men growin' rich
on graft, but nobody thinks of drawin' the distinction between honest
graft and dishonest graft. There's all the difference in the world between the two. Yes, many of our men have grown rich in politics. I
have myself. I've made a big fortune out of the game, and I'm gettin'
richer every day, but I've not gone in for dishonest graft—blackmailin'
gamblers, saloon-keepers, disorderly people, etc.—and neither has any
of the men who have made big fortunes in politics.

There's an honest graft, and I'm an example of how it works. I
might sum up the whole thing by sayin': 'I seen my opportunities and
I took 'em.'

Just let me explain by examples. My party's in power in the city,
and it's goin' to undertake a lot of public improvements. Well, I'm
tipped off, say, that they're going to lay out a new park at a certain
place.

I see my opportunity and I take it. I go to that place and I buy up
all the land I can in the neighborhood. Then the board of this or
that makes its plan public, and there is a rush to get my land, which
nobody cared particular for before.

Ain't it perfectly honest to charge a good price and make a profit on my investment and foresight? Of course, it is. Well, that's honest graft.

Or, supposin' it's a new bridge they're goin' to build. I get tipped off and I buy as much property as I can that has to be taken for approaches. I sell at my own price later on and drop some more money in the bank.

Wouldn't you? It's just like lookin' ahead in Wall Street or in the coffee or cotton market. It's honest graft, and I'm lookin' for it every day in the year. I will tell you frankly that I've got a good lot of it, too.

I'll tell you of one case. They were goin' to fix up a big park, no matter where. I got on to it, and went lookin' about for land in that neighborhood.

I could get nothin' at a bargain but a big piece of swamp, but I took it fast enough and held on to it. What turned out was just what I counted on. They couldn't make the park complete without Plunkitt's swamp, and they had to pay a good price for it. Anything dishonest in that? . . .

Another kind of honest graft. Tammany has raised a good many salaries. There was an awful howl by the reformers, but don't you know that Tammany gains ten votes for every one it lost by salary raisin'?

The Wall Street banker thinks it shameful to raise a department clerk's salary from $1500 to $1800 a year, but every man who draws a salary himself says: 'That's all right. I wish it was me.' And he feels very much like votin' the Tammany ticket on election day, just out of sympathy.

Tammany was beat in 1901 because the people were deceived into believin' that it worked dishonest graft. They didn't draw a distinction between dishonest and honest graft, but they saw that some Tammany men grew rich, and supposed they had been robbin' the city treasury or levyin' blackmail on disorderly houses, or workin' in with the gamblers and law-breakers.

As a matter of policy, if nothing else, why should the Tammany leaders go into such dirty business, when there is so much honest graft lyin' around when they are in power? Did you ever consider that?

Now, in conclusion, I want to say that I don't own a dishonest dollar. If my worst enemy was given the job of writin' my epitaph when I'm gone, he couldn't do more than write:

'George W. Plunkitt. He Seen His Opportunities, and He Took 'Em.' . . .

There's only one way to hold a district; you must study human nature and act accordin'. You can't study human nature in books. Books is a hindrance more than anything else. If you have been to college, so much the worse for you. You'll have to unlearn all you learned before you can get right down to human nature, and un-learnin' takes a lot of time. Some men can never forget what they learned at college. Such men may get to be district leaders by a fluke, but they never last.

To learn real human nature you have to go among the people, see them and be seen. I know every man, woman, and child in the Fif-teenth District, except them that's been born this summer—and I know some of them, too. I know what they like and what they don't like, what they are strong at and what they are weak in, and I reach them by approachin' at the right side.

For instance, here's how I gather in the young men. I hear of a young feller that's proud of his voice, thinks that he can sing fine. I ask him to come around to Washington Hall and join our Glee Club. He comes and sings, and he's a follower of Plunkitt for life. Another young feller gains a reputation as a base-ball player in a vacant lot. I bring him into our base-ball club. That fixes him. You'll find him workin' for my ticket at the polls next election day. Then there's the feller that likes rowin' on the river, the young feller that makes a name as a waltzer on his block, the young feller that's handy with his dukes—I rope them all in by givin' them opportunities to show themselves off. I don't trouble them with political arguments. I just study human nature and act accordin'.

But you may say this game won't work with the high-toned fellers, the fellers that go through college and then join the Citizens' Union. Of course it wouldn't work. I have a special treatment for them. I ain't like the patent medicine man that gives the same medicine for all diseases. The Citizens' Union kind of a young man! I love him! He's the daintiest morsel of the lot, and he don't often escape me.

Before telling you how I catch him, let me mention that before the election last year, the Citizens' Union said they had four hundred or five hundred enrolled voters in my district. They had a lovely headquarters, too, beautiful roll-top desks and the cutest rugs in the world. If I was accused of havin' contributed to fix up the nest for them, I wouldn't deny it under oath. What do I mean by that? Never mind. You can guess from the sequel, if you're sharp.

Well, election day came. The Citizens' Union's candidate for Senator, who ran against me, just polled five votes in the district, while I polled something more than 14,000 votes. What became of the 400 or 500 Citizens' Union enrolled voters in my district? Some people guessed that many of them were good Plunkitt men all along and worked with the Cits just to bring them into the Plunkitt camp by election day. You can guess that way, too, if you want to. I never contradict stories about me, especially in hot weather. I just call your attention to the fact that on last election day 395 Citizens' Union enrolled voters in my district were missin' and unaccounted for.

I tell you frankly, though, how I have captured some of the Citizens' Union's young men. I have a plan that never fails. I watch the City Record to see when there's civil service examinations for good things. Then I take my young Cit in hand, tell him all about the good thing and get him worked up till he goes and takes an examination. I don't bother about him any more. It's a cinch that he comes back to me in a few days and asks to join Tammany Hall. Come over to Washington Hall some night and I'll show you a list of names on our rolls marked 'C. S.' which means, 'bucked up against civil service.'

As to the older voters, I reach them, too. No, I don't send them campaign literature. That's rot. People can get all the political stuff they want to read—and a good deal more, too—in the papers. Who reads speeches, nowadays, anyhow? It's bad enough to listen to them. You ain't goin' to gain any votes by stuffin' the letter boxes with campaign documents. Like as not you'll lose votes, for there's nothin' a man hates more than to hear the letter-carrier ring his bell and go to the letter-box expectin' to find a letter he was lookin' for, and find only a lot of printed politics. I met a man this very mornin' who told me he voted the Democratic State ticket last year just because the Republicans kept crammin' his letter-box with campaign documents.

What tells in holdin' your grip on your district is to go right down among the poor families and help them in the different ways they need help. I've got a regular system for this. If there's a fire in Ninth,

Tenth, or Eleventh Avenue, for example, any hour of the day or night, I'm usually there with some of my election district captains as soon as the fire-engines. If a family is burned out I don't ask whether they are Republicans or Democrats, and I don't refer them to the Charity Organization Society, which would investigate their case in a month or two and decide they were worthy of help about the time they are dead from starvation. I just get quarters for them, buy clothes for them if their clothes were burned up, and fix them up till they get things runnin' again. It's philanthropy, but it's politics, too—mighty good politics. Who can tell how many votes one of these fires bring me? The poor are the most grateful people in the world, and, let me tell you, they have more friends in their neighborhoods than the rich have in theirs.

If there's a family in my district in want I know it before the charitable societies do, and me and my men are first on the ground. I have a special corps to look up such cases. The consequence is that the poor look up to George W. Plunkitt as a father, come to him in trouble—and don't forget him on election day.

Another thing, I can always get a job for a deservin' man. I make it a point to keep on the track of jobs, and it seldom happens that I don't have a few up my sleeve ready for use. I know every big employer in the district and in the whole city, for that matter, and they ain't in the habit of sayin' no to me when I ask them for a job.

And the children—the little roses of the district! Do I forget them? Oh, no! They know me, every one of them, and they know that a sight of Uncle George and candy means the same thing. Some of them are the best kind of vote-getters. I'll tell you a case. Last year a little Eleventh Avenue rosebud whose father is a Republican, caught hold of his whiskers on election day and said she wouldn't let go till he'd promise to vote for me. And she didn't.

I've been readin' a book by Lincoln Steffens on 'The Shame of the Cities.' Steffens means well but, like all reformers, he don't know how to make distinctions. He can't see no difference between honest graft and dishonest graft and, consequent, he gets things all mixed up. There's the biggest kind of a difference between political looters and politicians who make a fortune out of politics by keepin' their eyes wide open. The looter goes in for himself alone without considerin' his organization or his city. The politician looks after his own interests, the organization's interests, and the city's interests all at the same time. See the distinction? For instance, I ain't no looter. The looter hogs it. I never hogged. I made my pile in politics, but, at the same time, I served the organization and got more big improvements for New York City than any other livin' man. And I never monkeyed with the penal code.

The difference between a looter and a practical politician is the difference between the Philadelphia Republican gang and Tammany Hall. Steffens seems to think they're both about the same; but he's all wrong. The Philadelphia crowd runs up against the penal code. Tammany don't. The Philadelphians ain't satisfied with robbin' the bank of all its gold and paper money. They stay to pick up the nickels and pennies and the cop comes and nabs them. Tammany ain't no such fool. Why, I remember, about fifteen or twenty years ago, a Republican superintendent of the Philadelphia almshouse stole the zinc roof off the buildin' and sold it for junk. That was carryin' things to excess. There's a limit to everything, and the Philadelphia Republicans go beyond the limit. It seems like they can't be cool and moderate like real politicians. It ain't fair, therefore, to class Tammany men with the Philadelphia gang. Any man who undertakes to write political books should never for a moment lose sight of the distinction between honest graft and dishonest graft, which I explained in full in another talk. If he puts all kinds of graft on the same level, he'll make the fatal mistake that Steffens made and spoil his book.

A big city like New York or Philadephia or Chicago might be compared to a sort of Garden of Eden, from a political point of view. It's an orchard full of beautiful apple-trees. One of them has got a big sign on it, marked: 'Penal Code Tree—Poison.' The other trees have lots of apples on them for all. Yet, the fools go to the Penal Code Tree. Why? For the reason, I guess, that a cranky child refuses to eat good food and chews up a box of matches with relish. I never had any temptation to touch the Penal Code Tree. The other apples are good enough for me, and O Lord! how many of them there are in a big city!

Steffens made one good point in his book. He said he found that Philadelphia, ruled almost entirely by Americans, was more corrupt than New York, where the Irish do almost all the governin'. I could have told him that before he did any investigatin' if he had come to me. The Irish was born to rule, and they're the honestest people in the world. Show me the Irishman who would steal a roof off an alms-house! He don't exist. Of course, if an Irishman had the political pull and the roof was much worn, he might get the city authorities to put on a new one and get the contract for it himself, and buy the old roof at a bargain—but that's honest graft. It's goin' about the thing like a gentleman—and there's more money in it than in tearin' down an old roof and cartin' it to the junkman's—more money and no penal code.

One reason why the Irishman is more honest in politics than many Sons of the Revolution is that he is grateful to the country and the city that gave him protection and prosperity when he was driven by oppression from the Emerald Isle. Say, that sentence is fine, ain't it? I'm goin' to get some literary feller to work it over into poetry for next St. Patrick's Day dinner.

Yes, the Irishman is grateful. His one thought is to serve the city which gave him a home. He has this thought even before he lands in New York, for his friends here often have a good place in one of the city departments picked out for him while he is still in the old country. Is it any wonder that he has a tender spot in his heart for old New York when he is on its salary list the mornin' after he lands?

Now, a few words on the general subject of the so-called shame of cities. I don't believe that the government of our cities is any worse, in proportion to opportunities, than it was fifty years ago. I'll explain what I mean by 'in proportion to opportunities.' A half a century ago, our cities were small and poor. There wasn't many temptations lyin' around for politicians. There was hardly anything to steal, and hardly any opportunities for even honest graft. A city could count its money every night before goin' to bed, and if three cents was missin', all the fire-bells would be rung. What credit was there in bein' honest under them circumstances? It makes me tired to hear of old codgers back in the thirties or forties boastin' that they retired from politics without a dollar except what they earned in their profession or business. If they lived to-day, with all the existin' opportunities, they would be just the same as twentieth century politicians. There ain't any more honest people in the world just now than the convicts in Sing Sing. Not one of them steals anything. Why? Because they can't. See the application?

Understand, I ain't defendin' politicians of to-day who steal. The politician who steals is worse than a thief. He is a fool. With the grand opportunities all around for the man with a political pull, there's no excuse for stealin' a cent. The point I want to make is that if there is some stealin' in politics, it don't mean that the politicians of 1905 are, as a class, worse than them of 1835. It just means that the old-timers had nothin' to steal, while the politicians now are surrounded by all kinds of temptations and some of them naturally—the fool ones—buck up against the penal code.

(C). Woods

There are political virtues of different degrees, but the greatest of these is loyalty. Ward politics is built up out of racial, religious, industrial affiliations; out of blood kinship; out of childhood associations, youthful camaraderie, general neighborhood sociability. Party regularity is simply the coalescence of all these. It is the brightest star in the crown of a political veteran to have been "always regular." The frequent petty insurrections only show the power of this loyalty. They are family quarrels. The offending member is still more loved and even more trusted, so far as family interests are concerned, than any outsider. The very disinterestedness of the outsider makes the family recoil from him. The sudden way in which the most acrimonious political breaches are healed over shows the underlying fraternal bond. Ward politics is an amplified scheme of family communism—a modernized clan. Some day it may perhaps become apparent to the historian, looking back, that this clan life in the midst of civilization went with the industrial and social confusion of the time. The poor in our cities have as fierce a contest with industrial conditions as the barbarians had against wild nature. The similarity of social formation, of ethical standard, goes with the similarity of the facts of the two kinds of life. . . .

The street-corner gangs and a variety of loosely organized clubs form political groups, ready made to the hand of the ward heeler. In the North End certain political clubs leap into activity during campaign time. In the West End there is a remarkable political organization having rooms on the most prominent square in the ward. This club keeps up an active existence all the year round, and is the headquarters for the entire business of machine politics of the ward.

Apart from all formal organizations each ward is divided into several sections, and local lieutenants are appointed to hold together, and bring to the front at the proper time, the vote of their neighborhoods. The local lieutenant devotes himself unremittingly to the people of his section of the ward. He keeps himself acquainted with their whole round of life, and constitutes himself the adviser and helper of them all. By unresting vigilance, together with a careful and comprehensive system of political account keeping and statistics, he knows within a few votes just how much strength his section holds for the party ticket. As campaign time approaches committees are appointed, who divide among themselves the responsibility of seeing and making sure of all the voters in these sub-districts. . . .

Every imaginable supporter of the party has his name enrolled in a card catalogue. Every such person is visited in advance of the caucus, and to the utmost limit of the resources of the machine—with its knowledge of each man's ties, obligations, ambitions, necessities— satisfactorily "fixed." At the caucus, and again at election, voters, as they appear, are checked off by party representatives. . . .

Very special efforts have to be made to adapt political methods to the particular spirit and necessity of the different nationalities in these cosmopolitan wards. There is a constant tendency on the part of the Irish to move away to better favored parts of the city. . . . As the local political leaders are nearly all of Irish origin, and as the Irish are their surest and best reliance, they make determined efforts to re- tain in the ward the remnant of the Irish population. The Roman Catholic churches of these districts, which with enormous establish- ments are in danger of being left stranded, are working toward the same end. It is a fixed rule in Ward 8 that no man can receive a job without pledging himself to remain a voter in the ward as long as he holds the job.

The Jews and Italians are gradually becoming voters under pressure of leaders of their own, who show them the advantages of so doing. Nowadays, the Jew junk collector must have taken out citizenship papers before he can get a license, and the Italian laborer has no prospect of being engaged on city work unless he be an American citi- zen. Peddlers, junk dealers, fruit sellers, organ grinders, sewing-women, clothing manufacturers,—all must have dealings with public officials. Everybody knows, too, that by mistake or otherwise the laws of a strange country are easily broken. Under such circumstances the value of an accommodating expert in public administration is soon realized. The newcomer, in establishing his home, finds that some credit is necessary. The gas company requires security. The politician—not unknown to corporations—gives it. The politician expects votes in return. He has ways of enforcing his displeasure if the votes are not forthcoming. In each identical bearing of the social mechanism where oil is needed, it is possible to put sand.

WIDENING VISIONS OF POLITICS

Some immigrants from the start, and many more as time went on, realized that more was involved in control of the government than the simple disposition of favors. Through their actual involvement in the responsibilities of democracy, they came to perceive that state power offered important opportunities for the advancement of freedom and of the general welfare. In 1852, Carl Schurz, a young German who had come to the United States after the failure of the revolutions of 1848, explained the qualities of American democracy in a letter to a friend still in Europe.[4] In 1915, Alfred E. Smith, a member of the New York State Legislature, who spoke for the Irish immigrants of Manhattan, set forth his conception of what the government might do for the people. The selections from a number of his speeches that year point to a significant change in the direction of American government that would become clearer in the next thirty years.[5]

(A). *Schurz*

I have never before lived in a democratic country and been able to observe the conduct of a free people. I confess without a blush that until now I had only a faint conception of it. My political views have undergone a kind of internal revolution since I began to read the book that alone contains the truth—the book of reality. . . . It is true, indeed, that the first sight of this country fills one with dumb amazement. Here you see the principle of individual freedom carried to its ultimate consequences: voluntarily made laws treated with contempt; in another place you notice the crassest religious fanaticism venting itself in brutal acts. On the one hand you see the great mass

[4] Frederic Bancroft, ed., *Speeches, Correspondence and Political Papers of Carl Schurz* (New York, 1913), I, 5-8.
[5] Alfred E. Smith, *Progressive Democracy* (New York, 1928), 159-164.

of the laboring people in complete freedom striving for emancipation, and by their side the speculative spirit of capital plunging into unheard of enterprises. Here is a party that calls itself Democratic and is at the same time the mainstay of the institution of slavery. There another party thunders against slavery but bases all its arguments on the authority of the Bible and mentally is incredibly abject in its dependence,—at one time it displays an impetuous impulse for emancipation, while at another it has an active lust for oppression.—All these [forces] in complete liberty, [are] moving in a confused tumult, one with the other, one by the side of the other.

The democrat just arrived from Europe, who has so far lived in a world of ideas and has had no opportunity to see these ideas put into actual, sound practice will ask himself, hesitatingly, Is this, indeed, a free people? Is this a real democracy? Is democracy a fact if it shelters under one cloak such conflicting principles? Is this my ideal? Thus he will doubtingly question himself, as he steps into this new, really *new* world. He observes and reflects, gradually casting aside, one after the other, the prejudices with which Europe has burdened him and finally he will arrive at the solution of the problem.

Yes, this is humanity when it is free. Liberty breaks the chain of development. All strength, all weakness, all that is good, all that is bad, is here in full view and in free activity. The struggle of principles goes on unimpeded; outward freedom shows us which enemies have to be overcome before we can gain inner freedom. He who wishes liberty must not be surprised if men do not appear better than they are. Freedom is the only state in which it is possible for men to learn to know themselves, in which they show themselves as they really are. It is true, the ideal is not necessarily evolved, but it would be an unhappy thought to force the ideal in spite of humanity. Here they allow the Jesuits to manage their own affairs; they are not killed, they are not driven out, because democracy admits the liberty of every creed as long as it does not impair the civic liberty of others. They are not opposed with the weapon of official power but simply with that of public opinion. That is not only more democratic but also much more effective, for if the struggle of public opinion with mental subserviency is slow, it is only a sign that humanity is not more mature. This struggle has the advantage that it continually keeps pace with the point of view of the masses and for that reason its victories are less rapid, less brilliant, but more enduring and more decisive.

So it is here with everything. The European revolutionist becomes impatient at this and would like to apply some vigorous blows; but such is humanity that it does not like to be beaten even into reason, and such is true democracy that it will be governed by the public mind not as it ought to be but as it actually is. It is my firm conviction that the European revolutionists will drive the next revolution into a reaction merely through their lust for government, through their desire to improve things quickly and positively.

Every glance into the political life of America strengthens my convictions that the aim of a revolution can be nothing else than to make room for the will of the people—in other words, to break every authority which has its organization in the life of the state, and, as far as is possible, to overturn the barriers to individual liberty. The will of the people will have its fling and indulge in all kinds of foolishness —but that is its way; if you want to show it the way and then give it liberty of action, it will, nevertheless, commit its own follies. Each one of these follies clears away something, while the wisest thing that is done for the people accomplishes nothing until the popular judgment has progressed far enough to be able to do it for itself. Until then, conditions must stand *à force de l'autorité*, or they will totter. But if they exist by the force of authority, then democracy is in a bad way.

Here in America you can every day see how slightly a people needs to be governed. In fact, the thing that is not named in Europe without a shudder, anarchy, exists here in full bloom. Here are governments but no rulers—governors, but they are clerks. All the great educational establishments, the churches, the great means of transportation etc., that are being organized here—almost all of these things owe their existence not to official authority but to the spontaneous co-operation of private individuals. One has glimpses here into the productivity of liberty. Here you see a gorgeously built church; a stock company founded it. There a university; a wealthy man left a large endowment, which is its main capital, and the university is almost entirely supported by subscription. In another place you see an orphan asylum of white marble; a rich citizen built it. And so it goes with an endless list of things. It is only here that you realize how superfluous governments are in many affairs in which, in Europe, they are considered entirely indispensable, and how the possibility of doing something inspires a desire to do it.

(B). *Smith*

Mr. Speaker, in the recent campaign and in the campaign previous there was contained in the platforms of the two great parties a plank which pledged the parties to the conservation of our natural resources. As I see this bill and as I view the policy on the part of the State in reference to such matters, I am of the opinion that this bill should read, "An act to conserve the family life of the State." . . .

What new policy does this bill inaugurate? What new system does this bill inaugurate? The State of New York, under the provisions of this act, reaches out its strong arm to that widow and her children and says to them, "We recognize in you a resource to the State and we propose to take care of you, not as a matter of charity, but as a matter of government and public duty." What a different feeling that must put into the hearts of the mother and the children! What better citizens that policy must make! Why? Because it instills into those young hearts a love, a reverence, and devotion for the great State of New York and its sovereign power.

We are pledged to conserve the natural resources of the State. Millions of dollars of the taxpayers' money, untold and uncounted millions have been poured into that channel. We have been in a great hurry to legislate for the interests. We have been in a great hurry to conserve that which means to the State dollars and cents. We have been slow to legislate along the direction that means thanksgiving to the poorest man recorded in history—to Him who was born in the stable at Bethlehem.

We have been especially blessed by divine Providence in this State. He has seen fit to make it the great financial and the great commercial center of the western world. I believe it will in time be demonstrated that He intends to make it the market place of all the world; and by this legislation, by the adoption of this policy, we are sending up to Him a prayer of thanksgiving for the innumerable blessings that He has showered upon us, particularly in the light of the words of the Saviour Himself, who said: "Suffer little children to come unto me, and forbid them not, for of such is the kingdom of heaven." . . .

I am afraid that a lot of men have an entirely wrong idea about workmen's compensation. Nobody has ever been able to satisfy me that that is a privilege or an immunity. I am unable to figure how that comes into this discussion at all. My idea of workmen's compensation —and I may say it is the idea underlying the thoughts of the men who have suggested such a thing—is that workmen's compensation is an indirect tax upon the industry of the State for the purpose of relieving the shoulders of all the people from carrying the burden of the men injured or destroyed in the upbuilding of an industry. The only part of it that could be said to be a privilege is that part of it which makes all the people of the State pay the expenses of the commission. In order to cite to this convention that the men who drew it had that in mind, by the very provision of the act itself, it is provided that after the first day of December, in the year 1917, the cost of maintaining the commission is to be assessed back upon the State fund and the insurance companies as a further tax upon them for adjusting their business. Now where does that come under this proposal?

The labor laws—why, nobody believes that the labor laws are privileges. As I understand a privilege, it is a matter of favor. . . .

What is the State? Green fields and rivers and lakes and mountains and cities? Why, not at all. It is the people, all the people of the State, and anything that tends to make the members of the State strong and vigorous in turn helps to make the State so, and every one of these enactments has been for the general good and could in no way be described as a privilege.

American Politics and the Outer World

The immigrants could not forget the lands of their birth. Even after they had become American citizens, they retained an awareness of the interests of their friends and relatives, their former countrymen and co-religionists, who had stayed behind. Therefore, they remained concerned with European affairs; and they attempted to enlist support in the United States for the causes of the Old World. Yet, this effort did not involve a conflict of loyalties; the immigrants were simply reaffirming in their own way the general faith in freedom and democracy, in the

*right of self determination and tolerance, that other Americans
also held dearly. American statesmen frequently made this clear
with reference to the activities of Irish-Americans in the nineteenth century. A similar conclusion emerges from a petition forwarded, at the behest of some American Jews, by the Secretary
of State to be delivered to the Czar of Russia on July 15, 1903.*[6]

Secretary of State John Hay

[Mr. Hay to Mr. Riddle]

Department of State
Washington, D.C., July 15, 1903

Riddle, St. Petersburg:

You are instructed to ask an audience of the Minister of Foreign
Affairs and to make him the following communication:

EXCELLENCY: The Secretary of State instructs me to inform
you that the President has received from a large number of citizens of
the United States, of all religious affiliations and occupying the highest
positions in both public and private life, a respectful Petition relating
to the Jews and running as follows:

To His Imperial Majesty the Emperor of Russia

The cruel outrages perpetrated at Kishineff during Easter of 1903,
have excited horror and reprobation throughout the world. Until your
Majesty gave special and personal directions, the local authorities
failed to maintain order or suppress the rioting. The victims were
Jews and the assault was the result of race and religious prejudice. The
rioters violated the laws of Russia.

The local officials were derelict in the performance of their duty.

The Jews were the victims of indefensible lawlessness.

These facts are made plain by the official reports of, and by the
official acts following, the riot.

Under ordinary conditions the awful calamity would be deplored
without undue fear of a recurrence, but such is not the case in the
present instance. Your petitioners are advised that millions of Jews,

---

[6] Quoted in Cyrus Adler and Aaron N. Margalith, *With Firmness in the Right*
(New York, 1946), 268-270.

Russian subjects, dwelling in Southwestern Russia, are in constant dread of fresh outbreaks.

They feel that ignorance, superstition and bigotry, as exemplified by the rioters, are ever ready to persecute them; that the local officials, unless thereunto specially admonished, cannot be relied on as strenuous protectors of their peace and security; that a public sentiment of hostility has been engendered against them and hangs over them as a continuing menace.

Even if it be conceded that these fears are to some extent exaggerated, it is unquestionably true that they exist, that they are not groundless, and that they produce effects of great importance.

The westward migration of Russian Jews, which has proceeded for over twenty years, is being stimulated by these fears, and already that movement has become so great as to over-shadow in magnitude the expulsion of the Jews from Spain and to rank with the exodus from Egypt.

No estimate is possible of the misery suffered by the hapless Jews who feel driven to forsake their native land, to sever the most sacred ties, and to wander forth to strange countries.

Neither is it possible to estimate the misery suffered by those who are unwilling or unable to leave the land of their birth; who must part from friends and relatives, who emigrate; who remain in never-ending terror.

Religious persecution is more sinful and more fatuous than war. War is sometimes necessary, honorable and just; religious persecution is never defensible.

The sinfulness and folly which give impulse to unnecessary war received their greatest check when your Majesty's initiative resulted in an International Court of Peace.

With such an example before it, the civilized world cherishes the hope that upon the same initiative there shall be fixed in the early days of the twentieth century, the enduring principle of religious liberty; that by a gracious and convincing expression your Majesty will proclaim, not only for the government of your own subjects, but also for the guidance of all civilized men, that none shall suffer in person, property, liberty, honor or life, because of his religious belief; that the humblest subject or citizen may worship according to the dictates of his own conscience, and that government, whatever its form or agencies, must safeguard these rights and immunities by the exercise of all its powers.

Far removed from your Majesty's dominions, living under different conditions, and owing allegiance to another Government, your petitioners yet venture, in the name of civilization, to plead for religious liberty and tolerance; to plead that he who led his own people and all others to the shrine of peace, will add new luster to his reign and fame by leading a new movement that shall commit the whole world in opposition to religious persecution.

I am instructed to ask whether the Petition will be received by your Excellency to be submitted to the gracious consideration of his Majesty. In that case the Petition will be at once forwarded to St. Petersburg.

I avail myself, etc.,

You will report at the earliest possible moment your execution of this instruction.

Hay

6

Cultural Contributions

DESPITE THE
difficulties they encountered in the process of crossing to the
New World and of adjusting to American life, the immigrants
made substantial contributions to American culture. At the opening of the nineteenth century, the United States had achieved
political but not yet cultural independence from Europe. The
immense tasks of settling the continent, of developing the economy, and of making a fresh start in every field, absorbed the at-
tentions of the native Americans. They had not, furthermore,
the backlog of inherited traditions, knowledge and techniques
with which contemporary Europeans worked. Therefore, they
were long dependent for stimulus and assistance upon the forces
that emanated from the other side of the Atlantic.

Such influences crossed the ocean in a variety of ways. Americans, for instance, came to know English Romanticism, German
philosophy and French architecture through books and through
visits to the Old World. Extended tours on the Continent gave
some of them insight into new European ideas on education,

117

medicine and music. These contacts grew in importance through the nineteenth century.

But the immigrants also had a role in the transfer of culture. Although the great mass of newcomers were peasants and artisans, who themselves did not play a significant part in the process, there were among them also a small but significant element of exceptional men who established direct links with Europe. Some of these immigrants were themselves trained in the advanced techniques of the Old World. Engineers, sculptors, painters, and musicians who had passed through a European apprenticeship brought with them skills that were scarce and highly valued in the New World. They could immediately make their mark in the United States. Others among them had acquired useful bodies of knowledge which enabled them to teach; a significant number of scientists and scholars took their places on the faculties of American universities and helped to develop learning in the New World. Among still other Europeans, latent talents that would have remained hidden in Europe were brought to the surface in the migration to the New World. The sons of fishermen or of peasants who in Europe would have followed their fathers' callings here emerged into creative productivity as writers and artisans. Finally, there were some who in the course of migration were struck by the new conditions, and gained new insights to which they gave forceful and imaginative expression. These were the contributions of individuals, enabled by their migration to make better use of their talent, who, in doing so, enriched the country to which they came.

A cultural contribution of another sort was made, not by the exceptional individuals who happened to find themselves caught up in migration, but by the new groups in their entirety. Many immigrants who settled and developed their own way of life in the United States opened to the vision of Americans a new perspective on what culture might be like. The descendants of the older stocks, confronted entirely different people, and came to see and understand the passionate joys and sorrows of the Italians, the devotion to family life and good fellowship of the

Germans. That alone was a stimulus. But in addition, the immigrant communities themselves supported authentic cultural forms that would profoundly influence the native culture. These contributions ranged from changes in diet, dress, dance and folk music to influences upon the theater, literature, and art. Many of these influences are only just beginning to be felt in many areas of American life.

The European Scholar as a Teacher

At mid-century, the American college was still undeveloped by contrast with the universities of Europe. It was primarily a place where young boys passed through four years of moderate discipline to acquire a little rudimentary learning; and its teachers were men of little skill or ability. In the midst of these institutions there were planted a number of European scholars whose standards of learning inspired many who studied under them. In the selection which follows, George Herbert Palmer, a distinguished philosopher, looks back upon the influence of Evangelinus Apostolides Sophocles, his teacher of Greek at Harvard University.[1]

On the 14th of February, 1883, Evangelinus Apostolides Sophocles, Professor of Ancient, Byzantine, and Modern Greek in Harvard University, died at Cambridge, in the corner room of Holworthy Hall which he had occupied for nearly forty years. A past generation of American schoolboys knew him gratefully as the author of a compact and lucid Greek grammar. College students—probably as large a number as ever sat under an American professor—were introduced by him to the poets and historians of Greece. Scholars of a riper growth, both in Europe and America, have wondered at the precision and loving diligence with which, in his dictionary of the later and Bzyantine Greek, he assessed the corrupt literary coinage of his native land. His brief contributions to the *Nation* and other journals were always noticeable for exact knowledge and scrupulous literary honesty. As a great scholar, therefore, and one who through a long life labored to beget scholarship in others, Sophocles deserves well of America. At a

[1] George Herbert Palmer, *The Teacher* (Boston, 1908), 283-284, 289-293, 297-298, 300-303, 308.

time when Greek was usually studied as the schoolboy studies it, this strange Greek came among us, connected himself with our oldest university, and showed us an example of encyclopædic learning, and such familiar and living acquaintance with Homer and Æschylus—yes, even with Polybius, Lucian, and Athenæus—as we have with Tennyson and Shakespeare and Burke and Macaulay. More than this, he showed us how such learning is gathered. To a dozen generations of impressible college students he presented a type of an austere life directed to serene ends, a life sufficient for itself and filled with a never-hastening diligence which issued in vast mental stores. . . .

In his scheme, little things were kept small and great things large. What was the true reading in a passage of Aristophanes, what the usage of a certain word in Byzantine Greek,—these were matters on which a man might well reflect and labor. But of what consequence was it if the breakfast was slight or the coat worn? Accordingly, a single room, in which a light was seldom seen, sufficed him during his forty years of life in the college yard. It was totally bare of comforts. It contained no carpet, no stuffed furniture, no bookcase. The college library furnished the volumes he was at any time using, and these lay along the floor, beside his dictionary, his shoes, and the box that contained the sick chicken. A single bare table held the book he had just laid down, together with a Greek newspaper, a silver watch, a cravat, a paper package or two, and some scraps of bread. His simple meals were prepared by himself over a small open stove, which served at once for heat and cookery. Eating, however, was always treated as a subordinate and incidental business, deserving no fixed time, no dishes, nor the setting of a table. The peasants of the East, the monks of southern monasteries, live chiefly on bread and fruit, relished with a little wine; and Sophocles, in spite of Cambridge and America, was to the last a peasant and a monk. Such simple nutriments best fitted his constitution, for "they found their acquaintance there." The western world had come to him by accident, and was ignored; the East was in his blood, and ordered all his goings. Yet, as a grave man of the East might, he had his festivities, and could on occasion be gay. Among a few friends he could tell a capital story and enjoy a well-cooked dish. But his ordinary fare was meager in the extreme. For one of his heartier meals he would cut a piece of meat into bits and roast it on a spit, as Homer's people roasted theirs. "Why not use a gridiron?" I once asked. "It is not the same," he said. "The juice then runs into the fire. But when I turn my spit it bastes itself." His taste was more than usually sensitive, kept fine and discriminating by the restraint in which he held it. . . .

Unquestionably much of his disposition to remain aloof and to resist the on-coming intruder was bred by the experiences of his early youth. His native place, Tsangarada, is a village of eastern Thessaly, far up among the slopes of the Pindus. Thither, several centuries ago, an ancestor led a migration from the west coast of Greece, and sought a refuge from Turkish oppression. From generation to generation his fathers continued to be shepherds of their people, the office of Proëstos, or governor, being hereditary in the house. Sturdy men those ancestors must have been, and picturesque their times. In late winter afternoons, at 3 Holworthy, when the dusk began to settle among the elms about the yard, legends of these heroes and their far-off days would loiter through the exile's mind. At such times bloody doings would be narrated with all the coolness that appears in Caesar's Commentaries, and over the listener would come a sense of a fantastic world as different from our own as that of Bret Harte's Argonauts. "My great-grandfather was not easily disturbed. He was a young man and Proëstos. His stone house stood apart from the others. He was sitting in its great room one evening, and heard a noise. He looked around, and saw three men by the farther door. 'What are you here for?' 'We have come to assassinate you.' 'Who sent you?' 'Andreas.' It was a political enemy. 'How much did Andreas promise you?' 'A dollar.' 'I will promise you two dollars if you will go and assassinate Andreas.' So they turned, went, and assassinated Andreas. My great-grandfather went to Scyros the next day, and remained there five years. In five years these things are forgotten in Greece. Then he came back, and brought a wife from Scyros, and was Proëstos once more." . . .

This man, then, by birth, training, and temper a solitary; whose heritage was Mt. Olympus, and the monastery of Justinian, and the Greek quarter of Cairo, and the isles of Greece; whose intimates were Hesiod and Pindar and Arrian and Basilides,—this man it was who, from 1842 onward, was deputed to interpret to American college boys the hallowed writings of his race. Thirty years ago too, at the period when I sat on the green bench in front of the long-legged desk, college boys were boys indeed. They had no more knowledge than the high-school boy of today, and they were kept in order by much the same methods. Thus it happened, by some jocose perversity in the arrangement of human affairs, that throughout our Sophomore and Junior years we sportive youngsters were obliged to endure Sophocles, and Sophocles was obliged to endure us. No wonder if he treated us with a good deal of contempt. No wonder that his power of scorn, originally splendid, enriched itself from year to year. We learned, it is true, something about everything except Greek; and the best thing we learned was a new type of human nature. Who that was ever his pupil will forget the calm bearing, the occasional pinch of snuff, the averted eye, the murmur of the interior voice, and the stocky little figure with the lion's head? There in the corner he stood, as stranded and solitary as the Egyptian obelisk in the hurrying Place de la Concorde. In a curious sort of fashion he was faithful to what he must have felt an obnoxious duty. He was never absent from his post, nor did he cut short the hours, but he gave us only such attention as was nominated in the bond; . . .

In those easy-going days, when men were examined for entrance to college orally and in squads, there was a good deal of eagerness among the knowing ones to get into the squad of Sophocles; for it was believed that he admitted everybody, on the ground that none of us knew any Greek, and it was consequently unfair to discriminate. Fantastic stories were attributed to him, for whose truth or error none could vouch, and were handed on from class to class. "What does Philadelphia mean?" "Brotherly love," the student answers. "Yes! It is to remind us of Ptolemy Philadelphus, who killed his brother." . . . "Do you read your examination books?" he once asked a fellow instructor. "If they are better than you expect, the writers cheat; if they are no better, time is wasted." "Is today story day or contradiction day?" he is reported to have said to one who, in the war time, eagerly handed him a newspaper, and asked if he had seen the morning's news.

How much of this cynicism of conduct and of speech was genuine perhaps he knew as little as the rest of us; but certainly it imparted a pessimistic tinge to all he did and said. To hear him talk, one would suppose the world was ruled by accident or by an utterly irrational fate; for in his mind the two conceptions seemed closely to coincide. His words were never abusive; they were deliberate, peaceful even; but they made it very plain that so long as one lived there was no use in expecting anything. Paradoxes were a little more probable than ordered calculations; but even paradoxes would fail. Human beings were altogether impotent, though they fussed and strutted as if they could accomplish great things. How silly was trust in men's goodness and power, even in one's own! Most men were bad and stupid,—Germans especially so. The Americans knew nothing, and never could know. A wise man would not try to teach them. Yet some persons dreamed of establishing a university in America! Did they expect scholarship where there were politicians and business men? Evil influences were far too strong. They always were. The good were made expressly to suffer, the evil to succeed. Better leave the world alone, and keep one's self true. "Put a drop of milk into a gallon of ink; it will make no difference. Put a drop of ink into a gallon of milk; the whole is spoiled." . . .

All this whimsicality and pessimism would have been cheap enough, and little worth recording, had it stood alone. What lent it price and beauty was that it was the utterance of a singularly self-denying and tender soul. The incongruity between his bitter speech and his kind heart endeared both to those who knew him. Like his venerable cloak, his grotesque language often hid a bounty underneath. How many students have received his surly benefactions! In how many small tradesmen's shops did he have his appointed chair! His room was bare: but in his native town an aqueduct was built; his importunate and ungrateful relatives were pensioned; the monks of Mt. Sinai were protected against want; the children and grandchildren of those who had befriended his early years in America were watched over with a father's love; and by care for helpless creatures wherever they crossed his path he kept himself clean of selfishness. . . .

In the last days of his life, it is true, when his thoughts were oftener in Arabia than in Cambridge, he once or twice referred to "the ambition of learning" as the temptation which had drawn him out from the monastery, and had given him a life less holy than he might have led among the monks. But these were moods of humility rather than of regret. Habitually he maintained an elevation above circumstances, —was it Stoicism or Christianity?—which imparted to his behavior, even when most eccentric, an unshakable dignity. When I have found him in his room, curled up in shirt and drawers, reading the "Arabian Nights," the Greek service book, or the "Ladder of the Virtues" by John Klimakos, he has risen to receive me with the bearing of an Arab sheikh, and has laid by the Greek folio and motioned me to a

chair with a stateliness not natural to our land or century. It would
be clumsy to liken him to one of Plutarch's men; for though there
was much of the heroic and extraordinary in his character and manners, nothing about him suggested a suspicion of being on show. The
mold in which he was cast was formed earlier. In his bearing and
speech, and in a certain large simplicity of mental structure, he was
the most Homeric man I ever knew.

THE EUROPEAN AS AN IMPRESARIO

> *Musical taste in the United States began to take form be-*
> *tween 1830 and 1870. It matured slowly, hampered as it was by*
> *the undeveloped tastes of its audience, the unreliability of its*
> *performers, and the difficulties of concert life. In the process, a*
> *rather small number of European impresarios played a critical*
> *role. Among them was Theodore Thomas who had exerted a*
> *substantial influence upon music in the United States by the*
> *end of the nineteenth century. Born and trained in Germany,*
> *he helped to establish the symphony orchestra as an institution*
> *in America. The following account reveals some of the problems*
> *he encountered in the United States.*[2]

In 1862 I concluded to devote my energies to the cultivation of the
public taste for instrumental music. Our chamber concerts had created a spasmodic interest, our programs were reprinted as models of
their kind, even in Europe, and our performances had reached a high
standard. As a concert violinist, I was at that time popular, and
played much. But what this country needed most of all to make it
musical was a good orchestra, and plenty of concerts within reach of
the people. The Philharmonic Society, with a body of about sixty
players, and five yearly subscription concerts, was the only organized
orchestra which represented orchestral literature in this large country.

It is true that the public was admitted to a number of its rehearsals,
in addition to its concerts, but their influence was not salutary. The
orchestra was often incomplete. If a member had an engagement, he
would go to it instead of to the rehearsal. When one of the wind
choir was thus absent, his place would be filled for the occasion as
best it could. A clarinet or oboe part would be played on a violin, or a

---

[2] Theodore Thomas, *A Musical Autobiography*. George P. Upton, ed. (Chicago,
1905), I, 50-52, 54, 55-56, 73-74.

bassoon part on the 'cello, etc. The conductor therefore could not rehearse as he ought, and the audience talked at pleasure. Under these circumstances justice could not be done to the standard, much less to the modern and contemporary works. Such conditions debarred all progress.

I had been prominent before the public in chamber concerts, and as concertmeister (leader of the violins), of the opera since 1855, and during later years, also, as conductor of concerts and opera, and I thought the time had come to form an orchestra for concert purposes. I therefore called a meeting of the foremost orchestra musicians of New York, told them of my plans to popularize instrumental music, and asked their coöperation. I began by giving some concerts at Irving Hall, and conducted some Brooklyn Philharmonic concerts, alternating with Theodore Eisfeld; and in 1864 I gave my first series of Symphony Soirees, with an orchestra of about sixty men. These concerts were at once successful artistically but only moderately so financially. During the summer of 1865 a series of concerts was given in the afternoon at Belvedere Lion Park, One Hundred and Tenth Street, with an orchestra of thirty players.

During the winter of 1865-66 more concerts were given, and in the summer of 1866 a series of one hundred Summer Night Concerts was inaugurated at Terrace Garden, with enough success to give promise for the future. An audience had been collected and educated to enjoy that form of entertainment, and I had succeeded in finding a respectable occupation during the summer months for a small orchestra. During the season of 1866-67 several concerts were given, the number of which was increased by the opening of Steinway Hall. . . .

These concerts were very successful, and the programs had improved and advanced. It was in this season that some business men offered to build a hall for me, which would be suitable for summer concerts. The Terrace Garden concerts had always been given in the open air, the orchestra playing in an inclosure, while the audience were seated under the trees. When it rained there was a scramble for a hall in the adjacent building. We also had many little extravaganzas, which provoked much amusement. On one occasion, for instance, while playing the "Linnet Polka," I requested the piccolo players to climb up into the trees before the piece began. When they commenced playing from their exalted position in the branches, it made a sensation. I remember another funny incident which happened about this time. In the "Carnival of Venice" the tuba player had been sent, not up the trees, but back of the audience into the shrubbery. . . .

The thought of a permanent orchestra was natural and inevitable. The support of the public was growing, the orchestra was progressing in every way, and it had gained in size and quality of tone. For the Symphony Soirees, even as early as 1867, we had already increased the number of the orchestra to eighty men.

In the season of 1868-69, I began to travel with the orchestra. I found, however, that although New York and Brooklyn did not provide engagements enough to fill the necessary time of an orchestra, they nevertheless offered too many to permit us to go far from home. After the summer of 1869, therefore, I thought the orchestra was sufficiently well known over the whole country, and I decided, as the only means whereby I could keep my organization together, to devote our entire time to traveling. Accordingly I organized my orchestra on a permanent basis. . . .

The New York Philharmonic Society is the oldest orchestral organization in America, and has the great merit that it gave good music and an opportunity to hear the great master-works when no other society did so. Its endeavors were always for a noble cause—for art. Many misstatements and perversions of fact have been made, some with a sinister purpose and others ignorantly, with reference to the history of this society. It has been charged, for instance, that it was forced to elect me its conductor on account of my rivalry, and because I took away its best men for my orchestra. Except for these untruthful statements, I should not have alluded to the following facts, but I think I owe it to myself to give them to the public, and show that the reverse was the case.

My first instrumentalists were mostly brought over from Europe, and as long as I traveled I could offer them the inducement of a good engagement. I had the pick of the men, and had absolute control. I could make changes in my orchestra when I thought it necessary without consulting any one. The Philharmonic Society could not. This was, of course, to my advantage, but it was also for the benefit of the public, for it resulted in progress. Previous to Carl Bergmann's death, consultations had taken place between prominent members of the

Philharmonic Society and myself for the purpose of effecting a combination which would enable me to become its conductor. We could not come to an understanding, however, because they desired me to give up my Symphony Concerts. I refused to accept any conditions. In 1876, Bergmann died, and I was approached again, but as the same conditions were insisted upon, I again refused. Leopold Damrosch was thereupon elected conductor, and the season was financially disastrous. The following year I was elected conductor without any conditions, but later I voluntarily showed my respect for the society by discontinuing my Symphony Concerts, against the wishes and advice of my personal friends, because I thought it better for the cause of art that a society rather than an individual should be in authority. Besides this, during all the years that I was its conductor, I never drew the full amount of salary to which I was entitled by my contract.

An Immigrant Author

The immigrants produced an extensive literature of their own. But the barriers of language kept most native Americans ignorant of it, except for a few works that were so commanding as to deserve translation. Among those which quickly gained a wide general reputation was O. E. Rölvaag's Giants in the Earth. *Rölvaag composed this monumental novel out of his own observations of the migration to the New World. In the selection which follows, Lincoln Colcord gives a perceptive account of the influences which played upon this writer.*[3]

In Rölvaag we have a European author of our own—one who writes in America, about America, whose only aim is to tell of the contributions of his people to American life; and who yet must be translated for us out of a foreign tongue. . . .

There are certain points of technique and construction which show at a glance that the author of this book is not a native American. Rölvaag is primarily interested in psychology, in the unfolding of character; the native American writer is primarily interested in plot and incident. Rölvaag is preoccupied with the human cost of empire building, rather than with its glamour and romance. His chief char-

---

[3] Introduction by Lincoln Colcord to O. E. Rölvaag, *Giants in the Earth* (New York, 1929), xxiii-xxxiii.

acter, Beret, is a failure in terms of pioneer life; he aims to reveal a deeper side of the problem, by showing the distress of one who could not take root in new soil. Beret's homesickness is the dominant *motif* of the tale. Even Per Hansa, the natural-born pioneer, must give his life before the spirit of the prairie is appeased. This treatment reflects something of the gloomy fatalism of the Norse mind; but it also runs close to the grim reality of pioneering, a place the bravest art would want to occupy. *Giants In The Earth* never turns aside from the march of its sustained and inevitable tragedy. The story is told almost baldly at times, but with an unerring choice of simple human detail. When we lay it down we have gained a new insight into the founding of America.

Ole Edvart Rölvaag was born April 22, 1876, in a small settlement on the island of Dönna, in the district of Helgeland, just south of where the Arctic Circle cuts the coast of Norway. All the people in this settlement were fishermen. In summer they fished in small open boats, coming home every night; in winter they went in larger boats, carrying crews of from four to six men, to the historic fishing grounds off the Lofoten Islands, where the Maelstrom runs and the coast stretches away to North Cape and beyond. It was a life full of hardship and danger, with sorrow and poverty standing close at hand. The midnight sun shone on them for a season; during the winter they had the long darkness. . . . There Rölvaag's forebears had lived, going out to the fisheries, since time immemorial.

His father . . . is the image of a New England sea captain. The family must have been a remarkable one. An uncle, his father's brother, had broken away from the fishing life and made himself a teacher of prominence in a neighboring locality. An older brother had the mind of a scholar; but something happened—he went on with the fishing, and died long ago. There was a brilliant sister, also, who died young. These two evidently overshadowed Rölvaag while he was growing up; his case as a child seemed hopeless—he could not learn. Nevertheless, he had a little schooling, mostly of a semireligious nature. The school lay seven miles away, across the rocks and moors; that gave him a fourteen-mile walk for his daily education. He went to school nine weeks a year, for seven years. This ended at the age of fourteen, when his father finally told him that he was not worth educating. That was all the schooling he had in Norway.

Once during the period of childhood he was walking in the dusk with his mother; they had been gathering kelp on the rocks which they boiled and fed to the cattle; and now they were on their way home. His mother took him by the hand and asked him what he wanted to be when he grew up. "I want to be a poet," he told her. This was the only time he ever revealed himself to a member of his family. He remembers the quiet chuckle with which his mother received the news; she did not take him to task, nor try to show him how absurd it was, but she couldn't restrain a kindly chuckle as they went along the rock path together. That winter they had only potatoes and salt herring to eat, three times a day; his mother divided the potatoes carefully, for there were barely enough to go around.

In the place of education was the reading—for this was a reading family. The precinct had a good library, furnished by the state. Rölvaag had learned to read after a long struggle, and his head was always in a book. The first novel he ever read was Cooper's *The Last of the Mohicans* in the Norwegian. All of Cooper's novels followed, and the novels of Dickens and Captain Marryat and Bulwer-Lytton. Then came the works of Ingemann, the Danish historical novelist; the works of Zakarias Topelius, the great Swedish romanticist; the works of the German, Paul Heyse; and the complete works of their own great novelists, especially Björnson and Jonas Lie. For miscellaneous reading there were such things as the tales of Jules Verne and H. Rider Haggard and Alexandre Dumas, Carlyle's *The French Revolution*, and Stanley's *Across the Dark Continent*. Neither did they lack the usual assortment of dime novels and shilling-shockers, in paper covers. . . .

By this time Rölvaag had become a fisherman himself, like everyone else in the community. He went on his first trip to the Lofoten fishing grounds at the age of fifteen. In all, he fished five years, until he had just passed twenty. Every year he was growing more discontented. In the winter of 1893 a terrible storm devastated the fishing fleet, taking tragic toll among his friends and fellow fishermen. The boat he sailed in escaped only by a miracle. This experience killed his first romantic love of the fishing life; he sat down then and wrote to an uncle in South Dakota, asking him for a ticket to the United States. Not that he felt any particular call to go to America; he only thought of getting away. He longed for the unknown and untried—for something secret and inexpressible. Vaguely, stubbornly, he wanted the chance to fulfill himself before he died. But the uncle, doubtless influenced by Rölvaag's family reputation, refused to help him; and the fishing life went on.

Two more years passed, years of deepening revolt—when suddenly the uncle in South Dakota changed his mind. One day a ticket for America arrived. The way of escape was at hand. . . .

Rölvaag himself has told about the journey in his first book, *Amerika-Breve* (*Letters from America*), published in 1912, a work which is largely autobiographical and which struck home in a personal way to his Norwegian-American readers. He landed in New York in August of 1896. He was not even aware that he would require money for food during the railway trip; in his pocket were an American dime and a copper piece from Norway. For three days and nights, from New York to South Dakota, he lived on a single loaf of bread; the dime went for tobacco somewhere along the vast stretches unfolding before him. Through an error in calculation his uncle failed to meet him at the country station where he finally disembarked. He had no word of English with which to ask his way. The prairie spread on every hand; the sun was going down. He walked half the night, without food or water, until at last he found Norwegians who could direct him, reached his uncle's farm, and received a warm welcome.

Then began three years of farming. At the end of that time he knew that he did not like it; this was not the life for him. He had saved a little money, but had picked up only a smattering of English. A friend kept urging him to go to school. But his father's verdict, which so far had ruled his life, still had power over him; he firmly believed that it would be of no use, that he was not worth educating. Instead he went to Sioux City, Iowa, and tried to find work there—factory work, a chance to tend bar in a saloon, a job of washing dishes in a restaurant. But nothing offered; he was forced to return to the farm. He had now reached another crossroads in his life; a flat alternative faced him—farming or schooling. As the lesser of two evils, he entered Augustana College, a grammar or preparatory school in Canton, South Dakota, in the fall of 1899. At that time he was twenty-three years old.

Once at school, the fierce desire for knowledge, so long restrained, took him by storm. In a short while he discovered the cruel wrong that had been done him. His mind was mature and receptive; he was able to learn with amazing ease; in general reading, in grasp of life and strength of purpose, he was far in advance of his fellow students.

He graduated from Augustana in the spring of 1901; that fall he entered St. Olaf College, with forty dollars in his pocket. In four years he had worked his way through St. Olaf, graduating with honors in 1905, at the age of twenty-eight. On the promise of a faculty position at his *alma mater*, he borrowed five hundred dollars and sent himself for a year to the University of Oslo in Norway. Returning from this post-graduate work in 1906, he took up his teaching at St. Olaf College. . . .

He had married in 1908. In 1920 a tragedy occurred in his family— one of his children was drowned under terrible circumstances. This seems to have shaken him out of the war inertia and stirred his creative life again. That year he wrote and published his first strong novel, *To Tullinger* (*Two Fools*), the story of a rough, uncultivated couple, incapable of refinement, who gain success in America and develop the hoarding instinct to a fantastic degree. This book, too, made a sensation among Norwegian-Americans.

Then, in 1922, came *Laengselens Baat* (*The Ship of Longing*), which seems to have been Rölvaag's most introspective and poetical effort up to the present time. It is the study of a sensitive, artistic youth who comes to America from Norway full of dreams and ideals, expecting to find all that his soul longs for; he does not find it, with the result that his life goes down in disaster. Needless to say, this book was not popular with his Norwegian-American audience. The truth-teller of *To Tullinger* was now going a little too far.

All of these works were written and published in Norwegian. They were brought out under the imprint of the Augsburg Publishing House, of Minneapolis, and circulated only among those Norwegian-Americans who had retained the language of the old country. The reason why none of them had reached publication in Norway is characteristic. In 1912 the manuscript of *Amerika-Breve* had been submitted to Norwegian publishers. They had returned a favorable and even enthusiastic opinion, but had insisted on certain changes in the text. These changes Rölvaag had refused to concede, feeling that they marred the artistic unity of his work. In anger and disappointment, he had at once published with the local house; and with each successive volume the feeling of artistic umbrage had persisted—it had not seemed worth while to try to reach the larger field.

But in the spring of 1923, an item appeared in the Norwegian press to the effect that the great novelist Johan Bojer was about to visit the

United States, for the purpose of collecting material on the Norwegian-American immigration. He proposed to write an epic novel on the movement. This news excited Rölvaag tremendously; he felt that the inner truth of the Norwegian-American immigration could be written only by one who had experienced the transplanting of life, who shared the psychology of the settlers. His artistic ambition was up in arms; this was his own field.

He immediately obtained a year's leave of absence from St. Olaf College, and set to work. The first few sections of *Giants in the Earth* were written in a cabin in the north woods of Minnesota. Then he felt the need of visiting South Dakota again, to gather fresh material. In midwinter of that year he went abroad, locating temporarily in a cheap immigrant hotel in London, where he worked on the novel steadily. When spring opened in 1924, he went to Norway. There he met Bojer, visiting him at his country home. Bojer was delighted to learn that Rölvaag, of whom he had heard a great deal, was also working on a novel of the Norwegian-American settlement; the two men exchanged ideas generously. "How do you see the problem?" Rölvaag asked. The answer showed him that Bojer saw it from the viewpoint of Norway, not of America; to him it was mainly a problem of emigration. This greatly relieved Rölvaag's mind, for there was no real conflict; he set to work with renewed energy, and soon finished the first book of *Giants in the Earth*. . . .

Does Rölvaag's work belong legitimately to Norwegian or to American literature? The problem has unusual and interesting features. The volume . . . deals with American life, and with one of the most characteristically American episodes in our history. It opens on the western plains; its material is altogether American. Yet it was written in Norwegian, and gained its first recognition in Norway. Whatever we may decide, it has already become a part of Norwegian literature. Rölvaag's art seems mainly European; Rölvaag himself, as I have said, is typically American. His life and future are bound up in the New World; yet he will continue to write in a foreign language. Had he been born in America, would his art have been the same? It seems unlikely. On the other hand, had he remained in Norway—had he accepted the boat that fine, clear day in Nordland—how would his art have fared?

But such speculation, after all, is merely idle; these things do not matter. It has not yet been determined, even, what America is, or

whether she herself is strictly American. And any sincere art is international. Given the artist, our chief interest lies in trying to fathom
the sources of his art, and to recognize its sustaining impulses. What
were the forces which have now projected into American letters a
realist of the first quality writing in a foreign language a new tale of
the founding of America? It is obvious that these forces must have
been highly complex and that they will continue to be so throughout
his working life; but beyond that we cannot safely go. The rest is a
matter of opinion. When I have asked Rölvaag the simple question,
Did Norway or America teach you to write? he has invariably thrown
up his hands.

Grace as an Aspect of Culture

*On a somewhat different level, hundreds of young men and
women in the United States were trained in the social and
cultural graces by European teachers. In the selection which
follows, one such American recalls the influence of an Italian
dancing master who for many years helped to mold the society
of Boston.[4]*

Among the private academies in Boston in the nineteenth century
was one in which dancing and deportment were taught in perfection
and the memory of no citizen of this city is held in greater esteem than
that of Lorenzo Papanti, who was master of the academy from 1836
until his death in 1872, a period of almost forty years. . . .

Lorenzo Papanti was born in Leghorn, Italy, in 1799. Two years
before, Napoleon Bonaparte had marched his French troops to that
country and as young Papanti grew to manhood, a subject of the empire which soon followed, he became an officer in the bodyguard of
the restored Grand Duke of Tuscany. But he soon became involved in
revolutionary agitation that made a flight to the United States necessary and it is interesting that he came here in the summer of 1823 as
a member of the band of the frigate *Constitution* which is now being
restored to its original condition by the United States Government at

---

[4] Charles F. Read, "Lorenzo Papanti, Teacher of Dancing," *Proceedings of the
Bostonian Society at the Annual Meeting, January 17, 1928* (Boston, 1928), 41-
44.

the Charlestown Navy Yard. He soon obtained a position in the orchestra of the Federal Street Theatre and while so employed met an English actress who became his wife.

As he seemed to have been proficient in teaching dancing as well as being a musician, he passed early in life a summer at the West Point Military Academy teaching the young cadets the art of dancing and it is said that this opportunity was secured for him by Russell Sturgis, the eminent merchant, who was one of his earliest Boston friends. In this connection, it is interesting that two of his pupils were Jefferson Davis and Pierre G. T. Beauregard, who became prominent in the Southern Confederacy, the first as President, the other as a General.

It is said that young Mr. Papanti, to give him his adopted title, first taught dancing in a house situated on Allston Street; in 1829, however, the Boston Directory places him at 8 Montgomery Place. This was later the home of Dr. Oliver Wendell Holmes and it was here that the genial poet wrote "The Autocrat of the Breakfast Table." Referring again to the Directory, Papanti resided in several locations and is called musician, professor of music or dancing master. But in 1839 he is found at 22 Tremont Row, later designated as 23 Tremont Street, and here Boston's beloved Papanti's Dancing School remained until the year 1900 when its doors were closed. . . .

Papanti's Hall was on the third floor of one of the row of brick buildings on Tremont Street opposite to where the Boston Museum stood for many years. The hall was reached by two flights of narrow stairs and at the head of the stairs were the double doors which gave entrance to the hall; on the right was the boys' dressing room and on the left was the dressing room for girls; both were well fitted with lockers and hooks for clothing; doors led from both dressing rooms to the adjacent hall.

The hall itself was very attractive and extended from the front to the rear of the building. On each exterior wall there was a row of sofas on which the fond mothers, and perhaps fathers, sat to watch their offspring learn dancing and deportment. Over the entrance was a gallery where musicians played on occasion, and on the opposite wall in the center was a huge and beautiful mirror; on each side was a door which gave entrance to a long and narrow supper room. . . .

A large chandelier illuminated the hall and on its spring floor, said to have been the first one in the United States, we danced the cotil-

lions and the round dances. I shall never forget what was called the
Shawl Dance which occurred before the great mirror. It was danced
by one of the more proficient girls of the class, who held in both hands
a long gauzy scarf which she waved to and fro as she danced the
steps; I have never forgotten the beautiful music which accompanied
the dance. Nor have I forgotten how Mr. Papanti paired the boys and
girls so that all should dance. Gathering a group of boys in their
dressing room, who had rather play than dance, he would lead them
to the door of the girls' dressing room and select their partners from
the mortified girls who as yet had not found partners.

And what about Mr. Papanti and his ever present violin? He often
called me "Doctor" with the accent on the second syllable, for my
father was a physician. And, perhaps when he saw my mother as a
matron he thought of the little girl who had been a pupil in his school
almost forty years before.

THE PASSIONATE ITALIAN

*Americans early began to see the potentialities of a way of life
different from their own in contact with the immigrants around
them. For those brought up in relative isolation from Europe, it
was exciting to observe cultural values that contrasted markedly
with their own. A magazine writer in 1857 thus caught a glimpse,
in his encounter with some Italian refugees, of a style of belief
and behavior altogether unlike that of his own society.*[5]

An urbane violinist from Como, who led the orchestra in the
theater of my native town, first revealed to me the Epicurean side of
life. My elders of that austere community, were anxious plodders; they
did everything by rule; a thrifty, grave set, whose ideal was respectability, and their universal test common sense—formalists, utilitarians,
who ate, walked, transacted business, married and died, with little
apparent emotion, and in a perfectly decent but extremely uninter-
esting way. Sometimes a vague idea flitted across my overtasked brain,
that there was another kind of life somewhere on earth; and, as a
child, I wished myself Mungo Park, with that amiable Negress singing
to me in the African desert, Crusoe's man Friday, milking goats, or

[5] "Italians in America," *Putnam's Monthly*, IX (1857), 1-4.

even poor Belzoni, half-smothered in mummy-dust in an Egyptian catacomb at least, that I might try another mundane sphere.

But it was the jolly violinist who, apart from books, convinced me there was an absolutely enjoyable vein in the mere act of living, a way to take things easy, a possible art of being happy. He used to breakfast in a flowered *robe de chambre* at ten o'clock, chat, by the half hour, with any one who would stop with him at the street corner, take zestful pinches of snuff, pat boys on the head, laugh at mere trifles, look in at shop windows, nibble lumps of sugar, pet a canary, and, every night, flourish his bow with a good-will that was magnetic. All this was such a violation of the current philosophy of life, such a free, irresponsible, genial exception to the general rule, that it fairly bewildered me; and all the answer I could obtain, when trying to solve the problem by catechising my respectable fellow-citizens, was, "He's an Italian." Happy race, thought I, exempt from care, children of nature, living by music!

But there was one more specimen of the nation among us, whose demeanor quite contradicted my theory. Every afternoon he passed our house, looking so melancholy and abstracted that it made one pity his beautiful little greyhound, who followed as if afraid to gambol. That slender and sad figure was a perfect contrast to the round, chirping musician; and even the tinkle of his dog's silver bells was foreign to merriment. One day, when the hush and gloom of an impending thunder-storm made our quiet street more deserted than usual, he went by with a shadow, deeper than the heavens wore, on his pale forehead, and the dark eye below seemed alive with the latent fire of a mad resolve. He ascended the granite steps of a mansion, where we had often seen him keeping vigil in the summer moonlight; it was the home of a fair, wealthy pupil, whom he had wooed in vain. The servant hesitated to admit him; he rushed by, ascended to the lady's boudoir, demanded again to know her final answer to his irresistible passion, was once more calmly but firmly denied, placed a pistol to his breast and shot himself dead. His corpse stretched on the floor, with the little dog crouched upon the breathless chest, and moaning piteously, was a spectacle not to be erased from a young and appalled heart. This early experience of the actual comedy and tragedy of human life, identified both, to my imagination, with Italians. . . .

Italian refugees, without resources or education, suffer, here and elsewhere, the worst penalties of expatriation. The recent appeal of nine Tuscan peasants to the municipal authorities of New York, exposes the fraudulent means resorted to abroad, to shake off the irritating load of unprovided labor; and there is no class of emigrants, who, from their want of adaptation, strong home attachments, and inability to cope with a new climate and foreign habits, claim such ready sympathy. Among the large intermediate class, between the *contadini* and the highly cultivated, this natural inaptitude, sensitiveness, and ignorance of the world, produce some ludicrous contrasts of character and circumstances, they often prove the most difficult people to help, the most amiable of marplots, as a few sketches of my *protégés* will illustrate: . . .

The *Avocato* . . . had made a figure at the bar of Venice in his youth, and helped overhaul the treacherous archives of Austrian rule, when that romantic city fell into the hands of the revolutionists. He had what De Stael attributed to Gouverneur Morris, *l'air très imposant*; his iron-gray hair and lofty forehead, broad chest, deliberate carriage and distinct, emphatic speech, seemed to assure me that an exile of the rational school had now appeared. There was no impulse in his manner, look, or words; every idea he expressed was a formula; even words of mere courtesy were arranged like a proposition. All he had done and intended to do—from a programme of civil government to the choice of a lodging, from a system of tuition to the tie of a cravat—was logically stated. Instead of the exuberant, random blood of "Young Italy," here, I thought, was an old-fashioned formalist, whom it was only requisite to put in a satisfactory track, and he would jog on prosperously.

This view was encouraged by the definite aim and sensible expectations of the poor *Avocato*, whose scrupulously clean, but threadbare, apparel hinted too plainly the need of immediate employment. He proposed to find a situation as teacher of languages in a college, and there was that in his manners and appearance which carried with them a strong recommendation for such an office. Letters were, accordingly, written, professors consulted, testimonials forwarded, and interest made in every quarter; at last came an offer from Michigan, terms, situation, and prospects all that could be hoped for, and I soon had the pleasure to know that my dignified and argumentative friend was installed in a respectable and sufficiently lucrative post.

A few months elapsed, when he made his appearance once more, better dressed, more robust, and a little more lofty in his air; his salutation was, as usual, elaborate and exact. When concluded, he spoke of the weather, the last news from abroad, and other incidental topics, and, upon my inquiring the probable time of his absence from the college, he smiled sarcastically, and remarked that he had left never to return. I ventured to ask if there was any better place in view? "None whatever." "And pray, signor, may I inquire why you gave up so desirable a means of subsistence after the trouble we had in procuring it?" He drew himself up, raised his hand gracefully, and assumed that overwhelming look with which lawyers adduce final testimony or clinch an argument. I was prepared to hear of an invincible obstacle or an irreconcilable wrong. Solemnly, earnestly, and thrillingly spoke the *Avocato: "Per tre mesi, Signore, che io sono stato attacato a quel collegio, mi hanno dato brodo a pranzo tre volte soltante."* "During three months, sir, that I have been connected with that college, they gave me soup, at dinner, but three times!"

THE GOOD-NATURED GERMAN

In the same way, the image of the jolly, beer-drinking and sentimental, but good-natured German had a meaningful impact upon the Americans among whom they lived. In the popular poem which follows, Charles F. Adams, a New England writer, gives a Yankee impression of what the Germans liked.[6]

Vot I Like Und Don'd Like

I don'd dink mooch off dose fine shaps
    Vot lofe aboudt der schtreet,
Und nefer pays der landlady
    For vot dey haf to eat;
Who gifes der tailor notings,
    Und makes der laundress vait,
Und haf deir trinks off lager bier
    All "put ubon der schlate."

I don'd dink mooch off vimmin, too,
    Who dink it vas deir "schpeer"
To keep oup vine abbearances,

---

[6] Charles F. Adams, *Leedle Yawcob Strauss* (Boston, 1878), 119-122.

Und lif in "Grundy's" fear;
Who dress demselves mit vine array
  To flirt ubon der schtreet,
Und leaf deir moders at der tub
  To earn der bread dey eat.

I don'd like men dot feel so pig
  Ven dey haf plenty *geld*,
Who vas as Lucifer so broud,
  Und mit conceil vas schvelled.
Who dinks more off deir horse und dog
  As off a man dot's poor,
Und lets der schtarving und der sick
  Go hungry vrom der door.

I don'd dink mooch off dem dot holdt
  So tight ubon a tollar,
Dot, if 'tvas only shust alife,
  'Tvould make it shcream und holler.
Vy don'd dey keep it on der move,
  Not hide avay und lock it?
Dey gannot take it ven dey die:
  Der shroud don'd haf a pocket!

. . . . .

I like to see a hand dot's brown,
  Und not avraid off vork;
Dot gifes to dose vot air in need,
  Und nefer tries to schirk:
A man dot meets you mit a schmile,
  Und dakes you py der hand,
Shust like dey do vhere I vas born,
  In mine own vaterland,—

Vhere bier-saloons don'd keep a schlate;
  Vhere tailors get deir pay,
Und vashervimmin get der schtamps
  For vork dey dake avay;
Vhere *frauleins* schtick righdt to der vork

So schteady as a glock,
Und not go schtrutting droo der schtreets
Shust like a durkey-cock;
Vhere blenty und brosperity
Schmile ubon efery hand:
Dot ist der Deutscher's paradise;
Das ist das Vaterland.

REALISM IN THE YIDDISH THEATER

At the beginning of the twentieth century, some perceptive Americans began to be acquainted with the cultural forms that were developing within the immigrant communities. In the passage which follows, for instance, a reporter gives his impressions of the dramatic forms that had emerged in the Yiddish theater of New York and finds it marked by qualities very much lacking on the native American stage.[7]

In the three Yiddish theaters on the Bowery is expressed the world of the Ghetto—that New York City of Russian Jews, large, complex, with a full life and civilization. In the midst of the frivolous Bowery, devoted to tinsel variety shows, "dive" music-halls, fake museums, trivial amusement booths of all sorts, cheap lodging-houses, ten-cent shops and Irish-American tough saloons, the theaters of the chosen people alone present the serious as well as the trivial interests of an entire community. Into these three buildings crowd the Jews of all the Ghetto classes—the sweat-shop woman with her baby, the day-laborer, the small Hester Street shopkeeper, the Russian-Jewish anarchist and socialist, the Ghetto rabbi and scholar, the poet, the journalist. The poor and ignorant are in the great majority, but the learned, the intellectual and the progressive are also represented, and here, as elsewhere, exert a more than numerically proportionate influence on the character of the theatrical productions, which, nevertheless, remain essentially popular. The socialists and the literati create the demand that forces into the mass of vaudeville, light opera, historical and melodramatic plays a more serious art element, a simple

---

[7] Hutchins Hapgood, *The Spirit of the Ghetto* (New York, 1902), 113-116, 135, 137, 140-142. 149.

transcript from life or the theatric presentation of a Ghetto problem. But this more serious element is so saturated with the simple manners, humor and pathos of the life of the poor Jew, that it is seldom above the heartfelt understanding of the crowd.

The audiences vary in character from night to night rather more than in an uptown theater. On the evenings of the first four weekdays, the theater is let to a guild or club, many hundreds of which exist among the working people of the east side. Many are labor organizations representing the different trades, many are purely social, and others are in the nature of secret societies. Some of these clubs are formed on the basis of a common home in Russia. The people, for instance, who came from Vilna, a city in the old country, have organized a Vilna Club in the Ghetto. Then, too, the anarchists have a society; there are many socialistic orders; the newspapers of the Ghetto have their constituency, which sometimes hires the theater. Two or three hundred dollars is paid to the theater by the guild, which then sells the tickets among the faithful for a good price. Every member of the society is forced to buy, whether he wants to see the play or not, and the money made over and above the expenses of hiring the theater is for the benefit of the guild. These performances are therefore called "benefits." The widespread existence of such a custom is a striking indication of the growing sense of corporate interests among the laboring classes of the Jewish East Side. It is an expression of the socialistic spirit which is marked everywhere in the Ghetto.

On Friday, Saturday and Sunday nights the theater is not let, for these are the Jewish holidays, and the house is always completely sold out, although prices range from twenty-five cents to a dollar. Friday night is, properly speaking, the gala occasion of the week. That is the legitimate Jewish holiday, the night before the Sabbath. Orthodox Jews, as well as others, may then amuse themselves. Saturday, although the day of worship, is also of holiday character in the Ghetto. This is due to the Christian influences, to which the Jews are more and more sensitive. Through economic necessity Jewish workingmen are compelled to work on Saturday, and, like other workingmen, look upon Saturday night as a holiday, in spite of the frown of the Orthodox. Into Sunday, too, they extend their freedom, and so in the Ghetto there are now three popularly recognized nights on which to go with all the world to the theater.

On those nights the theater presents a peculiarly picturesque sight. Poor workingmen and women with their babies of all ages fill the theater. Great enthusiasm is manifested, sincere laughter and tears accompany the sincere acting on the stage. Pedlars of soda-water, candy, of fantastic gew-gaws of many kinds, mix freely with the audience between the acts. Conversation during the play is received with strenuous hisses, but the falling of the curtain is the signal for groups of friends to get together and gossip about the play or the affairs of the week. Introductions are not necessary, and the Yiddish community can then be seen and approached with great freedom. . . .

The distinctive thing about the intellectual and artistic life of the Russian Jews of the New York Ghetto, the spirit of realism, is noticeable even on the popular stage. The most interesting plays are those in which the realistic spirit predominates, and the best among the actors and playwrights are the realists. The realistic element, too, is the latest one in the history of the Yiddish stage. The Jewish theaters in other parts of the world, which, compared with the three in New York, are unorganized, present only anachronistic and fantastic historical and Biblical plays, or comic opera with vaudeville specialties attached. These things . . . are, to be sure, given in the Yiddish theaters on the Bowery too, but there are also plays which in part at least portray the customs and problems of the Ghetto community, and are of comparatively recent origin. . . .

In almost every play given on the Bowery all the elements are represented. Vaudeville, history, realism, comic opera, are generally mixed together. Even in the plays of Gordin there are clownish and operatic intrusions, inserted as a conscious condition of success. On the other hand, even in the distinctively formless plays, in comic opera and melodrama, there are striking illustrations of the popular feeling for realism,—bits of dialogue, happy strokes of characterization of well-known Ghetto types, sordid scenes faithful to the life of the people.

It is the acting which gives even to the plays having no intrinsic relation to reality a frequent quality of naturalness. The Yiddish players, even the poorer among them, act with remarkable sincerity. Entirely lacking in self-consciousness, they attain almost from the outset to a direct and forcible expressiveness. They, like the audience, rejoice in what they deem the truth. In the general lack of really good plays they yet succeed in introducing the note of realism. To be true to nature is their strongest passion, and even in a conventional melodrama their sincerity, or their characterization in the comic episodes, often redeems the play from utter barrenness. . . .

When we turn to Jacob Gordin's plays, to other plays of similar character and to the audiences to which they specifically appeal, we have realism worked out consciously in art, the desire to express life as it is, and at the same time the frequent expression of revolt against the reality of things, and particularly against the actual system of society. Consequently the "problem" play has its representation in the Ghetto. It presents the hideous conditions of life in the Ghetto—the poverty, the sordid constant reference to money, the immediate sensuality, the jocular callousness—and underlying the mere statement of the facts an intellectual and passionate revolt. . . .

The *Beggar of Odessa* [for instance] was . . . an adaptation of the *Ragpicker of Paris*, a play by Felix Piot, the Anarchistic agitator of the French Commune in 1871. The features of the play particularly interesting to the audience were those emphasizing the clashing of social classes. The old ragpicker, a model man, clever, brilliant, and good, is a philosopher too, and says many things warmly welcomed by the audience. As he picks up his rags he sings about how even the clothing of the great comes but to dust. His adopted daughter is poor, and consequently noble and sweet. The villains are all rich; all the very poor characters are good.

Another play, *Vogele*, is partly a satire of the rich Jew by the poor Jew. "The rich Jews," sang the comedian, "toil not, neither do they spin. They work not, they suffer not,—why then do they live on this earth?" This unthinking revolt is the opposite pole to the unthinking vaudeville and melodrama. In many of the plays referred to roughly as of the Gordin-Adler type—although they were not all written by Gordin nor played by Adler—we find a realism more true in feeling and cast in stronger dramatic form. In some of these plays there is no problem element; in a few is that element so prominent as essentially to interfere with the character of the play as a presentation of life. . . .

The Slaughter, written by Gordin, and with the main masculine character taken by David Kessler, an actor of occasionally great realistic strength, is the story of the symbolic murder of a fragile young girl by her parents, who force her to marry a rich man who has all the vices and whom she hates. The picture of the poor house, of the old mother and father and half-witted stepson with whom the girl is

unconsciously in love, in its faithfulness to life is typical of scenes in
many of these plays. It is rich in character and *milieu* drawing. There
is another scene of miserable life in the second act. The girl is married and living with the rich brute. In the same house is his mistress,
curt and cold, and two children by a former wife. The old parents
come to see the wife; she meets them with the joy of starved affection.
But the husband enters and changes the scene to one of hate and
violence. The old mother tells him, however, of the heir that is to
come. Then there is a superb scene of naïve joy in the midst of all the
sordid gloom. There is rapturous delight of the old people, turbulent
triumph of the husband, and satisfaction of the young wife. They make
a holiday of it. Wine is brought. They all love one another for the
time. The scene is representative of the way the poor Jews welcome
their offspring. But indescribable violence and abuse follow, and the
wife finally kills her husband, in a scene where realism riots into burlesque, as it frequently does on the Yiddish stage.

But for absolute, intense realism Gordin's *Wild Man*, unrelieved
by a problem idea, is unrivaled. An idiot boy falls in love with his
stepmother without knowing what love is. He is abused by his father
and brother, beaten on account of his ineptitudes. His sister and another brother take his side, and the two camps revile each other in
unmistakable language. The father marries again; his new wife is a
heartless, faithless woman, and she and the daughter quarrel. After
repeated scenes of brutality to the idiot, the daughter is driven out to
make her own living. Adler's portraiture of the idiot is a great bit of
technical acting. The poor fellow is filled with the mysterious won-
derings of an incapable mind. His shadow terrifies and interests him.
He philosophizes about life and death. He is puzzled and worried by
everything; the slightest sound preys on him. Physically alert, his
senses serve only to trouble and terrify the mind which cannot interpret what they present. The burlesque which Mr. Adler puts into
the part was inserted to please the crowd, but increases the horror of
it, as when Lear went mad; for the Elizabethan audiences laughed,
and had their souls wrung at the same time. The idiot ludicrously
describes his growing love. In pantomime he tells a long story. It is
evident, even without words, that he is constructing a complicated
symbolism to express what he does not know. He falls into epilepsy
and joins stiffly in the riotous dance. The play ends so fearfully that
it shades into mere burlesque.

This horrible element in so many of these plays marks the point where realism passes into fantastic sensationalism. The facts of life in the Ghetto are in themselves unpleasant, and consequently it is natural that a dramatic exaggeration of them results in something poignantly disagreeable. The intense seriousness of the Russian Jew, which accounts for what is excellent in these plays, explains also the rasping falseness of the extreme situations. It is a curious fact that idiots, often introduced in the Yiddish plays, amuse the Jewish audience as much as they used to the Elizabethan mob. . . .

Some of the more striking of the realistic plays on the Ghetto stage have been partly described, but realism in the details of character and setting appears in all of them, even in comic opera and melodrama. In many the element of revolt, even if it is not the basis of the play, is expressed in occasional dialogues. Burlesque runs through them all, but burlesque, after all, is a comment on the facts of life. And all these points are emphasized and driven home by sincere and forcible acting.

Crude in form as these plays are, and unpleasant as they often are in subject and in the life portrayed, they are yet refreshing to persons who have been bored by the empty farce and inane cheerfulness of the uptown theaters.

❦ 7 ❧

Conceptions of Americanization

differences of opinion as to how successful immigrant adjustment
had been sprang from deeper differences as to the meaning of
"adjustment." At the opening of the twentieth century one could
discover three rival interpretations of Americanization. It was in
terms of such dissimilar criteria that the opponents and defenders
of unrestricted immigration argued.

Since well back in the eighteenth century Americans had been
disposed to think of themselves as new men, not simply replicas
of any European folk, but a new stock produced by an amalgam
of many different strains. Through the nineteenth century the
open policy that had admitted any comers to the nation had been
justified by the certainty that all could be absorbed and that all
could contribute to an emerging national character.

After a century of experience, some Americans began to wonder whether the image of the melting pot actually described the
process of immigrant adjustment. Such observers insisted that a
healthy social order did not depend upon assimilation in the
sense of a total fusion of all the elements in the population into

146

a homogeneous mass. They argued, rather, that the valuable cultural qualities each immigrant group brought with it ought to be preserved; and that adjustment meant the achievement of a kind of harmony among diverse national elements, each of which retained its own distinctive identity. This viewpoint was formulated in the conception of cultural pluralism.

In part, the supporters of the idea of cultural pluralism were moved to take the position they did because the melting pot theory was already under attack from the other extreme by men who argued that the immigrants could not assimilate. Before the end of the nineteenth century, the notion that the United States was an amalgam continually changing was being challenged by some Americans who argued that national character was already fixed. The American was basically Anglo-Saxon, an offspring of the English people, and it was the obligation of many new arrivals to conform to the patterns of life and to institutions that already existed here. They were to be assimilated within the national character already formed and already fixed. If they could not meet that demand, they were unfit for admission to the New World.

AMERICA AS A MELTING POT

Even before the Revolution, an eloquent writer, himself born in France, had lucidly explained the basis upon which American immigration policy would rest for the next century and a half. The "Letters from an American Farmer" pointed out that the American was, and would be, a new man, shaped not by his ancestral heritage, but by the free institutions under which he lived.[1] A century later, pride in the record of the United States as a haven of refuge moved a poet to compose the lines of welcome, to be inscribed on the base of the Statue of Liberty.[2] In the first decade of the twentieth century, an English dramatist still

---

[1] Michel Guillaume St. Jean de Crèvecoeur, *Letters from an American Farmer* (London, 1782), 45-59, 62-6, 69-80, 121-5, 130-1, 146-8, 150-8, 162-7, 170-1, 176-8, 182-98, 201-3.

[2] Emma Lazarus, "The New Colossus" (1883), *Poems* (Boston, 1889), I, 202-03.

*found the melting pot an attractive theme, and gave it forceful ex-
pression in the last act of his play of that name.[3] At about the
same time, the Anglican pastor of the Church of the Ascension
in New York still found the idea in accord with the noblest
American ideals.[4]*

(A). An American Farmer

Whence came all these people? They are a mixture of English,
Scotch, Irish, French, Dutch, Germans, and Swedes. From this pro-
miscuous breed, that race, now called Americans, have arisen. In this
great American asylum, the poor of Europe have by some means met
together. . . . To what purpose should they ask one another what
countrymen they are? Alas, two-thirds of them had no country. Can a
wretch, who wanders about, who works and starves, whose life is a
continual scene of sore affliction or pinching penury; can that man
call England or any other kingdom his country, a country that had no
bread for him, whose fields produced him no harvest; who met with
nothing but the frowns of the rich, the severity of the laws, with jails
and punishments; who owned not a single foot of the extensive surface of this planet? No! Urged by a variety of motives, here they came.
Everything has tended to regenerate them: new laws, a new mode of
living, a new social system. Here they are become men. In Europe they
were so many useless plants, wanting vegetative mold and refreshing
showers. They withered, and were mowed down by want, hunger, and
war. But now, by the power of transplantation, like all other plants,
they have taken root and flourish! Formerly they were not numbered
in any civil lists of their country, except in those of the poor; here
they rank as citizens.

By what invisible power has this surprising metamorphosis been
performed? By that of the laws and that of . . . [the people's] industry. The laws, the indulgent laws, protect them as they arrive,
stamping on them the symbol of adoption. They receive ample rewards for their labors; these accumulated rewards procure them lands;
those lands confer on them the title of freemen; and to that title

[3] Israel Zangwill, *The Melting-Pot* (New York, 1909), 198-199. By permission
of The Jewish Publication Society of America.
[4] Percy Stickney Grant, "American Ideals and Race Mixture," *North American
Review,* CXCV (1912), 513-535.

every benefit is affixed which men can possibly require. This is the
great operation daily performed by our laws. Whence proceed these
laws? From our government. Whence that government? It is derived
from the original genius and the strong desire of the people ratified
and confirmed by the Crown.

What attachment can a poor European emigrant have for a country where he had nothing? The knowledge of the language, the love of
a few kindred as poor as himself, were the only cords that tied him.
His country is now that which gives him land, bread, protection, and
consequence. . . . He is either a European, or the descendant of a
European; hence, that strange mixture of blood, which you will find
in no other country. . . . *He* is an American, who, leaving behind
him all his ancient prejudices and manners, receives new ones from the
new mode of life he has embraced, the new government he obeys, and
the new rank he holds. . . . Here individuals of all nations are melted
into a new race of men, whose labors and posterity will one day cause
great changes in the world. Americans are the western pilgrims, who
are carrying along with them that great mass of arts, sciences, vigor,
and industry, which began long since in the east. They will finish the
great circle.

The Americans were once scattered all over Europe. Here they are
incorporated into one of the finest systems of population which has
ever appeared, and which will hereafter become distinct by the power
of the different climates they inhabit. The American is a new man,
who acts upon new principles; he must therefore entertain new ideas
and form new opinions. From involuntary idleness, servile dependence, penury, and useless labor, he has passed to toils of a very different nature, rewarded by ample substistence.—This is an American.

(B). *The New Colossus*

Not like the brazen giant of Greek fame,
With conquering limbs astride from land to la**nd**
Here at our sea-washed, sunset gates shall sta**nd**
A mighty woman with a torch, whose flame
Is the imprisoned lightening, and her na**me**
Mother of Exiles. From her beacon-handed
Glows world-wide welcome; her mild eyes comma**nd**

The air-bridged harbor that twin cities frame
"Keep, ancient lands, your storied pomp!" cries she
With silent lips. "Give me your tired, your poor,
Your huddled masses yearning to breathe free,
The wretched refuse of your teeming shore.
Send these, the homeless, tempest-tost to me,
I lift my lamp beside the golden door!"

(C). *The Melting-Pot*

It is the fires of God round His Crucible.

There she lies, the great Melting-Pot—listen! Can't you hear the
roaring and the bubbling? There gapes her mouth—the harbour
where a thousand mammoth feeders come from the ends of the world
to pour in their human freight. Ah, what a stirring and a seething! Celt
and Latin, Slav and Teuton, Greek and Syrian,—black and yellow—
Jew and Gentile—

Yes, East and West, and North and South, the palm and the pine,
the pole and the equator, the crescent and the cross—how the great
Alchemist melts and fuses them with his purging flame! Here shall
they all unite to build the Republic of Man and the Kingdom of God.
Ah, Vera, what is the glory of Rome and Jerusalem where all nations
and races come to worship and look back, compared with the glory
of America, where all races and nations come to labour and look forward!

Peace, peace, to all ye unborn millions, fated to fill this giant continent—the God of our children give you Peace.

(D). *Percy S. Grant*

The rapidity with which the democratic ideas are taken on by immigrants under the influence of our institutions is remarkable. I have
personally had experiences with French-Canadians, Portuguese, He-
brews, and Italians. These races have certainly taken advantage of
their opportunities among us in a fashion to promise well for their
final effect upon this country. The French-Canadian has become a

sufficiently good American to have given up his earlier program of turning New England into a new France—that is, into a Catholic province or of returning to the Province of Quebec. He is seeing something better than a racial or religious ideal in the freedom of American citizenship; and on one or two occasions, when he had political power in two municipalities, he refrained from exercising it to the detriment of the public-school system. He has added a gracious manner and a new feeling for beauty to New England traits.

The Portuguese have taken up neglected or abandoned New England agricultural land and have turned it to productive and valuable use. Both the French-Canadian and the Portuguese have come to us by way of the New England textile mills.

The actual physical machinery of civilization—cotton-mills, woolen-mills, iron-mills, etc.—lock up a great deal of human energy, physical and mental, just as one hundred years ago the farms did, from which later sprang most of the members of our dominant industrial class. A better organization of society, by which machinery would do still more and afford a freer play for mental and physical energy and organization, would find a response from classes that are now looked upon as not contributing to our American culture; would unlock the high potentialities in the laboring classes, now unguessed and unexpended.

The intellectual problems and the advanced thinking of the Hebrew, his fondness for study, and his freedom on the whole from wasteful forms of dissipation, sport, and mental stagnation, constitute him a more fortunate acquisition for this country than are thousands of the descendants of colonial settlers. In short, we must reconstruct our idea of democracy—of American democracy. This done, we must construct a new picture of citizenship. If we do these things we shall welcome the rugged strength of the peasant or the subtle thought of the man of the Ghetto in our reconsidered American ideals. After all, what are these American ideals we boast so much about? Shall we say public schools, the ballot, freedom? The American stock use private schools when they can afford them; they too often leave town on election day; as for freedom, competent observers believe it is disappearing. The conservators and believers in American ideals seem to be our immigrants. To the Russian Jew, Abraham Lincoln is a god. If American ideals are such as pay honor to the intellectual and to the spiritual, or foster human brotherhood or love culture and promote liberty, then they are safe with our new citizens who are eager for these things.

Not only do these races bring with them most desirable qualities, but they themselves are subjected to new environment and strongly influential conditions. Just here arise duties for the present masters of America. Ought they not to create an industrial, social, and educational environment of the most uplifting sort for our foreign-born citizens?

If working-people are obliged to live in unhealthful tenements situated in slums or marsh land, if the saloon is allowed to be their only social center, if they are fought by the rich in every effort to improve their condition, we may expect any misfortune to happen to them and also any fate to befall the state.

What improved *milieu* can do to improving the physique is easily seen on all sides. The increase in the height and weight of Americans in the last few decades is conspicuous. Even the size of American girls and boys has increased, and this increase in size is commonly attributed to the more comfortable conditions of life, to better food, and especially to the popularity of all forms of athletics, and the extension, as in the last twenty-five or thirty years, of the out-of-door and country life. If these factors have made so marked and visible a change in the physique of the children of native-born Americans, why may not the same conditions also contribute an improvement to the more recent immigrant stock?

Our question, then, as to the effect of race mixture is not the rather supercilious one: What are we admitting into America that may possibly injure American ideals? but, What are the old American races doing to perpetuate these ideals? And is not our future as a race, largely by our own fault, in the hands of the peasant races of Europe?

Indifference, prejudice, illiteracy, segregation of recent immigrants by parochial schools, by a native colonial press, bad physical and social environment, and the low American ideals of citizenship held by those the immigrant sees or hears most about, obstruct race assimilation; but all these can be changed. Yes, it is the keeping up of difference and class isolation that destroys and deteriorates. Fusion is a law of progress.

Every act of religious or civil tyranny, every economic wrong done to races in all the world, becomes the burden of the nation to which the oppressed flee for relief and opportunity. And the beauty of democracy is that it is a method by which these needs may freely express themselves and bring about what the oppressed have prayed for and have been denied. Let us be careful not to put America into the class of the oppressors. Let us rise to an eminence higher than that occupied by Washington or Lincoln, to a new Americanism which is not afraid of the blending in the western world of races seeking freedom. Our present problem is the greatest in our history. Not colonial independence, not federal unity, but racial amalgamation is the heroic problem of the present, with all it implies in purification and revision of old social, religious, and political ideals, with all it demands in new sympathy outside of blood and race, and in a willingness to forego old-time privileges.

CULTURAL PLURALISM

The proponents of cultural pluralism were unwilling to accept the assumption, implicit in the melting-pot idea, that all the peoples who came to the United States would ultimately fuse in a homogeneous mass. In an influential series of articles in 1915, the philosopher Horace M. Kallen set forth the thesis that American society constituted a federation of cultures. He denied that it was possible or desirable for the immigrant groups to lose their identity and argued that our culture had much to gain by permitting each of them to develop its own particular tendencies.[5] In a review of two contemporary works on immigration four years later, just after the war, Carl H. Grabo pointed, in addition, to the wide international implications of America's treatment of its immigrants.[6]

(A). H. M. Kallen

We are, in fact, at the parting of the ways. A genuine social alternative is before us, either of which parts we may realize if we will. . . . What do we will to make of the United States—a unison, singing the old Anglo-Saxon theme "America," the America of the New England

---

[5] Horace M. Kallen, "Democracy Versus the Melting-Pot," *The Nation*, C (1915), 219-220.

[6] Carl H. Grabo, "Americanizing the Immigrants," *The Dial*, LXVI (1919). 539-541.

school, or a harmony, in which that theme shall be dominant, perhaps, among others, but one among many, not the only one? . . .

The attainment of . . . a harmony . . . requires concerted public action. But the action . . . would seek simply to eliminate the waste and the stupidity of our social organization, by way of freeing and strengthening the strong forces actually in operation. Starting with our existing ethnic and cultural groups, it would seek to provide conditions under which each may attain the perfection that is proper to its kind. The provision of such conditions is the primary intent of our fundamental law and the function of our institutions. And the various nationalities which compose our commonwelath must learn first of all this fact, which is perhaps, to most minds, the outstanding ideal content of "Americanism"—that democracy means self-realization through self-control, self-government, and that one is impossible without the other. . . .

What is inalienable in the life of mankind is its intrinsic positive quality—its psychophysical inheritance. Men may change their clothes, their politics, their wives, their religions, their philosophies, to a greater or lesser extent: they cannot change their grandfathers. Jews or Poles or Anglo-Saxons, in order to cease being Jews or Poles or Anglo-Saxons, would have to cease to be. The selfhood which is inalienable in them, and for the realization of which they require "inalienable" liberty, is ancestrally determined, and the happiness which they pursue has its form implied in ancestral endowment. This is what, actually, democracy in operation assumes. There are human capacities which it is the function of the state to liberate and to protect; and the failure of the state as a government means its abolition. . . . As intelligence and wisdom prevail over "politics" and special interests, as the steady and continuous pressure of the inalienable qualities and purposes of human groups more and more dominate the confusion of our common life, the outlines of a possible great and truly democratic commonwealth become discernible.

Its form is that of the Federal republic; its substance a democracy of nationalities, co-operating voluntarily and autonomously in the enterprise of self-realization through the perfection of men according to their kind. The common language of the commonwealth, the language of its great political tradition, is English, but each nationality expresses its emotional and voluntary life in its own language, in its own inevitable aesthetic and intellectual forms. The common life of the commonwealth is politico-economic, and serves as the foundation and background for the realization of the distinctive individuality of each *natio* that composes it. Thus "American civilization" may come to mean the perfection of the cooperative harmonies of "European civilization," the waste, the squalor, and the distress of Europe being eliminated—a multiplicity in a unity, an orchestration of mankind. As in an orchestra, every type of instrument has its specific timbre and tonality, founded in its substance and form; as every type has its appropriate theme and melody in the whole symphony, so in society each ethnic group is the natural instrument, its spirit and culture are its theme and melody, and the harmony and dissonances and discords of them all make the symphony of civilization, with this difference: a musical symphony is written before it is played; in the symphony of civilization the playing is the writing, so that there is nothing so fixed and inevitable about its progressions as in music, so that within the limits set by nature they may vary at will, and the range and variety of the harmonies may become wider and richer and more beautiful.

But the question is, do the dominant classes in America want such a society?

(B). C. H. Grabo

It is somewhat unjust to the Rev. Enrico C. Sartorio in quoting from his book, *Social and Religious Life of Italians in America* . . . to emphasize his criticisms of the country of his adoption, for he is ardently patriotic and sanguine of the future. So too in citing from Mr. Horace J. Bridges' essays, *On Becoming an American* . . . , for Mr. Bridges sees more clearly than nine out of ten of the native-born whatever is great and good in the American spirit and tradition. Yet in both it is from their strictures and their suggestions of amendment that we can derive most profit, particularly at this time when there is under way a widespread movement to Americanize the immigrant more efficiently than in the past. For in how few quarters is there any clear notion of what Americanization means. . . .

Despite the fine work done by Hull House in Chicago, and similar agencies, we do not as a people make any effort to understand our immigrants or to aid them. . . . The American point of view is compactly expressed in the remark cited from the report of a group of social workers: "Not yet Americanized; still eating Italian food." . . .

Mr. Sartorio's suggestion of one means whereby in the naturalizing process, which now affects almost solely the second generation, much needless pain, cultural loss, and even criminality may be obviated will doubtless fall coldly upon the ears of those patriotic Americans who feel that the best and quickest way to naturalize the foreigner is as soon as possible to make him forget his native speech, substituting therefor, in the public schools, commercial Spanish in view of the commercial possibilities (somewhat dubious) of Latín America:

> The children of foreign extraction learn English and, as very little is done in school to make them keep up the language of their parents, they soon forget it, with the result that their home life is destroyed. . . . It is sad to notice the patronizing attitude that the child assumes towards his father and mother after a few months in the public school. . . . When I discuss the matter with teachers in the public schools, I become aware that they possess a holy horror of teaching children the language and history of Italy. In my opinion the way to preserve the home life of the children of immigrants is to teach through the language and history of their fathers that in every country men and women have always been ready to sacrifice their personal interest for the sake of their country. By making these children realize that they are connected by blood with a race of glorious traditions, and by adoption have come to belong to a country which has also a glorious past, the love for America will be kept in their hearts without their acquiring a feeling of contempt for their fathers' country.

Mr. Bridges, English born and trained in the English tradition, making his home in the United States only when he was mature, and after careful consideration, conceives it to be the "business of America to produce a new type of national character and civilization by the cross-fertilization of the many cultural types which the Republic has absorbed and is absorbing." This thesis he develops at length, it being his conviction that hybrid civilizations have always, as history shows, been culturally the most rich. In the United States we have now, undeveloped and unappreciated, the materials for a new and richer civilization than the world has yet seen:

> It is an astonishment to me that so few Americans seem aware of the great educational opportunity which lies at their doors, through contact with their fellow-citizen of alien origin. One would have ex-

pected *a priori* that familiarity with foreign languages would be more general among Americans than among any other people. Yet the fact, I fear, is precisely the opposite of this. My impression, tested on a fairly large scale, is that among native-born Americans there are comparatively few who are really at home in the language and literatures of continental Europe. . . . We blame our foreigners for their clannishness. We resent the fact that they sequester themselves among people of their own race, and do not take the trouble to understand our language or our history and institutions; but we are guilty of an exactly analogous piece of provincialism when we betray our unwillingness to learn from them, while expecting them to learn from us.

Mr. Bridges objects to our favorite figure of speech, "the melting pot," as one utterly unsuited to define the Americanizing process. "There is," he observes, "no such thing as humanity-in-general, into which the definite, heterogeneous, living creature can be melted down. . . . There is no human mould in America to which the spiritual stuff of the immigrant is to be patterned. Not only is there as yet no fixed and final type, but there never can be." He adds that "the very genius of democracy, moreover, must lead us to desire the widest possible range of variability, the greatest attainable differentiation of individuality, among our population. . . . The business of America is to get rid of mechanical uniformity, and, by encouraging the utmost possible differentiation through mental and psychic cross-fertilization, to attain to a higher level of humanity."

Mr. Bridges would have the foreign-language press fostered rather than discouraged, not only to afford Americans an opportunity to learn of their neighbors, for he would have every American read at least one foreign language paper, but also as a means to genuine Americanization of the foreign-born and their acquaintance with the spirit and ideals of the Republic. Foreign societies are likewise one of the best means to Americanization and serve another purpose only less important:

> Let them keep alive Italian and German music and literature, Balkan handicrafts, and the folk-lore and folk dances of the Old World; —not for the sake of the Old World, but as elements contributory to American culture. Let them spend as much time in bringing the spirit and meaning of American institutions home to their members as in bringing home to Americans the spirit and meaning of their European traditions.

As a specific means to "cultural cross-fertilization" Mr. Bridges suggests that every immigrant be a member not only of a society of his own national origin, but "also a member of an international society composed of representatives of as many different peoples as possible." The native-born, likewise, for the good of his soul and the eradication of his provincialism, should be a member of an international society. Intermarriage between persons of different national descent, which is also advocated, can be safely left, one imagines, to take care of itself. But the establishment of municipal theaters in which plays in all languages shall be presented, a useful and timely suggestion, will need to be pushed if it is to be realized. . . .

More is involved in this problem of Americanization than the cultural enrichment of our national life and the conversion of our present provincial spirit. In the internationalism which is coming, peace among the nations and their cooperation to the larger ends of a world civilization are dependent upon the good will and reciprocal understanding among men of diverse stocks and cultures. If we are to work with Russian, Frenchman, Italian, and German to the attainment of our common welfare and security, the first step to that end is a greater sympathy with and appreciation of the foreigners now among us. If we truly absorb them, and are modified by contact with them as they by us, we shall be better prepared to assume our duties in the League of Nations.

Advocates of Assimilation

The melting-pot theory was also rejected by those who believed that adjustment should simply take the form of the assimilation of the newcomers to the existing society. From this point of view, American character was already formed and was not to be modified by the immigrants. An influential work by the sociologist Richmond Mayo-Smith, first published in 1890, early set forth that argument.[7] Many widely-read works thereafter also made the point that it was the task of the immigrants simply to rid themselves of their old habits and culture in order to become American.

---

[7] Richmond Mayo-Smith, *Emigration and Immigration. A Study in Social Science* (New York, 1904), 62-64, 71-76, 77-78.

R. Mayo-Smith

A much more important subject of study, however, is the effect of this immigration on the ethnical or race composition of our population. If it at present consisted merely of the descendants of the people who were here in 1790, with slight additions from year to year of immigrants from Europe, we should be, with the exception of the blacks, a remarkably homogeneous people. Notwithstanding the fact that among the original colonists were to be found Dutch, Germans, Swedes and French, yet the dominating element was the English. This is seen in the fact that the language has remained English, and that the institutions are English. The long connection of all the colonies with England, whatever the original home of the colonists, accounts for this in large measure. The revolutionary struggle united the people and gave them the feeling of one nationality. Free institutions have worked in the same way, until we find the native born Americans, however widely separated by distance, exhibiting very much the same traits. In later years the means of communication, the common interest in the common government, and still more the commercial intercourse unhindered by tax-barriers and facilitated by the same language, the same money and similar commercial law have unified the whole. There is less difference in language, customs and feeling between the inhabitants of distant portions of the United States than there is often between counties or provinces of European States, which have had different historical development. This influence has been so strong that it has enabled us to assimilate many elements of different quality, and has leavened, at least to a certain extent, the whole lump.

But during the last forty years the immigration has been so large that the process of assimilation has become more difficult, and the addition of foreign elements has been so rapid that it has made the race composition of our population essentially different from what it would have been if we had been left to our own natural growth. These foreign elements are now so prominent that it is worth our while to consider the actual composition of our population as it presents itself to-day. . . .

The strength of this foreign element is disclosed if we take a typical

state and study the make-up of its population more closely. Massachusetts is commonly thought of as peculiarly an American community,
where the population is largely composed of descendants of the Puri-
tans. It was found in 1885 that over 27 per cent of the inhabitants
of that commonwealth were of foreign birth, and that over one-half of
all the inhabitants were of foreign parentage. Nearly 30 per cent were
of Irish parentage alone.

The persons of foreign birth in the United States seem to seek the
large cities. In 1880 more than 34 per cent were found therein. Of
the Irish, 45 per cent settle in the large cities; of the Germans, 38 per
cent; of the English and Scotch, 30 per cent; of the Italians, 60 per
cent. In the city of Boston in 1885 only 31 per cent of the inhabitants
were of native (*i.e.* born in the United States) parentage; the rest
were of foreign parentage. In the city of Lowell only 30 per cent were
of native parentage; in Lawrence, 22 per cent; in Fall River, 17 per
cent; and in the city of Holyoke, only 16 per cent. Many of our factory towns and cities are really foreign so far as the nationality of
their inhabitants goes.

These statistics show that in certain parts of the country the foreign
element in our population has become very powerful and is in fact
overshadowing the native. Especially in the cities it shows its strength.
But it always tends to concentrate. This is due to several causes. One
is that the immigrants naturally seek that portion of the country
where they can find employment in their particular trades. The miners from Wales and England naturally go to the mines of Pennsylvania. The lumbermen from Canada seek the forests of the Northern
States. The unskilled labor remains in the large city where it is employed in the rougher parts of building trades, or seeks the factory
town where it can soon learn to manage the simple operations of
industrial machinery. Another great influence is the presence of
friends or countrymen upon whom the newly arrived immigrants can
depend for help and counsel. Many come at the solicitation of friends
or relatives, or with the aid of money sent by them, and naturally go
to them on their arrival.

There are, fortunately, certain forces which tend to counteract this
exclusiveness on the part of the immigrants and gradually to fuse the
different elements into one American nationality. Two of these we
have already mentioned, viz., economic prosperity and the practice of
free political institutions. The former widens the circle of wants of

the new citizen and leads him to imitate the higher style of living which he sees about him. This separates him from the habits and traditions of his native country and he adopts new standards which are associated in his mind with the new domicile, and which produce a feeling of superiority when he revisits the old home or comes into contact with later arrivals. It differentiates him, so to speak, from the immigrant, and gives him a feeling of attachment to the country where he has prospered. This feeling increases with his children and grandchildren until they become fully identified with our customs, manner of living and habits of thought, and are thoroughly Americanized.

The exercise of political rights, to which many of the immigrants are strange, tends to differentiate them in much the same way. It makes them of importance to the political leaders. It gives them a higher position than they were accustomed to at home, and this naturally attaches them to the new country. However much our politics may suffer from the addition of this vote, much of it ignorant and some of it depraved, there is no doubt as to the educational and nationalizing effect of the suffrage on the immigrants themselves. However attached the Irishman may be to the cause of home rule for Ireland, or however proud the Germany may be of the military glory of the empire, his feelings must gradually and unconsciously gravitate to the country where he has found economic prosperity and political recognition. He may still observe the national feast days and wave the old flag, but if it ever came to a contest, he would probably find that he was more of an American than an Irishman or a German.

Another great fusing force has been the dominance of one language, —the English. In the great mass of cases the immigrant has found it necessary or desirable to adopt that language. Where he has not done it himself, his children have; and in many cases it has become the mother tongue if not the only tongue of the descendants. As soon as that happens, the man of foreign descent is irreparably separated from his former home. In some cases thickly settled communities have managed to maintain the foreign speech and the old religion for several generations. But the disintegrating forces are at work all about them. The moment the young man ventures out into the world he is obliged to learn English. The moment he aspires to the higher education or to political or commercial position he must recognize the prevailing tongue. The children learn it in the school. The parents recognize that it is desirable for the children if not for themselves. It is impossible to isolate the little community completely and it is gradually undermined.

It is eminently desirable that it should be so. We must have one speech in this country. We must insist that English shall be taught in the schools and that it shall be the fundamental language of future generations. It must be everywhere the official language of the courts and the laws. German clergymen and educated men sometimes regret that the immigrants and their descendants should lose this connection with the old country and access to the great literature of the German tongue. But it is better that a man should have one country and not divide his allegiance. If we are to build up in this country one nationality we must insist upon one speech.

There is one other way in which the foreign elements might amalgamate with each other and with the native, so as in the course of time to form one homogeneous people,—that is by intermarriage. In the case of the blacks there is the insuperable color obstacle in the way of their fusion with the whites. But in the case of the immigrants this does not exist, and the impediments of difference in language, customs, and even religion may gradually be removed. It is a question of great interest how far such a fusion of blood is actually occurring in the United States.

The statistics on this point are not very encouraging to those persons who believe that mixture of blood in the United States will finally produce a race different from and superior to any of the older nationalities. It appears that where a particular nationality is concentrated in any one locality, the men choose wives of their own race. . . .

It is possible that the future generations of different blood may intermarry more freely. But even here it is seen how desirable it is to break up the concentration of immigrants of the same nationality in one place, so that by intermarriage with the natives and with people of other nationality this process of fusion and amalgamation may be hastened.

It is one of the favorite theories of social philosophers that mixed races are the strongest. And it is true as a matter of history that the most progressive peoples of Europe are mixed in blood. The American people of the future will be a race composed of many different elements, and it is possible that this mixture will have produced a people possessing the best characteristics displayed by these various elements. It seems, however, that there are two things that ought to be carefully considered. One is that the constituent elements of this amalgamation should themselves be of desirable quality. It is scarcely probable that by taking the dregs of Europe we shall produce a people of high social intelligence and morality. The second is that we must see to it that the opportunity for amalgamation is really given. Simply placing these discordant elements in juxtaposition will not make a compact and solid whole. On the contrary it will give rise to an atomistic weakness which will make any homogeneous and harmonious development impossible. A nation is great, not on account of the number of individuals contained within its boundaries, but through the strength begotten of common national ideals and aspirations. No nation can exist and be powerful that is not homogeneous in this sense. And the great ethnic problem we have before us is to fuse these diverse elements into one common nationality, having one language, one political practice, one patriotism and one ideal of social development.

The Immigrant Views His Own Adjustment

The ideas of theorists were often so general as to lose contact with reality. Their problems did not particularly trouble the immigrants themselves. From the point of view of the newcomers, adjustment meant the ability to enter soundly upon those aspects of American life with which they had contact. As a letter from a Polish immigrant showed, that meant primarily the ability to find a good job and to learn English.[8] But it meant also the opportunity for their children, through education, to grow up as future citizens of the New World.[9]

(A). A Polish Immigrant

I'm in this country four months (from 14 Mai 1913—Noniton—Antverpen).

---

[8] "Letter of an Anonymous Polish Immigrant to the Massachusetts Commission on Immigration, August, 1914," *Report of the Commission on the Problem of Immigration in Massachusetts* (Boston, 1914), 134.

[9] A. R. Dugmore, "New Citizens for the Republic," *The World's Work*, April, 1903, 3323-6.

I am polish man. I want be american citizen—and took here first paper in 12 June N 625. But my friends are polish people—I must live with them—I work in the shoes-shop with polish people—I stay all the time with them—at home—in the shop—anywhere.

I want live with american people, but I do not know anybody of american. I go 4 times to teacher and must pay $2 weekly. I wanted take board in english house, but I could not, for I earn only $5 or 6 in a week, and when I pay teacher $2, I have only $4—$3—and now english board house is too dear for me. Better job to get is very hard for me, because I do not speak well english and I cannot understand what they say to me. The teacher teach me—but when I come home —I must speak polish and in the shop also. In this way I can live in your country many years—like my friends—and never speak—write well english—and never be good american citizen. I know here many persons, they live here 10 or moore years, and they are not citizens, they don't speak well english, they don't know geography and history of this country, they don't know constitution of America.—nothing. I don't like be like them I wanted they help me in english—they could not—because they knew nothing. I want go from them away. But where? Not in the country, because I want go in the city, free evening schools and lern. I'm looking for help. If somebody could give me another job between american people, help me live with them and lern english—and could tell me the best way how I can fast lern —it would be very, very good for me. Perhaps you have somebody, here he could help me?

If you can help me, I please you.

I wrote this letter by myself and I know no good—but I hope you will understand whate I mean.

Excuse me,
F.N.

(B). A. R. *Dugmore*

At the corner of Catharine and Henry Streets in New York is a large white building that overlooks and dominates its neighborhood. Placed in the middle of a region of tawdry flathouses and dirty streets, it stands out preëminent because of its solid cleanliness and unpretentiousness. It is the home of Public School No. 1. In it are centred all the hopes of the miserably poor polyglot population of the surrounding district—for its pupils the scene of their greatest interest and endeavor, and for their parents an earnest of the freedom they have come far and worked hard to attain.

The child of American parentage is the exception in this school. The pupils are of the different nationalities or races that have their separate quarters in the immediate neighborhood. If they were to be divided according to their parental nationality, there would be twenty-five or more groups. The majority of the pupils, however, are Swedes, Austrians, Greeks, Russians, English, Irish, Scotch, Welsh, Rumanians, Italians, Poles, Hungarians, Canadians, Armenians, Germans and Chinese. The Germans, Russians and Polish predominate, for there are a very large number of Jewish pupils.

The most noticeable thing in the school is the perfectly friendly equality in which all these races mix; no prejudice is noticeable. The different races are so scattered that there is no chance for organization and its attendant cliques and small school politics. This is particularly interesting in the face of the fact that the one thing more than any other which binds the boys together is their intense common interest in party and city politics. All political news is followed and every question is heatedly debated in and out of class. This interest in politics and the training in argument and oratory it brings is probably due in large measure to the parents. To them this opportunity for political discussion is an evidence of the freedom of the new country which has replaced the tyranny of the old. The lack of organization and the lack of prejudice is shown by the fact that the "captain" or elected leader of a class composed with one exception of Jewish lads is the solitary exception—an Irish boy. In another class the "captain" is Chinese.

The interest in politics is only one of the evidences of a great desire to "get along in the world." Another is the fact that many of the boys are self-supporting. The number of boys working their way through can only be guessed. They are reluctant to tell anything about their home life or conditions. It is known, however, that about one hundred and twenty of the six hundred odd boys in the grammar department are self-supporting. A little Italian boy was late one morning and was asked for his excuse by the principal. After much questioning he told his story: His mother was dead, and his father, who worked on the railways, and consequently was away from home most of the time, could send him only enough money to pay the rent of the two small rooms in which he and a smaller brother and sister lived. To pay for their food and clothing he and his brother sold papers after school hours, making about $4 a week. The sister did the cooking and the housework. This particular morning she had been ill and unable to leave her bed, and it had taken him so long to care for her and attend to her work that he had been late. This was told quietly and quite as a matter of course. The boy was fourteen years old. He had no idea that his story seemed extraordinary. He had never thought of trying to get help of any kind. This earnestness is carried into all the school work. The boys, because of the sacrifices their schooling brings, realize more keenly how valuable it is to them. . . .

It is a large task that schools of this kind are doing, taking the raw, law-class foreign boys of many nationalities and molding them into self-supporting, self-respecting citizens of the republic. The amount of this work done by the public schools in New York is indicated by the figures of the immigration bureau, for of the great body of foreigners who come into this country, more than two-thirds come through the port of New York, beyond which most of them rarely get. The results shown by the public schools seem little short of marvelous. There are many things in which, as a rule, the public consider that the public schools fail, but the one thing that cannot be denied —and it is the greatest—is that these boys and girls of foreign parentage catch readily the simple American ideas of independence and individual work and, with them, social progress.

·§ 8 ·§·

Restriction

that put an end to the immigration movement was adopted after
a quarter century of agitation. The action finally taken was
shaped by two factors: First, by the nationalistic sentiments of
the war years and after; and also, by the restrictionist ideas developed and spread in the long debate since the question was first
raised.

Several distinct elements coalesced in the restrictionist campaign. The West Coast anti-Oriental battle had a profound influence, for it was there the notion took hold that there were
categories of humanity altogether unfit to become Americans and
therefore altogether to be excluded. In the 1870's and 1880's, the
Chinese were the predominant target; in the years after 1900, the
Japanese.

The restrictionists could also draw upon the support of religious prejudice. Among American Protestants there had long
been latent the fear that the bulk of the immigrants, Catholic or
Jewish, by heritage, might subtly undermine the traditional

167

American religious forms. It was no coincidence that the years in which the new immigration legislation was enacted were also the years in which the Ku Klux Klan was building up its membership of 5,000,000.

The developing conception of racism added further strength to the drive for closing the gates. In the early years of the twentieth century many sociologists and anthropologists had accepted the idea that mankind was divided into biologically distinct races, that any intermixture was undesirable, and that Americans ought to aim at a population that was pure and Aryan.

Through most of the campaign the argument revolved about the literacy test that would have barred any immigrant incapable of reading in any language. It was hoped such a measure would cut down the total numbers and select the superior applicants. The Immigration Restriction League, an organization particularly strong in New England, sponsored the measure in the hope that it would allow the English-speaking groups to retain their predominance. The proposal was also aimed to attract the support of the "old" immigrants from northern and western Europe who were sedulously courted with the assurance they were different from and better than the "new" immigrants from southern and eastern Europe. In addition the literacy test drew the support of the organized labor movement anxious to retain its favored position in the American economy.

Enactment of the measure in 1917 did not end the restrictionist movement. Indeed the Immigration Restriction League was spurred by its initial success to renewed efforts toward a more complete restriction. And it could now draw upon the dark hatreds and fears of wartime for support.

THE ORIENTALS AND COLOR PREJUDICE

Writing shortly after the event, but with scholarly detachment, Mary R. Coolidge presented an acute analysis of the causes and significance of the California campaign against Chi-

nese immigration. The first selection below is taken from her book published in 1909.[1]

An enlightening account of the anti-Japanese agitation comes in the second selection, from a modern discussion of the problem by Carey McWilliams, a sympathetic student of American racial problems and himself experienced as a California state official in dealing with the diversified population of that commonwealth.[2]

(A). Coolidge

Throughout this year and a half of financial depression [1875-1876], stagnation and social agitation, much had been threatened and done against the Chinese; yet it may be doubted whether Chinese immigration was, after all, the storm center of the disturbance. Rather, it appears that a mushroom prosperity and great extremes of fortune, arising from speculation and chance rather than legitimate industry, and the gathering of heterogeneous idlers under the leadership of demagogues, had brought to the surface all the elements of jealousy, envy and lawlessness which, inherent in human nature, now surged and frothed about the more stable elements of society. The indifference to public welfare characteristic of a society based on the pursuit of money alone, was bearing its legitimate fruits in a general disorder.

Of this unfortunate situation the Chinese were the victims rather than the fundamental cause; they were so many, so thrifty, so uncomplaining, so glad to work at any price, and above all so alien, so strange—so "heathenish." To the followers of the Workingmen's Party they seemed such a facile tool for the greedy capitalist that it was only natural to suppose that they were the chief cause both of his riches, and of their own hardships. Yet the Chinese had not caused drought, nor decline of mineral production, nor speculation and panic in stocks and real estate, nor land monopoly nor even the labor movement which was world-wide and which had taken on a special and violent phase in San Francisco. . . .

That the Workingmen's Party was now a serious factor to be reckoned with was recognized by both political parties. . . . The old-line

---

[1] Mary R. Coolidge, *Chinese Immigration* (New York, 1909), 116-121.

[2] Quoted by permission of the author from Carey McWilliams, *Prejudice, Japanese-Americans: Symbol of Racial Intolerance* (Boston, Little, Brown & Company, 1944), 18-33.

politicians were already dismayed by the sweeping victories of the Workingmen's Party; and in view of the election of delegates to the Constitutional Convention upon which the political interest of the whole State was now centered, they arranged a strong fusion ticket of Republicans, Democrats and non-partisans in the State at large. The Workingmen's Party, in which could now be discerned two factions, offered to the voters a lengthy programme of reform, in which opposition to the Chinese—not to employ them or to buy from them or sell to them—stood first, and opposition to land monopoly stood second.

When the Constitutional Convention assembled it was almost equally divided between the two old parties, but the predominance of workingmen from San Francisco, and of farmers representing the Granger element of the country districts who stood together on some of the most extreme propositions, gave the radicals the balance of power and produced the most extraordinary state constitution known in the history of the United States. By this time even conservative citizens were so desperate at the lawlessness of the Workingmen's Party that they were ready to concede anything for the sake of industrial peace. The constitution, formed under this intimidation of the extreme laboring and agricultural classes, was permeated with two main ideas: hostility to capital, expressed in measures of taxation and limitation, and hostility to the Chinese, expressed in measures for cutting off their means of livelihood. . . .

The Workingmen's delegation brought in a series of anti-Chinese propositions of which the more important were as follows: aliens should not be allowed to hold property; Chinese should not be allowed to trade, peddle or carry on any mercantile business; no person not eligible to be a citizen should be allowed to settle in the State, and any person encouraging such should be fined; aliens, ineligible to citizenship, should be prohibited from bearing arms, giving testimony in the courts in cases involving white persons, from fishing in the inland waters of the State and from employment on public works; a per capita tax of $250.00 should be levied on each Chinese immigrant.

These propositions were remarkable not only for their display of rancor and ignorance, but for their total inapplicability to the problem to be solved. Their tone is inhuman in its disregard of the common rights of men, as well as of the protection guaranteed to the Chinese under the Burlingame Treaty. At least two-thirds of them were on their face violations of the Federal Constitution, and several had been passed and declared invalid in previous years. And yet they were seriously proposed although it had become thoroughly understood in the ten years of previous agitation that no limitation or prohibition of Chinese immigration was possible except by Congressional legislation and treaty negotiation. . . .

Article Nineteen gave the Legislature power to regulate the immigration of paupers, criminals, diseased persons and aliens otherwise dangerous or detrimental to the State, and to impose the conditions of their residence or removal. It forbade corporations to employ any Mongolian, nor could they be engaged on any public works. Coolie contracts were declared void and companies importing them, whether formed in this or any foreign country, were to be penalized. The Legislature was even empowered to remove the Chinese beyond the limits of cities and towns and to prohibit their introduction into the State. . . .

Nevertheless, most of the sections finally incorporated in Article Nineteen were adopted almost unanimously and many of the injustices to the Chinese were thus given a sort of constitutional approval.

(B). McWilliams

The campaign was launched on February 23, 1905 . . . by a series of sensational and highly inflammatory articles in the San Francisco Chronicle. Some of the captions on these articles were: Crime and Poverty Go Hand in Hand with Asiatic Labor; Brown Men Are an Evil in the Public Schools; Japanese a Menace to American Women; Brown Asiatics Steal Brains of Whites. "Every one of these immigrants," said the Chronicle, "so far as his service is desired, is a Japanese spy." Just why the Chronicle should have launched this attack has never been determined. But the owner of the Chronicle, M. H. DeYoung, had been a candidate for the United States Senate a few years previously and some observers construed these vicious articles as a renewal of his candidacy. . . .

Following the appearance of the Chronicle articles, the California legislature, on March 1, 1905, by a vote of twenty-eight to nothing in the Senate and seventy to nothing in the Assembly, passed a resolution urging Congress to exclude the Japanese. Two months later, the Japanese and Korean Exclusion League was formed in San Francisco. Within a year, this organization had a membership of 78,500 (three fourths of its membership being located in the San Francisco Bay area). By 1905 the fight had been narrowed down to the Japanese. "The Chinese," the Chronicle observed, "are faithful laborers and do not buy land. The Japanese are unfaithful laborers and do buy land." At this time, however, California was, as David Starr Jordan pointed out, "by no means a unit on the question of the immigration of Japanese laborers. The fruit growers openly welcome it. Business men generally, quietly, favor it; and, outside of San Francisco and the labor unions, it is not clear that a majority of the people are opposed to the free admission of Japanese laborers or even of Chinese." The southern part of the state and the rural areas generally were not favorable to the agitation. Furthermore, the whole movement received a definite setback in President Theodore Roosevelt's message to Congress of December 1, 1905, in which he spoke out most emphatically in favor of a nondiscriminatory policy. . . .

[Political developments in San Francisco, however, lent an impetus to the campaign.] As an aftermath to a great teamsters' strike in July, 1901, the Union Labor Party [had] succeeded in electing Eugene E. Schmitz as mayor of San Francisco. In campaigning against Mayor James D. Phelan, Schmitz had forced such antilabor publications as the San Francisco Chronical [sic] and Call to compete for the "anti-Oriental" vote. Thus the violently prolabor and the violently antilabor forces both sought to exploit anti-Oriental sentiment. Formerly a bassoon player in a San Francisco orchestra, Schmitz was the henchman of Abe Ruef, an exceedingly able and notoriously corrupt politician. In the years following the victory of the Union Labor Party, San Francisco wallowed in corruption. . . . Although he had been reelected as Mayor of San Francisco, Schmitz was facing indictment in 1906 for his many crimes. Hard-pressed for an effective diversionary issue, Schmitz and Ruef saw an opportunity to save themselves by whipping up a Japanese pogrom.

At about this time, other groups in California . . . became actively interested in the anti-Oriental movement. A glance at the list of prominent leaders of the anti-Oriental agitation in California from 1907 to 1941 will show that most of these men were members and in most cases officials of the Native Sons of the Golden West. Hiram

Johnson, James D. Phelan, U. S. Webb, V. S. McClatchy (the doyen of all anti-Oriental leaders in California), J. M. Inman (State Senator and President of the California Oriental Exclusion League), Mayor Eugene E. Schmitz, Abe Ruef, Aaron Altman and James L. Gallagher (members of the San Francisco Board of Education in 1906), Anthony Caminetti (formerly a State Senator and United States Commissioner-General of Immigration in 1913)—all of these leaders of the anti-Oriental agitation were members and officials of the Native Sons. They were also active and successful political figures in California. As a matter of fact, scores of legislators, judges, state officials, Congressmen, and Senators received their initial support and owed their election (or appointment) to public office in California in the years 1907-1924 to the Native Sons of the Golden West. The organization, in turn, acquired its great political potency by cleverly using anti-Oriental feeling to solidify its own ranks and to build a compact political organization.

While glorifying the state of California, its history and traditions, the Native Sons has always been a strictly "lily-white" organization. Although making birth in California a condition of membership, the organization always excepted Chinese, Japanese, Negroes, and Mexicans (although a few elegant pseudo-Mexicans of the "early" and therefore the "best" families were admitted to membership). According to its philosophy, the State of California should remain what "it has always been and God Himself intended it shall always be—the White Man's Paradise." It has always been committed to the interesting proposition that the "31st Star shall never become dim or yellow." For years it maintained that citizenship should be restricted to "native-born Californians of the white male race." . . .

On May 6, 1905, the school board had gone on record in favor of segregating Oriental students in the San Francisco schools, but, for lack of funds, the resolution had been tabled. Now, on October 11, 1906, on the eve of the indictment of Messrs. Schmitz and Ruef for sundry felonies, the school board suddenly decided to carry the resolution into effect: it ordered all Oriental students to attend a segregated school in Chinatown. Not only were the graft investigations pending at the time, but a state election was scheduled for November. The conclusion is inescapable that the school board, which was completely dominated by Ruef and Schmitz, acted at this time to divert public attention from the graft scandals. There were only ninety-three

Japanese students out of a total school population of 25,000. A contemporary observer has stated that "no oral or written protests were ever made against the Japanese pupils by the parents of white pupils"; and, furthermore, educators throughout the state joined in voicing an emphatic protest.

"When word of this action reached Japan, there swept over the country," writes Dr. Bailey, "a wave of resentment against what was commonly spoken of as both a treaty violation and an insult." That the action violated the treaty of 1894 with Japan, there can be no doubt. Secretary of State Elihu Root admitted as much when he cabled our ambassador in Tokyo that "the United States will not for a moment entertain the idea of any treatment of the Japanese people other than that accorded to the people of the most friendly European nations." From this time forward, America ceased to be Dai On Jin, "the Great Friendly People," in the eyes of the Japanese masses. So intense was popular indignation in Japan that one newspaper, the Mainichi Shimbum, exclaimed editorially: "Why do we not insist on sending ships?" While it cannot be determined how much of this resentment was spontaneous and how much was inspired, it is apparent that the Japan government took advantage of the incident to create a diversion at Washington and to create popular sentiment in Japan in favor of increased military and naval appropriations.

When formal protests were filed in Washington, the Japanese in San Francisco immediately called a mass meeting and began to raise funds to fight the issue. In the meantime, Japanese parents refused to send their children to the segregated school. There is good reason to believe that this action on the part of the resident Japanese was in large part instigated by the Japanese consul in San Francisco. The Japanese vernacular press in San Francisco proceeded to publish, at this time, some extremely foolish and highly inflammatory editorials. "When National dignity is called to question," read one of these editorials, "the sword of Masamune is unsheathed for action." For the next twenty-five years these editorials were quoted in California as proof of the menacing character of the resident Japanese. One can at least draw an inference, however, that these editorials were inspired by the consul, whose influence was admittedly great with the editors of both publications. In retrospect, it seems altogether unlikely that such provocative statements would have been made without the approval of the consul.

Faced with this crisis, President Roosevelt promptly dispatched Secretary of Commerce and Labor, V. H. Metcalf (a Californian), to the Coast to make a thorough investigation. Without waiting for a report, however, he sent a message to Congress on December 3, 1906, in which he condemned the action of the San Francisco School Board as "a wicked absurdity." In the same message, he urged Congress to make it possible for the Japanese to become citizens and suggested that the President should be authorized to protect the treaty rights of aliens.

The Metcalf Report (dated December 18, 1906) clearly established that there was no factual justification for the action of the school board. It also documented some nineteen cases involving serious assaults against Japanese residents of San Francisco. The action of the school board was, in fact, merely the first of a long series of discriminatory measures adopted in California for the purpose of forcing Congress to exclude Japanese immigration. None of these acts was aimed at correcting a particular situation; they were all deliberately provocative in character. "The school question," said the Coast Seamen's Journal, "is a mere incident in our campaign for Japanese exclusion."

Coming soon after the Treaty of Portsmouth, the school-board affair proved most embarrassing to the national government, and it remained a source of embarrassment since no effective remedy was available to the government. On January 17, 1907, the federal government filed two suits in California by which it sought to enjoin the school board from carrying its order into effect. Had these suits ever been pressed to trial (they were later dismissed), it is extremely doubtful whether the federal government could have prevailed. For by 1907 the Supreme Court stood firmly committed to the notion that segregation, on the basis of race, is not unconstitutional, if equal and separate facilities are provided. This strange constitutional doctrine had been developed as part of the campaign to emasculate the Fourteenth Amendment in the years immediately subsequent to the Civil War.

Discussion of the San Francisco School Board "incident" on the floor of Congress showed clearly enough that the Japanese question in California was intimately related to the Negro question in the Deep South. "Because of their Negro problem, southerners were in sympathy with San Francisco's views; southern congressmen as a whole were decidedly with California in her race struggle." Congressman Burnett of Alabama stated that "we have suffered enough already from one race question" and similar views were echoed by Senator Bacon of Georgia, Senator Tillman of South Carolina, Senator Underwood of Alabama, Senator Burgess of Texas, and Senator Williams of Mississippi. One congressman from Mississippi stated:—

> I stand with the State of California in opposition to mixed schools. [Applause] I stand with Californians in favor of the proposition that we want a homogeneous and assimilable population of white people in the Republic. [Applause]

While these gentlemen were Democrats and doubtless aware of the fact that the Republican President faced re-election in 1908, the real basis of their action was obviously the racial situation in the South. In attempting to cope with California, President Roosevelt suddenly discovered that he faced the opposition of the Solid South.

In defying the President of the United States, California stood on firm legal grounds. . . . If the federal government could force California to abandon its policy of segregation, it could force compliance with the same policy in the South.

At a large mass meeting called in San Francisco, just before Christmas, Mayor Schmitz shouted defiance of the federal government; claimed that he was being unjustly prosecuted in the courts; and contended that he had been indicted, not for his crimes (which were legion), but because of his anti-Japanese views. In the course of this speech, the Mayor stated that, if necessary, he would lay down his life in battle with the Japanese. The Los Angeles Times was prompted to remark that "it is a notable fact that his Honor has never laid down anything of value. His promise, however, would almost reconcile anyone to a war with Japan." In the November elections of 1906, California politicians were volunteering by the score to fight Japan. "If we are to have a war with Japan," advised Congressman E. A. Hayes, "let's have it right away. We are ready and they are not." P. H. McCarthy believed that the "states west of the Rockies could whip Japan at a moment's notice."

Suggesting that the ordinance be suspended, Mr. Roosevelt invited the school board to Washington. It took Mayor Schmitz a full week to decide whether he would permit the board to accept the invitation. When he finally agreed, he decided to accompany them himself. In

February, 1907, the party left for Washington amidst much excite-
ment and fanfare. The Mayor's followers, according to Franklin
Hitchborn, "were frankly delighted with prospect of the indicted
Mayor returning from the national capitol covered with glory and
acclaimed the savior of the country from a war with Japan."

It would be difficult, indeed, to imagine a more ludicrous spectacle.
Heading the delegation was the Mayor, a bassoon player by profession, under indictment for numerous crimes. He was accompanied
by the Superintendent of Schools, Roncovieri, a trombone player,
close personal friend of the Mayor, and by Aaron Altman, President
of the School Board, a brother-in-law of Abe Ruef. Here were Altman,
Schmitz, and Roncovieri—all descendants of recent immigrants to
the United States, all members in good standing of the Native Sons,
one of them under indictment—going to "treat with" the President
of the United States as though they were the ministers of a sovereign
political power. . . .

As Mayor Schmitz and party neared Washington, the newspapers
carried sensational headlines about the "inevitable" conflict with
Japan. Throughout this period, Captain Richmond P. Hobson was
conducting an inflammatory anti-Japanese campaign, on the lecture
platform, in Congress (1907-1915), and in the press. "We know," he
wrote, "that the Japanese in California are soldiers organized into
companies, regiments, and brigades." While the Mayor was en route
to Washington, the California legislature convened and the usual
spate of anti-Japanese legislation was promptly introduced. By direct
appeals to Governor Gillett, President Roosevelt managed to have
these bills tabled while he was negotiating a settlement with California's ambassadors. The agreement finally reached in Washington
provided that the school board would withdraw the offensive ordinance and that the President would negotiate with Japan for a sus-
pension of further immigration. On March 17, 1907, the ordinance
was withdrawn; and shortly afterwards the President, by executive
order, stopped further Japanese immigration by way of Hawaii, Canada, or Mexico. The moment this agreement was announced, the anti-
Japanese forces in California attacked Mayor Schmitz as a traitor—
even the Catholic Archbishop of San Francisco felt that he had been
"betrayed."

Religious Intolerance

*A brief survey of the development of American anti-Semitism
and of its connection with immigration comes from an account
by the editor. An extract from it follows in the first selection.*[3]
*Although agitators had threatened Americans with the menace
of the Pope for more than a century, anti-Catholic agitation
reached a high pitch after 1919 with the growth of the Ku Klux
Klan. Klansmen's objections to Catholics were stated in The
Fiery Cross, February 8, 1924. It was one of the organization's
official publications. The second selection is taken from it.*[4]

(A). *Handlin*

By 1920, a full-fledged racial ideology colored the thinking of many
Americans. The conquest of opinion was by no means complete; the
traditional American attitude of tolerance still acted as a brake upon
the headlong sweep of these new ideas. What was ominous was the
support the ideas received from occasional incidents at the practical
level.

Significantly, in practice, as in the theory, the Jews were not alone
singled out. The racist found equally his enemies all the colored peoples, the Latins, and the Slavs. If the Jews were often the first to draw
fire, that was because local circumstances sometimes made them the
most prominent targets.

The Pattern of Exclusion. Social mobility has always been an important characteristic of the American scheme for living. A great deal
of freedom in the economic structure has made room for the free play
of talents and has permitted newcomers to make their way from the
lower to the higher rungs in the occupational ladder. In the absence
of an hereditary aristocracy, social position has generally accompanied
economic position.

Those who occupied the higher places of course always resented

---

[3] Oscar and Mary F. Handlin, *Danger in Discord.* (New York, 1948), 24-29.
Published in the Freedom pamphlet Series by the Anti-Defamation League of
B'nai B'rith, New York 10, New York.

[4] Cited in Michael Williams, *The Shadow of the Pope.* (New York, McGraw-
Hill, 1932), 313-314.

the competition from those who climbed out of the lower places. More than a hundred years ago, newspapers were already carrying the injunction over their help-wanted ads, "No Irish Need Apply!"

But the democratic nature of American society made it difficult permanently to establish such barriers. In the nineteenth century these artificial restraints had always broken down beneath the pressure of the necessity for cooperation at all levels in the community. Furthermore, constant expansion in the economic and social structure of the nation made room for newcomers without lowering the position of those already well established. In fact, it often happened that a rise in the level of the immigrants and their children lifted even higher the positions of all those above them.

The earliest encounters of the Jews with this feature of the American social system were not unlike those of members of other ethnic groups who passed through the same process. In adjusting to the American economy, some groups moved upward much more rapidly than others. The Jews were among those who advanced most quickly in earning power and in social position. Their special difficulties arose from the circumstance that they seemed singularly to rise faster than other peoples of recent immigration origin. This success in mobility came at a time when the earlier immigrant groups of the later eighteenth and early nineteenth centuries had chosen to forget their own swift rise and extraordinary accumulation of the great fortunes characteristically found among them.

All who mounted the economic ladder earned the resentment of the well-established; but, in their rapid climb, the Jews seemed interlopers, out of place, more often than earlier outsiders moving in the same direction.

Economic power in America was usually enveloped in certain symbols of prestige and position—good family, membership in the appropriate churches and associations, residence in select districts, and participation in communal activities. Success by Jews was resented, not only because the success of every new arrival seemed to leave less room for those already entrenched, but also because success in their case was not graced with the proper symbols, did not take the proper form.

Furthermore, the rapidity of the climb heightened the sense of difference between Jews and non-Jews at the upper economic levels. Some Jews reached positions of economic power and influence within

a single generation, a time-interval not long enough for adequate social adaptation. The contrast in behavior was therefore particularly
noticeable. "High society" and its lowlier imitators, uncomfortable at
the entrance of any newcomers, in the case of these, could ascribe its
discomforts to the difference in manners rather than to an inherent
unwillingness to make room for competitors. As in every manifesta-
tion of prejudice, the Jew was in the same category as other minorities
discriminated against. But his exceptional mobility made him the
more prominent and the more vulnerable target.

Exclusion was first prominently expressed in areas that involved the
use of leisure time facilities, that is, in vacation places, in clubs, and
in social groups of various kinds. Such activities, being less formalized
than, say, the activities of business or politics, were open to intimate
personal contacts, and therefore felt the strangers' presence more sen-
sitively. What is more, these activities involved the whole family.
Unlike the office or the workshop, where each man could deal im-
personally and almost anonymously with individuals as individuals,
the resort or dance drew in the members of his family and made him
more conscious of questions of background and origin.

Toward the end of the nineteenth century, many places began to
close their doors to Jews. The incident in Saratoga Springs in 1877
when Joseph Seligman was refused accommodations at the Grand
Union Hotel was a dramatic precursor of a pattern that would become more familiar in succeeding decades. In the 1890's also appeared
a large number of hereditary prestige societies, which based their
membership upon descent from eighteenth-century American ancestors, and which had the effect of excluding most Jews as well as most
other Americans, who were descended from immigrants who arrived
after 1800.

These social slights ultimately had an effect upon other activities,
of course. To the extent that business and political contacts often
were made within the realm of the club or society, those who were
excluded from the club or society were automatically discriminated
against.

And soon that discrimination became more direct. After 1910, as
the sons of the immigrant Jews entered more keenly and more notice-
ably into competition for professional and white collar places in the
American economic system, the weight of such prejudice became formal and more open. Newspaper advertisements began specifically to

exclude Jews from consideration for certain positions. Access to many professions was arbitrarily if informally limited.

Uneasily many Americans accepted this pattern of discrimination. Although not a few were still conscious enough of their heritage of freedom and equality to protest against the tendency, all too many, lulled by the racist justification of ineradicable differences, were disposed to acquiesce. The formation of the American Jewish Committee in 1906 and of the Anti-Defamation League of B'nai B'rith in 1913 to fight these trends indicated a growing awareness of the seriousness of the problem.

Georgia Blood Bath. What drew attention to the potential menace of all these developments was a sudden eruption that displayed the ugly turn the forces of racism could take. Appropriately enough the eruption came in the South, the source of so much of the festering venom; and appropriately enough it came in the New, not the Old South, in industrial Atlanta rather than in the romantic plantation.

Among the disorganized masses of men thrown together in the American cities, seeming grievances with no hope of redress from "legal" channels often led to violent outbursts of mob action. Many people did not trust their governments, were ready to believe that their police department and courts had sold out to special interests, and, under provocation, were willing to take direct action themselves.

Distinctive minorities were particularly subject to violent reprisals when their actions seemed to run against the cherished patterns of the community, yet involved no clear infraction of the law. In the 1890's, Italians in New Orleans and Irishmen in Boston had suffered the harsh effects of mob violence.

In 1915 the blow fell upon Leo Frank, a Jewish resident of Atlanta, Georgia. Accused of the murder of a fourteen-year-old girl and convicted on the flimsiest grounds, he was taken from jail and lynched the day after the governor of the state had commuted his sentence.

Many factors combined to draw the web of hatred around Frank's neck. He was a Northerner and an employer of labor, and earned a full share of mistrust on those grounds alone. As a Jew he inherited all the dislikes stirred up by the racist writers of the period, and also the murky suspicions about Jewish blood murders left over from agitation of the Beiliss case a few years earlier. Finally the indignation everywhere outside the state that followed his conviction, and the ultimate commutation of the sentence by the governor, raised the suspicion that justice was being frustrated through the intercession of powerful hostile outsiders. Under skillful manipulation, these became the goads that prodded the mob into action.

The manipulation came from Tom Watson. By 1913 this man had a long political career behind him. A sympathizer with the cause of the poor in his own region, he had been prominent as a populist and as a leader in the progressive movements at the turn of the century. But the years after 1900 were a long series of frustrations not only, or not so much, in terms of personal ambitions, but in terms of the success of the program for which he fought. "The world is plunging Hellward," he complained.

In common with many other men of his period, Watson blamed this deterioration upon the interference of outside interests. At first, his hostility focused upon the traditional objective of fundamentalist America, the Roman Catholic Church, and he engaged in a long, bitter campaign of vilification through his journals and books.

But in practice as in theory, prejudice was not easily limited to one group. The Frank case offered an alternative, and Watson transferred the identical arguments he was using against the Catholics to the Jews. He rallied his followers with the slogan that Frank must be executed to eliminate outside Jewish interference from Georgia.

In an immediate sense, Watson was successful. Frank died and Watson himself rode to continued political power on the basis of his leadership in the anti-Semitic campaign. Local bitterness raised by the issue persisted for many years.

Yet the very violence of the terms Watson used, the very barbarousness of the methods of his mob, revolted the great mass of Americans outside his state. The rude gallows at Marietta, Georgia, cast a sombre shadow across the land, a premonitory warning of what might develop.

(B). *The Fiery Cross*

Old stock Americans have become restless. . . . They are dissatisfied with the denationalizing forces at work in the country. There is something wrong and the American people know there is something wrong, and they are talking among themselves as to where the trouble is. They know the arrogant claims of the Papacy to temporal power and that the Romish church is not in sympathy with American ideals and institutions. They know that Rome is in politics, and that she often drives the thin edge of her wedge with a muffled hammer; they have seen the results of her activities in other lands. They know the facts as to Rome's opposition to the Bible in our public schools and to our public school system itself. They know she is opposed to a free press, free speech, and to other democratic principles.

These old stock Americans are coming to believe that the Jews dominate the economic life of the nation, while the Catholics are determined to dominate the political and religious life. And they have apprehensions that the vast alien immigration is at the root an attack upon Protestant religion with its freedom of conscience, and is therefore a menace to American liberties.

They have seen Roman canon law come into conflict with American law, and they are not willing to have a foreign power dictate to them, or pursue a policy destructive to true Americanism. Many of these American patriots have heard about a great building now being erected in Washington in preparation as the residence of the Pope transferred from the Vatican to the national capital. And whether this is true or false, it is believed by a large number of citizens. At any rate, the American people know there is something wrong. They are afraid of the race groups that adhere to their own language and race prejudice and religious superstitions, and have no sympathy with our Americanism. They have their forebodings as to the union of Jews and Catholics in their opposition to the Bible in our public schools. And they are determined that Romanism, with its political ambitions and with whatever allies it may have, shall not carry out any plot against our free institutions and against the very government itself.

RACISM

The full ideology of racism was set forth in 1916 by a well-known anthropologist at the American Museum of Natural History in a phenomenally popular book from which the following selection is drawn.[5]

---

[5] Madison Grant, *The Passing of the Great Race*, 3rd ed., 86-92. Copyright 1916 by Charles Scribner's Sons, 1944 by DeForest Grant; used by permission of the publishers.

Race consciousness . . . in the United States, down to and including the Mexican War, seems to have been very strongly developed among native Americans and it still remains in full vigor today in the South, where the presence of a large Negro population forces this question upon the daily attention of the whites.

In New England, however, whether through the decline of Calvinism or the growth of altruism, there appeared early in the last century a wave of sentimentalism, which at that time took up the cause of the Negro and in so doing apparently destroyed, to a large extent, pride and consciousness of race in the North. The agitation over slavery was inimical to the Nordic race, because it thrust aside all national opposition to the intrusion of hordes of immigrants of inferior racial value and prevented the fixing of a definite American type. . . .

The native American by the middle of the nineteenth century was rapidly acquiring distinct characteristics. . . . The Civil War, however, put a severe, perhaps fatal, check to the development and expansion of this splendid type by destroying great numbers of the best breeding stock on both sides and by breaking up the home ties of many more. If the war had not occurred these same men with their descendants would have populated the Western States instead of the racial nondescripts who are now flocking there. . . .

The prosperity that followed the war attracted hordes of newcomers who were welcomed by the native Americans to operate factories, build railroads and fill up the waste spaces—"developing the country" it was called.

These new immigrants were no longer exclusively members of the Nordic race as were the earlier ones who came of their own impulse to improve their social conditions. The transportation lines advertised America as a land flowing with milk and honey and the European governments took the opportunity to unload upon careless, wealthy and hospitable America the sweepings of their jails and asylums. The result was that the new immigration . . . contained a large and increasing number of the weak, the broken and the mentally crippled of all races drawn from the lowest stratum of the Mediterranean basin and the Balkans, together with hordes of the wretched, submerged populations of the Polish Ghettos. Our jails, insane asylums and almshouses are filled with this human flotsam and the whole tone of American life, social, moral and political has been lowered and vulgarized by them.

With a pathetic and fatuous belief in the efficacy of American institutions and environment to reverse or obliterate immemorial hereditary tendencies, these newcomers were welcomed and given a share in our land and prosperity. The American taxed himself to sanitate and educate these poor helots and as soon as they could speak English, encouraged them to enter into the political life, first of municipalities and then of the nation. . . .

These immigrants adopt the language of the native American, they wear his clothes, they steal his name and they are beginning to take his women, but they seldom adopt his religion or understand his ideals and while he is being elbowed out of his own home the American looks calmly abroad and urges on others the suicidal ethics which are exterminating his own race. . . .

As to what the future mixture will be it is evident that in large sections of the country the native American will entirely disappear. He will not intermarry with inferior races and he cannot compete in the sweat shop and in the street trench with the newcomers. Large cities from the days of Rome, Alexandria, and Byzantium have always been gathering points of diverse races, but New York is becoming a *cloaca gentium* which will produce many amazing racial hybrids and some ethnic horrors that will be beyond the powers of future anthropologists to unravel.

One thing is certain: in any such mixture, the surviving traits will be determined by competition between the lowest and most primitive elements and the specialized traits of Nordic man; his stature, his light colored eyes, his fair skin and light colored hair, his straight nose and his splendid fighting and moral qualities, will have little part in the resultant mixture.

THE LITERACY TEST DEFENDED

The first effort to restrict immigration was through the literacy test vigorously advocated by Prescott F. Hall and the Immigration Restriction League. The reasons why organized labor supported the literacy test are explained in a letter of May 16, 1902, from Samuel Gompers, president of the American Federation of Labor, to James E. Watson, Representative from Georgia.[6]

---

[6] Quoted in the *Publications of the Immigration Restriction League*, no. 35.

Gompers

I have observed with much pleasure your activity in the cause of the regulation of immigration, and in particular your introduction of a bill providing that no adult immigrant shall be admitted to our country till he has acquired the first rudiments of education. It is for this reason that I now address you with regard to pending and prospective legislation.

The organized workers of the country feel that the existing immigration laws, while not without their value, are of trifling effect compared with the needs and the just demands of American labor. . . .

The strength of this country is in the intelligence and prosperity of our working people. But both the intelligence and the prosperity of our working people are endangered by the present immigration. Cheap labor, ignorant labor, takes our jobs and cuts our wages.

The fittest survive; that is, those that fit the conditions best. But it is the economically weak, not the economically strong, that fit the conditions of the labor market. They fit best because they can be got to work cheapest. Women and children drive out men, unless either law or labor organization stops it. In just the same way the Chinaman and others drive out the American, the German, the Irishman.

The tariff keeps out cheap foreign goods. It is employers, not workingmen, that have goods to sell. Workingmen sell labor, and cheap labor is not kept out by the tariff. The protection that would directly help the workers is protection against the cheap labor itself.

The Nashville convention of the American Federation of Labor, by a vote of 1,858 to 352, pronounced in favor of an educational test for immigrants. Such a measure would check immigration in a moderate degree, and those who would be kept out by it are those whose competition in the labor market is most injurious to American workers. No other measure which would have any important effect of this kind is seriously proposed.

The need of regulation may be less sharply felt at the present time, when there are less men out of work than there were a few years ago. But the flood of cheap labor is increasing, and its effect at the slightest stagnation in industry or in any crisis will be fearful to the American workmen.

A fall in wages or a relative fall of wages makes the workers unable to buy as large a share as before of the goods they produce. This hastens the time when overproduction or underconsumption will show itself. That means hard times; and when hard times come, the mass of immigrants that prosperity attracted will be here to increase the burden of unemployment.

For these reasons the American Federation of Labor believes that the present opportunity ought not to be allowed to pass without the adoption of an effective measure for the protection of American labor.

I earnestly hope that you will be able to procure the embodiment of an illiteracy test for immigrants in the bill (H.R. 12199) which the House now has under consideration.

THE LITERACY TEST CONDEMNED

Despite heavy pressures upon him, President Wilson refused to accede to the demands of the restrictionists and vetoed the bill in 1915 and in 1917, as Presidents Cleveland and Taft had done before him. In 1917, however, the Act was passed over his veto. His message of January 28, 1915, explained his objections to the proposed law.[7]

In two particulars of vital consequence this bill embodies a radical departure from the traditional and long-established policy of this country, a policy in which our people have conceived the very character of their Government to be expressed, the very mission and spirit of the nation in respect of its relations to the peoples of the world outside their borders. It seeks to all but close entirely the gates of asylum which have always been open to those who could find nowhere else the right and opportunity of constitutional agitation for what they conceived to be the natural and inalienable rights of men; and it excludes those to whom the opportunities of elementary education have been denied, without regard to their character, their purposes, or their natural capacity.

Restrictions like these, adopted earlier in our history as a Nation, would very materially have altered the course and cooled the humane ardors of our politics. The right of political asylum has brought to

---

[7] Albert Shaw, ed., *Messages and Papers of Woodrow Wilson.* (New York, 1924), I, 95, 96

this country many a man of noble character and elevated purpose who was marked as an outlaw in his own less fortunate land, and who has yet become an ornament to our citizenship and to our public councils. The children and the compatriots of these illustrious Americans must stand amazed to see the representatives of their Nation now resolved, in the fullness of our national strength and at the maturity of our great institutions, to risk turning such men back from our shores without test of quality or purpose. It is difficult for me to believe that the full effect of this feature of the bill was realized when it was framed and adopted, and it is impossible for me to assent to it in the form in which it is here cast.

The literacy test and the tests and restrictions which accompany it constitute an even more radical change in the policy of the Nation. Hitherto we have generously kept our doors open to all who were not unfitted by reason of disease or incapacity for self-support or such personal records and antecedents as were likely to make them a menace to our peace and order or to the wholesome and essential relationships of life. In this bill it is proposed to turn away from tests of character and of quality and impose tests which exclude and restrict; for the new tests here embodied are not tests of quality or of character or of personal fitness, but tests of opportunity. Those who come seeking opportunity are not to be admitted unless they have already had one of the chief of the opportunities they seek, the opportunity of education. The object of such provisions is restriction, not selection.

If the people of this country have made up their minds to limit the number of immigrants by arbitrary tests and so reverse the policy of all the generations of Americans that have gone before them, it is their right to do so. I am their servant and have no license to stand in their way. But I do not believe that they have. I respectfully submit that no one can quote their mandate to that effect. Has any political party ever avowed a policy of restriction in this fundamental matter, gone to the country on it, and been commissioned to control its legislation? Does this bill rest upon the conscious and universal assent and desire of the American people? I doubt it. It is because I doubt it that I make bold to dissent from it. I am willing to abide by the verdict, but not until it has been rendered. Let the platforms of parties speak out upon this policy and the people pronounce their wish. The matter is too fundamental to be settled otherwise.

EFFECTS OF THE WAR

The World War into which the United States found itself plunged stirred up violent nationalistic feelings and stimulated distrust of everything foreign. During the debates over neutrality that had preceded American entry into the conflict, the charge of hyphenism and of potential disloyalty had frequently been hurled at the foreign-born. Although the war itself supplied no justification for these fears, the suspicion by then aroused did not readily subside. In any case, the disappointments of the post war period induced many Americans to long for a complete separation from Europe. It is against the background of such sentiments that one must understand the final development of the present immigration policy of the United States.

The passage of the literacy test over President Wilson's veto had by no means satisfied the restrictionists, who resolved at once to push on toward a more rigid policy. A professor of geology at Harvard University, long prominent in the restrictionist movement, set forth in May 1919 the reasons why new legislation was necessary. In addition to old arguments, he emphasized the danger of radicalism among the foreigners—the danger that seemed particularly important as the Red scare gathered momentum.[8]

The balance of expert opinion on the question of our probable immigration in the years immediately ahead is that, as soon as ocean transportation is again fully established, there will be a far larger immigration than ever before. It is the opinion of American diplomatic and consular officers in Europe, and of competent correspondents who have recently traveled extensively abroad, that there is everywhere a more widespread desire than ever to "go to America." All the arguments which may be urged in favor of a decreased immigration, based on the need of labor for reconstruction and for agriculture abroad, collapse when we remember that the great magnet of "America" will continue to draw immigrants to this "promised land." Our part in feeding and caring for vast numbers of people abroad, and in helping to win the war as liberators of the oppressed,

---

[8] Robert De C. Ward, "Americanization and Immigration," *American Review of Reviews*, LIX, 513-516.

and as ready to sacrifice, if necessary, any number of lives and endless sums of money for an ideal, will prove new incentives.

Immigration is essentially a matter of economic conditions here and abroad. As the late Gen. Francis A. Walker so well put it, "the stream of immigration will flow on as long as there is any difference in economic level between the United States and the most degraded communities abroad." A recent writer, after considerable study of the subject, has put the probable annual number of immigrants who will soon be coming here at 2,000,000. Be that as it may, the most enthusiastic believer in the success of the Americanization movement can hardly face the prospect of a steady annual immigration of even only several hundred thousands without doubt and discouragement. To hope to accomplish successful Americanization when the supply of aliens keeps up is to have an optimism "beyond all bounds of reason." A real restriction of immigration is a necessary and a logical part of the Americanization program. . . .

Our present Immigration Act, after having been twice vetoed by President Wilson, was passed over the veto by both Senate and House, and became law on February 5, 1917, about two months before this country declared war. The new statute became effective on May 1, 1917. It is by far the most comprehensive immigration legislation ever enacted in this country, and if properly enforced would be of immense benefit to our future race.

If any further arguments were needed to show the value and importance of this new legislation the war has supplied them. This law is our only breakwater against the advancing tide of alien immigration, which will be both increased in quantity and lowered in quality. Everything should be done to secure the effective administration of the new law, which has not yet had to stand the test of a large immigration. Its rigid enforcement will unquestionably result in an improvement in the mental, physical and moral qualities of immigrants even if not designed to reduce greatly their numbers. . . .

The new Immigration Act, while a great advance on previous legislation, goes only a very little way toward remedying the conditions here referred to. This act is qualitatively selective, not quantitatively restrictive. It will not greatly reduce the numbers of our immigrants.

Our newspapers have lately been making much of the deportation of alien anarchists and of other groups of agitators. Such deportation, while most desirable in every way for the internal peace and safety of the country, is not a large or important factor in our immigration policy. It concerns a few thousand persons only. These deportations are made under the provisions of the Immigration Act of 1917, as expanded and strengthened by a supplementary Act of October 16, 1918. Under this legislation, the United States may expel and deport at any time after their landing, anarchists and similar classes of aliens who preach or practise the use of violence against persons, property or organized government.

The almost certain prospect of a greatly increased immigration closely following the ending of the war; the manifest injustice of exposing our returning soldiers and sailors to competition with the low-priced labor of Europe and of Western Asia, and the conviction that our present immigration law is selective rather than numerically restrictive, have naturally resulted in a widespread demand for immediate further legislation which shall really limit the numbers of our alien immigrants. During the Short Session of the Congress which ended on March 4, 1919, the Immigration Committee of the House of Representatives reported a bill . . . suspending immigration for four years, with many exceptions in the cases of certain professional classes; the near relatives of aliens now in, or who have become citizens of the United States; aliens from Canada, Newfoundland, Cuba and Mexico; aliens who are refugees because of various kinds of persecution, and aliens admitted temporarily under regulations to be prescribed. No action was taken on this bill.

At the hearings which were given by the House Committee on Immigration, the bill was strongly advocated by the American Federation of Labor and by other organizations which stand for the maintenance of American wages and of American standards of living, and which, especially in view of demobilization and of the dangers of unemployment, wish to prevent, at least temporarily, the influx of large numbers of alien workers. . . .

That a further real *restriction* of immigration is necessary for the best interests of American labor, and for the proper assimilation and Americanization of our heterogeneous population, has long been obvious to the large majority of those, both Americans and foreigners, who have impartially studied our immigration problems.

Our attitude on this question of immigration should be clearly defined. Sentiment will never solve this, or any other great national problem. There is no place here for the idealist who shudders at the mere thought of a further regulation of immigration, and who, holding fast to the vision of the universal brotherhood of man, calls "ungenerous" and "un-American" anyone who suggests any further immigration legislation. . . .

Not immigration restriction but indiscriminate hospitality to immigrants is the "ungenerous" and "un-American policy." To grant free admission to all who want to come may give us, for the moment, a comfortable feeling that we are providing a "refuge for the oppressed." But it is in the highest degree "ungenerous" in us, the custodians of the future heritage of our race, to permit to land on our shores mental, physical and moral defectives, who, themselves and through their descendants, will not only lower the standards of our own people, but will tremendously increase all future problems of public and private philanthropy. It is in the highest degree "un-American" for us to permit any such influx of alien immigrants as will make the process of Americanization any more difficult than it already is.

The Quota System and Its Effects

The quota system satisfied all the accumulated demands of the restrictionists. Ultimately the "National Origins" device set up a basis of selection that embodied the racist ideas of its proponents. It ranked all the nations of the earth according to an order of precedence and assigned the largest number of admissions to those that were presumed to be closest in racial heritage to the original settlers of the United States. It thus favored the "old" at the expense of the "new" immigrants.

The effects of the legislation were far reaching. Not only were the total of admissions sharply reduced; the ultimate consequence was to put an end to the flow of free immigration. For the restrictive pattern of these laws and the discrimination embodied in them helped to destroy the old European image of America as the land of opportunity. Before the decade of the 1920's the number of applicants had dropped sharply and after 1930 there were years in which more people left than entered the United States. The great migrations which had been so much a part of American history by then had come to a close. A quarter of a century after the laws were passed, William S. Bernard, an as-

tute student of immigration, wrote a sober assessment of their effects.[9]

The quota system was enacted into law not as a comprehensive plan of immigration control but primarily as a method of regulating European immigration. Immigration from the (independent) countries of the Western Hemisphere has remained free from quota restriction, in part as a gesture of friendship to neighboring peoples, in part because immigration from this area was not considered a major problem. Asiatic immigration, as we have seen, had already been barred, and quotas created for countries in Asia were in most cases set up for the use not of native people but of members of the white race born there. The pivotal function of the quota system has thus been the restriction of European immigration, and the basic problem has been that of distributing quotas among the countries of Europe.

Pressure for cutting down immigration . . . was aimed particularly at the new groups from southern and eastern Europe. . . . When in 1921, after the slump resulting from the First World War, the total stream of immigrants started to rise rapidly as did the proportion represented by southern and eastern Europeans, the demand for a stricter method of restriction became more insistent. As a consequence in 1921 the quota law was enacted (in temporary form), setting for European countries and other areas numerical limits based on the proportions of foreign born in our population coming from each country. This method of computing quotas met with favor because it allotted the lion's share of the total to the countries of northern and western Europe and only a small part to the countries of southern and eastern Europe.

The notion of a quota system had been suggested as early as 1911 by Senator William P. Dillingham of Vermont, chairman of the special United States Immigration Commission. The report of the Commission included among its suggested methods of restriction "the limitation of the number of each race arriving each year to a certain percentage of the average of that race arriving during a given period of years." In the Congressional Immigration Committee hearings of 1919-1921 the principle of allotting quotas on the basis of the pro-

---

[9] *American Immigration Policy—a Reappraisal.* (New York, Harper & Brothers, 1950), 23-34. Reprinted by permission.

portion represented by various nationalities in our foreign-born population, or the "percentage quota principle," was introduced by Dr. Sidney L. Gulick, a former missionary in Asia. At the hearings Dr. Gulick represented the National Committee on Constructive Immigration Legislation, an organization originally founded by the Federal Council of Churches of Christ in America though no longer operating under its auspices. Dr. Gulick's chief objective was to devise an over-all system of immigration control which would obviate the need for offensive bans on Asiatics. Ironically enough, the plan adopted did not include quotas for Asiatics and these people continued to be banned. Other features of his plan were likewise discarded. He proposed that quotas be based on the foreign born of each nationality, together with their native-born children, and urged that the principle of "differential assimilation" be adopted, using the naturalization rate as an index. Since this principle met with objections and difficulties, he made the concrete suggestion that immigrants from any country be limited annually to a quota of three per cent of the number of their countrymen present in the United States in 1910.

The quota principle was embodied in a number of temporary acts before it evolved into its present form. The Quota Law of 1921, the Johnson Act, was signed by President Harding after being vetoed by President Wilson in his final days in office. It was designed as a temporary measure and, following Dr. Gulick's formula, provided that the number of aliens of any nationality to be admitted in any year be limited to three per cent of the number of foreign born of such nationality resident in the United States in 1910, according to that year's Census. This law was extended in 1922 and continued in force until 1924. A new system was adopted in 1924, and our present version went into effect in 1929.

The temporary 1921 quotas favored immigrants from northern and western Europe over those from southern and eastern Europe, though to a lesser degree than did later versions. Of a total quota of 358,000 the former received an annual total of about 200,000 as compared to 155,000 for the latter. This meant a reversal of the previous trend of immigration, since immigration from southern and eastern Europe had been more than four times as large as that from northern and western Europe in the years before the First World War. The average yearly immigration from northern and western Europe had been only 183,000, or less than the total quota allotted to the countries involved, whereas the average annual immigration from southern and eastern Europe had been 783,000, or five times as large as the total quota assigned to the countries in this region.

After three years these first emergency quotas were judged by Congress to be insufficiently restrictive; total immigration had risen to over 700,000 in the year 1923-1924. New quotas were therefore devised. The Immigration Act of 1924 set up another set of quotas representing two per cent of each foreign-born group resident in the United States in 1890. The intent of this law was not only to reduce the total quota (which was cut to 165,000) but also to cut down further the proportion represented by immigrants from southern and eastern Europe by using an earlier base year when this element had been much smaller. This use of outdated population statistics was the most flagrantly discriminatory device of any employed in quota calculation, and it made particularly obvious the motives which were behind the quota legislation. The total quota for northern and western European countries was cut by only 29 per cent, whereas that for southern and eastern Europe suffered a cut of 87 per cent. The quota for Italy, for instance, was reduced from 42,057 to 3,845; Poland's from 30,977 to 5,982; Turkey's from 2,654 to 100.

The "two per cent quotas" established in 1924, however, were set up for only temporary use until new quotas based on the national origins of our total population, both native and foreign-born, could be calculated. The 1924 Act provided that after July, 1927, each country should receive as a yearly quota a number which bore the same relation to the total quota of 150,000 as the number of people derived from that country by birth or descent bore to our total population in 1920. In other words, the total quota was apportioned among the various countries to which the Act applied according to their relative contribution to the American population as enumerated in 1920. Since the Act provided that the minimum quota for each country should be 100, the total quota has exceeded 150,000 by as much as the minimum quotas of 100 exceeded the quotas which would have been assigned to these countries by the simple formula above. . . .

Although the term "national origin" was used to describe this quota plan, actually the belief in racial differences was employed as a justification for the differential treatment it established. The opinions offered before Congress preceding the enactment of the National Origins Law sought to build up the notion of the innate inferiority of the "new" immigration. Some of the testimony dealt with the newly devised intelligence tests which had been used on an extensive scale for the first time in the United States Army. These tests, administered and interpreted in a literal and crude form, failed to take into account language and other environmental differences between various groups. Nevertheless, the lower scores of some of the new immigrants were offered as evidence of the group's innate inferiority. (It should be noted that careful tests given to children of immigrants in later years have resulted in scores that are as high as or higher than those of children of the native born.)

An indication of the scientific weakness of the quota system, even within the objectives which the law itself sets, is given by its imperfections and inconsistencies. Neither the national origins quotas nor those preceding have been established on a genuine nationality-group or culture-group basis. With a few minor exceptions the quotas have been set up according to the country of birth, and many countries of Europe contain a variety of different nationalities and culture groups, all of whom are eligible for the same quota. Poles, Czechs, and a number of other nationalities born in Germany are eligible for the German quota. Similarly, within the shifting boundaries of Poland, former natives of Austria, Russia, and Germany have been included. Thus the relationship between our quotas and the national origins of our population in 1920 is itself problematical.

Another obvious weakness is the fact that quotas do not take account of population transfers or changes of boundaries which continually alter the ethnic composition of European countries. Actually, when quotas were first established, the map of Europe had just undergone profound alterations which could only be roughly approximated in quota calculations. Only eight countries emerged after the First World War with the same boundaries, and nine new nations had been created (among them Czechoslovakia and Jugoslavia) from which immigrants had been previously admitted as natives of Austria-Hungary or some other dismembered nation. Boundary changes and population shifts effected during and after the Second World War have further invalidated the bases of the old quotas. The law includes a provision for adjusting quotas to take cognizance of territorial changes, but the obstacles are so great and the procedure so complex that this provision has had little practical effect. Only a few very obvious changes have been taken into account by such adjustments. No provision had been made, at least by the end of 1948, for the profound nationality and population changes resulting from the Second World War. Thus our quota law, even for the purpose for which it was intended, is to a considerable degree anachronistic.

Any critique of the quota system must recognize that it forms only one part of our total immigration regulation and functions in relationship to other features of our law. The quota plan was established to operate in conjunction with our basic immigration law as enacted in the Immigration Act of 1917 and not in substitution for it. All immigrants, whether quota or non-quota, must meet the qualifications set up by our statutes barring mentally, physically, and morally undesirable classes and persons likely to become a public charge. The last of these grounds for exclusion has been used to cut the size of immigration to a minimum in times of depression by setting up strict economic tests as the basis of eligibility. It is often argued that the framework for restricting and screening immigration without recourse to nationality-group quotas exists in statutes promoting selection of desirable immigrants on an individual basis.

The visa requirement established by the Immigration Act of 1924 is in itself an important regulative device. All immigrants, non-quota as well as quota, must have an immigration visa issued by a United States consul abroad before they can be admitted to the United States. In order to secure a visa an immigrant must have established his eligibility to enter the United States, a process requiring many documents with respect to the identity, character, and financial standing of the applicant. The overseas issuance of visas has proved an effective means of controlling the use of quotas and of screening immigrants prior to entry. On the other hand it has tended to involve excessive red tape, which has proved a handicap in times of emergency when speed was essential, such as during the years of Nazi persecution in Europe. . . .

It is evident that during the period since the enactment of quota controls immigration has been sharply reduced in volume. It is difficult, however, to estimate with precision the effect of the quota laws on the volume of immigration because during most of the intervening years other powerful influences have been at work cutting down movement and distorting immigration patterns. The chief of these forces have been the world-wide depression of the 1930's and the Second World War and its preliminaries. . . .

The depression reduced immigration to the point where the restrictive function of the quotas was dubious indeed. Reduction of immigration during the depression resulted in part from the automatic decline of immigration which in our history has always accompanied depressions. In addition, in accordance with presidential instructions issued in September, 1930, consular officials began rigidly to apply the clause in our general law excluding persons likely to become a public charge, and this further reduced the numbers admitted. The use of that provision was extremely effective in cutting immigration to a minimum for it was applied to all immigration, including non-quota immigration from the Western Hemisphere. The large portion of most quotas left unused showed that the quotas in themselves were actually restricting movement only from areas which had very small quotas. Immigrant admissions reached a low point of 23,000 in 1932.

Strict interpretation of the likely-to-become-a-public-charge clause remained in effect up to the outbreak of the Second World War. The flow of immigrants to the United States rose slightly after 1934 because of the flight of refugees from Nazi Europe, and immigration reached about 83,000 in 1939. No alteration was made in existing immigration regulations for the benefit of refugees, and no refugees were admitted without guarantees either from individuals or from private welfare agencies against their becoming public charges. Refugee immigration never became a large-scale movement; it is estimated by reliable authorities that less than 250,000 refugees were admitted to this country as immigrants during the whole period 1933 and 1944. The period of so-called refugee immigration was thus characterized by the smallest flow of immigration for any comparable period since 1830.

Immigration dropped rapidly with the outbreak of the Second World War in 1939 and the entry of the United States into the war in 1941. During the five years of our participation in the war immigration averaged under 30,000 (deducting departures of aliens, the net immigration was even smaller). The years after the close of hostilities showed the first rise of immigration over the 100,000 mark since 1930. In the fiscal year 1946 (ending June 30) 108,721 were admitted, 147,292 in 1947, and 170,570 in 1948. G.I. brides and their offspring represented nearly one-half of the total in 1946 and continued to bulk large in 1947 and 1948. The admission of some 40,000 displaced persons in 1947 and 1948 was also responsible for part of the increase.

During the whole period from 1924 through 1947, immigration has totaled only 2,718,006, and when departures of aliens are deducted the net increase to our population has been only 1,734,521. Thus the total for the whole 23-year period represented about the same increase as that sustained in any two years in the period immediately preceding the First World War. Totals for the years since 1929 are even more strikingly small. From that year through 1947 immigrant admissions totaled 1,197,096 for the eighteen-year period, and when departures were deducted the net immigration totaled only 603,357, or an average of about 33,000 yearly.

9

The Aftermath

a decade since the end of World War II, there has been no reversal of the immigration policy established in 1924. Two temporary measures permitted the United States to offer asylum to some of the refugees of war-torn Europe. But the restrictive quota system has remained unchanged, and was indeed codified and made more rigid by the McCarran-Walter Act of 1952. Nor, despite the evident weaknesses of that law, can one be optimistic as to the prospect of a change in the near future. The mood of 1924, in this respect, remains significant today.

The America of 1924 was a far different place from the America of 1783 in which Crèvecoeur had once proclaimed, "This is every man's country." In the century and a half that had intervened a vast continent had been filled, teeming cities had sprung up, and a young society that had welcomed experiment had given way to a more cautious one that sought stability and feared change. The difference between the old and the new accounted for the difference in attitudes toward immigration.

Whether it was necessarily so is a fit subject for speculation.

The men who labored for the new restrictive legislation often argued that the new policy was dictated by the altered circumstances of the environment. The disappearance of the frontier and the expansion of population no longer left room for unlimited growth; the United States had outreached its capacity to expand. That assumption itself reflected a want of confidence and showed the width of the distance between themselves and their adventurous forefathers who had not allowed the environment to dictate to them.

The end of immigration altered many of the problems that confronted American society. But it did not relieve Americans of all problems. The failures of the economic order, the difficulties with the labor force, poverty, insecurity, intemperance, political corruption, and crime continued to demand drastic remedies. And shortly, as a great depression approached many Americans came to realize that to end immigration had brought them no nearer a solution to the fundamental issues posed by the life of the new America. Later still the coming of the refugees showed that the question of immigration policy was relevant even in the cold war period.

AMERICA—A LAND OF IMMIGRANTS

In considering the problems of future policy it will be helpful to have in mind the summary considerations advanced by a Commission appointed by President Harry S. Truman after the McCarran-Walter Act had been passed over his veto.[1]

In a short period of human history the people of the United States built this country from a wilderness to one of the most powerful and prosperous nations in the world. The people who built America were forty million immigrants who have come since the Mayflower, and their descendants. We are still a vigorous and growing nation, and

---

[1] *Whom We Shall Welcome. Report of the President's Commission on Immigration and Naturalization* (Washington, 1953), 23-32.

the economic, social and other benefits available to us, the descendants of immigrant forebears, are constantly expanding.

Our remarkable national development testifies to the wisdom of our early and continuing belief in immigration. One of the causes of the American Revolution, as stated in the Declaration of Independence, was the fact that England hindered free immigration into the colonies.

Our growth as a nation has been achieved, in large measure, through the genius and industry of immigrants of every race and from every quarter of the world. The story of their pursuit of happiness is the saga of America. Their brains and their brawn helped to settle our land, to advance our agriculture, to build our industries, to develop our commerce, to produce new inventions and, in general, to make us the leading nation that we now are.

Immigration brought wealth to the United States, many billions of dollars. The immigrants did not bring this wealth in their baggage—many arrived penniless and in debt—but in their skills, their trades, and their willingness to work. In his testimony to the Commission, Dr. Louis I. Dublin, statistician and second vice president of the Metropolitan Life Insurance Company, pointed out that a young adult immigrant of eighteen years today is worth to the nation at least $10,000, since that is what it costs to raise the average American. The average net worth of such a person to the economy of the United States falls between $30,000 and $80,000, depending on his potential earning power. Throughout our history immigrants have in this way represented additional wealth to our country. . . .

In the 145 years of unrestricted immigration into the United States, from 1776 to 1921, immigrants generally came when and where they were needed. There is no evidence that their arrival caused either unemployment or impoverishment. . . . In the period of unrestricted immigration, the volume of immigration rose during prosperity but rapidly disappeared in times of depression when it would have contributed to unemployment. . . . In general, immigrants came when they were needed and stayed away when they were not. Before quota restrictions were imposed, immigration was large in periods of full employment, small in times of unemployment. . . .

The great depression of the 1930's began almost a decade after the passage of restrictive immigration legislation. The unemployment of the 1930's therefore could hardly be attributed to immigration. On the contrary, a number of distinguished economists believe the restriction of immigration to have been one cause of the depression. Throughout American history rapid increase of population had provided a constantly expanding market for our products. The decline in population growth incident to reduction of immigration and to the declining birth rate in the 1920's removed one factor contributing to our expanding economy.

During the depression, quota restrictions were of no significance— even the small quotas for Southern and Eastern Europe were unfilled. As in the earlier periods, with or without quotas and restrictive devices, prospective immigrants had no incentive or desire to come to this country in time of depression. In fact, in the depression years from 1931 through 1936, a total of 240,000 more aliens left than were admitted. The Commission finds no evidence that immigration either caused or aggravated the depression.

Historically speaking, therefore, immigration has supplied much of the brain and sinew, the human resources that have created our nation. It has come when and where manpower was in demand to build up America and raise its standard of living, but it has not, of itself, caused depression and unemployment. The new immigrant has helped to enrich the native descendants of earlier immigration.

In reviewing the history of debates on the problem of immigration, the Commission was impressed by the fact that those opposing immigration appear to have been influenced . . . by a pessimistic outlook regarding the future economic growth of the United States. The nation was barely founded before a Congressman rose to say on the floor of the House of Representatives in 1797 that while a liberal immigration policy was satisfactory when the country was new and unsettled, now that the United States had reached maturity and was fully populated, further immigration should be stopped.

However, such views have continued throughout our history. In 1921, the Immigration Committee of the House of Representatives again recommended complete termination of all immigration. By the 1920's there was widespread fear that the country could not profitably absorb immigration in the volume received before World War I. The territorial frontier was gone. The country was "filled up" in the sense that the good agricultural land was almost fully occupied and under cultivation. The economy was rapidly becoming industrialized, a "mature" economy was emerging, and therefore, it was argued, immigration had to be drastically curtailed.

With the 1921 Quota Act, originally designed for a one-year emergency, there began a wholly new departure in American law; a limitation on the number of immigrants that could be admitted into the United States. The Immigration Act of 1924 not only carried into permanent law the concept of a limitation on numbers, but also initiated the formula of selection on the basis of race and nationality. The Immigration and Nationality [McCarran-Walter] Act of 1952 continued and strengthened the same principles.

The onset of the depression in 1929 seemed to validate the views of those who feared that economic maturity meant the end of economic growth in the United States. This did not prove to be the case.

Our economy has expanded by leaps and bounds. Our gross national product in 1924 of $140 billion (in 1951 dollars) grew to $329 billion in 1951; foreign exports of goods expanded from $6½ billion (1951 dollars) in 1924 to $15 billion in 1951; manufacturing production increased by 140 per cent, and agricultural output by 51 per cent between 1924 and 1951. Our farmers had an average per capita income from farming of only $302 in 1924 (in terms of 1951 purchasing power), which rose to $760 per capita in 1951. These are but a few examples of growth since the 1920's, and of the dynamic nature of our economy.

This economic expansion required an expanding labor force. The demands were met, as in the past, partly through natural growth and partly from migration. The labor force increased from 41.2 million in 1920 to 66 million in 1951. When the normal sources of European immigration were substantially cut off by our legislation of the 1920's, our industries had to seek other sources of labor. This they found in three ways: (1) by enormous migration from our own rural areas in the United States; (2) by increased immigration from Puerto Rico, the West Indies, and the nonquota countries of the Western Hemisphere; and (3) by special legislation providing for temporary immigration from neighboring countries.

During World War II, and after, many hundreds of thousands of workers were drawn from the farms to man the factories and other establishments of our urban centers. Since 1940 over one and a half million southern Negroes moved to the cities of the North and West to fill the manpower shortages. The Negro population of the North and West more than doubled through this migration. But this was not enough. This source of manpower had to be supplemented by some 200,000 Puerto Ricans, and other West Indians. Quite aside from the movements of native white people in the United States, there were nearly 2 million total migrants who moved into the northern and western States from these internal sources in the decade 1940-50, and the movement continues unabated.

During the same period there was a net foreign immigration of one and a half million people that went chiefly to the industrial areas of the country. Thus, the total migration to the North and West from the South and from abroad during the forties was at least as large as the net immigration in the decade 1890-1900, the third largest decade of European immigration in our history. In other words, the northern cities continued to need immigrants but had to get them mainly from elsewhere than Europe.

But even this was not enough to meet the demands of our growing economy. Congress also found it necessary to enact special immigration legislation admitting certain groups of immigrants temporarily to meet the manpower shortages, both in agricultural and non-agricultural employment.

As a result of acute labor shortages in agriculture during World War II, special programs for recruitment of seasonal and temporary workers from Western Hemisphere countries were undertaken by intergovernmental agreements. Large numbers of aliens were involved in these programs, both during the war and after. The greatest number of Mexican farm workers legally in the United States for this purpose at any one time during World War II was 67,860 around August 1, 1944. As many as 21,000 Jamaicans and 6,000 Bahamans, as well as small numbers of Canadians and other North Americans, entered the United States under similar programs from time to time during this period. After the war, and under a law enacted in 1948, this recruitment of immigrant agricultural workers was continued on a peacetime basis. During the year 1951, some 191,000 Mexican nationals were admitted temporarily for agricultural work. Even this movement of immigrants, authorized by Congress, is overshadowed by the illegal entry each year of over half million Mexican "wetbacks."

Specific agricultural activities have sometimes received explicit Congressional exemption from restrictive immigration provisions. Two enactments have authorized the granting of special quota immigration visas to skilled sheepherders, to be charged against future quotas. Under 1950 legislation, 250 were permitted to enter, of whom 125 were admitted during the fiscal year 1951. Another statute in 1952 authorized the admission of 500 more sheepherders.

In the original 1948 Displaced Persons Act, Congress provided a 40 per cent preference for agricultural labor, a further indication of Congressional recognition of immigration as a potential source of agricultural manpower.

During the war a manpower gap also appeared in the nonagricultural occupations. A total of 135,283 Mexican nationals worked on railroads in the United States from May 1943 to August 1945. More might have been used, but the Mexican government imposed a maximum ceiling of 75,000 who could be permitted in this country at any particular time. During the fiscal year 1951 some 10,000 Canadian woodsmen were permitted entry into Maine, Vermont, New Hampshire, and New York to fill a need for manpower not otherwise available. . . .

In the light of this experience under the restrictive limitations on immigration under the laws in effect since 1924, the Commission finds that immigration continues to be what it has always been in our history, a source of necessary manpower. Despite the efforts to change this situation by shutting off immigration from its customary sources, the American economy still continues to demand some form of immigration to meet the manpower demands of a growing and vigorous nation.

C

The Eyewitness Accounts of American History Series

The Classics in History Series